AF512410

A FIELD GUIDE TO FISHES

A Field Guide to FISHES

(Chilika Lake, Orissa, East Coast of India)

D.V. Rao

AKANSHA PUBLISHING HOUSE
NEW DELHI - 110002 (INDIA)

AKANSHA PUBLISHING HOUSE
4649-B,Ansari Road,
Daryaganj, New Dellii-11 0002
Phones:23268193, 9811582579, 09435116718
Email: ektabooks@yahoo.com
visit us: www.akanshapublishinghouse.com

A Field Guide to Fishes (Chilika Lake Orissa, East Coast of India)
© Author

First Published 2009

ISBN 978-81-8370-199-0

[All rights reserved. No part of this publication may be reproduced or transmitted, in any form or by any means, without prior permission of the editors. Any person who does any unauthorised act in relation to this publication may be liable to criminal prosecution and civil claims for damages.]

PRINTED IN INDIA

Published by Akansha Publishing House, New Delhi-110002 and printed at Mehra Offset Press, Delhi.

Foreword

With increasing utilisation of fish as a resource of protein throughout the world almost all water bodies including seas, estuaries, rivers, lakes, reservoirs, and streams are exploited up to a maximum extent and some of them are even overexploited led to the local extinction of many species. The situation is not exceptional in Indian water bodies. The Chilika Lake is one such biggest brackish water lake situated on the east coast of Orissa. The lake is home to a rich diversity of plants and animals including large number of migratory birds. Also it is an abode of many threatened species of plants and animals. In recent decades the physico-chemical characteristics of the lake was drastically changed and brought to alarming state due to several anthropogenic factors. Chilika Lake was designated the first Indian wetland of international importance under the *Ramsar Convention* during 1981. Due to uncontrolled fishing activities over a long period, the fish landings are stagnating in the Chilika Lake and brought the socioeconomic scenario of the people, living in and around the lake, to a controversial state. Sustainable utelisation of fish stocks need meticulous study and conservation by issuing guidelines on total permissible catches, by limiting mesh sizes, declaring fishing sanctuaries, discouraging use of mechanized craft, by encouraging traditional methods of fishing etc.

A prerequisite for these is the knowledge of the species composition of fish resources of the water bodies. A comprehensive publication on the fish diversity of the lake is need of the hour. The efforts made by the author to bring out such comprehensive illustrated Field Guide to Fisheries with emphasis on Chilika Lake fishes is welcoming step and I congratulate the author for his commendable job. The guide book in hand describes about 259 fish species of Chilika Lake with over 135 colour illustrations. It will assist fishery institutions and research scholars in a safe identification of commercial and noncommercial fish species thus creating the basis for an efficient fishery development in the brackish waters.

Date: 06.05.2009
Place: New Delhi

Dr. P.K. Talwar
Retd. Joint Director
Zoological Survey of India

Preface

Fishing in multispecies large lagoons is followed by changes in productivity of the system in long run. Therefore, the management and development of multispecies fisheries requires detailed analysis of species composition of the landings and scientific sampling. In tropical waters, taxonomists find it difficult to sort a multispecies catch as many of them are similar in appearance.

There are several FAO species identification sheets for Fishery Purposes and other publications on fish taxonomy are made available covering a wide area. But it seems worthwhile to produce identification tools tailored to the local needs of fishery research. Therefore efforts have been made to give more detailed description of the morphological characters, habitat and distribution of the various fish species found in the brackish areas of eastern India w.s.r. to Chilika Lake along with colour illustrations in order to make easy the identification. The present guide is not meant strictly as a scientific publication but as means to facilitate the easy identification of fish diversity by the field workers, taxonomists, amateur fishery biologists and fishery managers to manage their fishery resources in a broad and productive manner working in the area.

—Dr. D.V. Rao

Acknowledgements

I wish to express my sincere thanks to Dr. Ramakrishna, Director, Zoological Survey of India for encouragement. I am also thankful to Dr. L.Kosigyn Singh, Scientist-C, Smt. Kamla Devi, Sr. Zool. Asstt., Shri P. Verma, Photographer of Zoological Survey of India and Shri G.N. Indresha, Scientist-C of Regional Museum of Natural History, Bhubaneswar and many others who generously spared some photographs appeared in this guide. Also thankfully acknowledged The CDA (Chilika Development Authority), Orissa for some of the information utelised from their website.

–Dr. D.V. Rao

Contents

Glossary

A : Symbol for anal fin (Used in fin formula).

Abdomen: The belly or lower surface of a fish.

Adipose eyelid: Fatty, transluscent tissue that partially covers the eye ball in some fishes.

Adipose fin: Small fatty fin located on posterior part of 1st dorsal fin, lacking spines or rays.

Anadromus: Migrating from the sea into freshwater to spawn.

Anal fin: The median fin located undersurface, just behind the anus.

Anus: The external pening of intestine or vent.

Auxiliary scales: Small scales superimposed on surface of large scales.

Axil: The inner base of a pectoral fin.

Axillary scale: Scale in pectoral or ventral fin axil.

Barbel: An elongate fleshy whisker-like projection found near mouth or on lower surface of head.

Bifurcate: Branched or forked.

Canine: A pointed, conical sharp tooth, usually longer than the surrounding teeth.

Cartilaginous: Made of cartilage. (*Ex*. Shark skeleton).

Caudal fin: A median fin at the rear of the body; the tail fin.

Caudal peduncle: The narrower part of body just before the caudal fin; refer the part of a fish between the rear of anal fin and the base of caudal fin.

Cirrus (*pl*. cirri): A small thin flap of skin or appendage that located anywhere on the body of fish.

Compressed: Flattened from side to side.

Ctenoid: One type of scale; the rear edge of each scale is toothed, making the scale rough to touch.

Cycloid: Another type of scale; with a smooth ear edge, which makes thenscale smooth to touch.

D: Symbol for dorsal fin (Used in fin formula).

Dorsal fin: A median rayed fin on the back, often notched or fully divided into two fins.

Filamentous: Thread like, usually refers to elongated fin rays.

Fin spine: Hard unbranched ray in a fin.

Finlet: A small rayed fin, usually in a series, and often following the dorsal and anal fins.

Gill arch: The bony support to which the gill filaments and gill rakers are attached.

Gill chamber: The cavity where the gill are located.

Gill cover: The bony flap that covers the outside of the gill chamber.

Gill rakers: Bony, tooth like projections from the front edge of the gill arch., opposite the gill filaments.

Gills: The respiratory organs in fishes.

Head length: The length measured from the tip of the snout to the rear edge of the gill cover.

Interorbital: Between the eyes.

Keel: A horizontal bony ridge, often located at the base of caudal fin.

Lateral line (Ll.): A row of pore like openings on head and lateral side of body.

Lateral: On the side.

Ls.: Lateral scales series.

Maxillary: A bone in the upper jaw.

Meristics: Countable characters (eg. Finrays, spines, gill rakers etc.).

Morphometrics: Measuarble characters (ex. Total lemgth, eye diameter, caudal length etc.).

Naked: Smooth or unscaled.

Nostril: A nasal pening.

Notched: Indented; refers to a fin in which some rays ae shorter.

Opercle: The thin bone forming most of the the gill cover.

Orbit: The bony eye socket.

P. Symbol for Pectoral fin (Used in fin formula)

Papilla: A small fleshy knob or projection.

Pectoral fin: One of a pair of fins that are attached to the shoulder girdle, behind the head.

Pelvic fins: One of a pair of fins on the lower surface of the body, located below the pectoral fins.

Posterior: Towards the rear.

Preopercle: A chek bone, at the front of the gill cover.

Rostral: Pertaining to snout; a beaklike extension at the tip of the snout.

Scute: A horny projection, often a modified scale.

Snout: The part of head in front of eyes.

Soft dorsal fin: A median fin on the back composed of soft rays.

Spine: A bony projection usually on head.

Spiracles: The opening that leads to gill chamber in sharks and rays.

Suborbital: Bone below the eyes.

Tail: The part of body behind anus.

V. Symbol for ventral or pelvic fin (Used in fin formula)

Ventral: On the lower surface or on the belly.

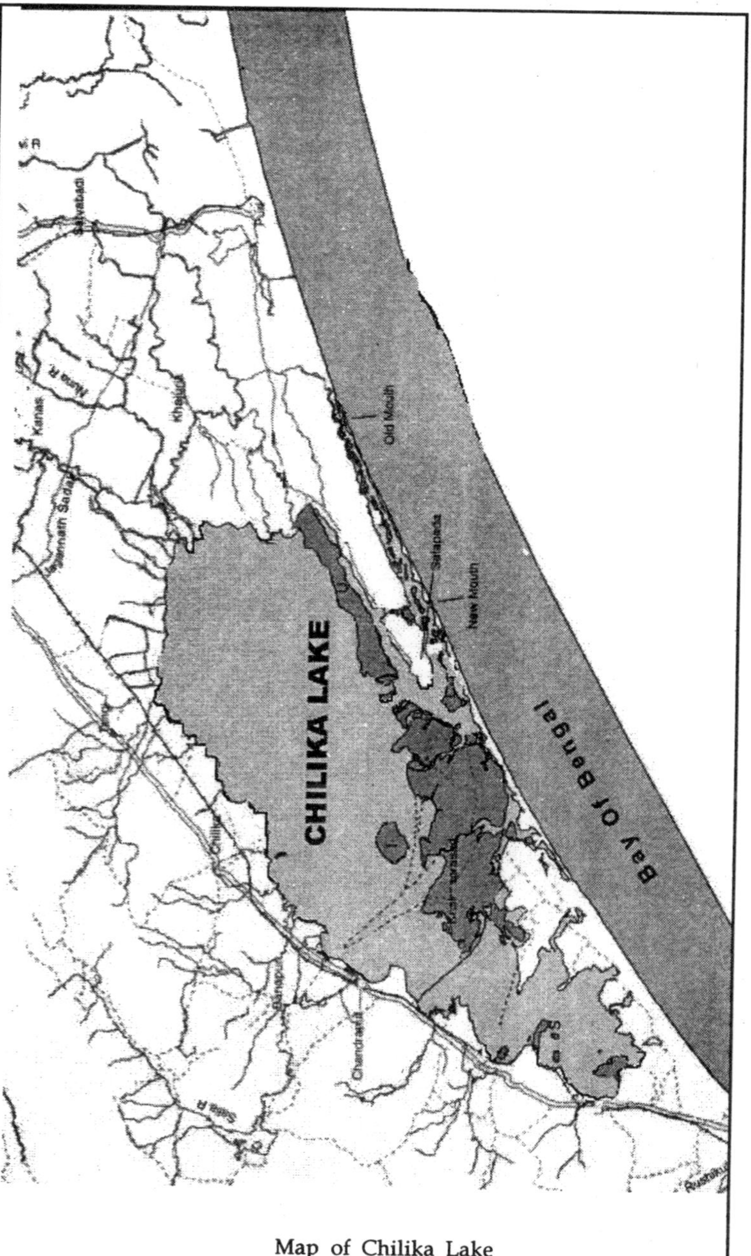

Map of Chilika Lake

Introduction

The Chilika Lake is a brackish water coastal lake situated on the east coast of India in Orissa State, located between $19^0 28'$-$19^0 45'$ N and $85^0 05'$-$85^0 38'$ E. It is the largest coastal lake in India and second largest lagoon in the world extends from the Bhusandpur, southeast corner of Puri District in the north to Palur in Ganjam District in the south. Due to the silting action of the Mahanadi River which drains into the northern end of the lake, and the sand bar formed due to northerly currents of the Bay of Bengal along the eastern shore leading to the formation of a shallow lagoon. The lake is pear-shaped and has a maximum length of 64.3 km with a mean width of 20.1 km, wider in the northern part and gradually narrowed towards southern end. It is separated from the sea by a long sand bar of over 60 km length in the foreshore area. The total area of the lake varies from 1165 km^2 in the monsoon season period to 906 km^2 in the summer season. The lake is shallow and the depth is ranging from 50cm to 3.7m. studded with many islands. The larger islands, separated by shallow channels, lie between the sandbar and the lake, thus acts as a natural barrier between sea and lake. The major islands are Parikud, Phulbari, Berahpura, Nuapara, Nalbana, and Tampara. These islands, together with the peninsula of Malud, constitute the Krishnaprasad Revenue Block of Puri District. But the lake is connected to the sea by a narrow, zig-zag channel near Arakhuda. The channel does not join directly from the sea, but ran parallel for some distance and divides into two branches, one merges in a network of swamps and narrow waterways and the other joined at a point of lake known as Mugger Mukh which is a very shallow point. Due to this, the incursion of sea water in to lake is poor. As a result the lake waters always remain brackish for most part of the year. In addition to the entry of sea water, large number of tributaries of major rivers joining the lake on northern and western sides bringing huge amount of silt laden freshwater. Due to siltation, the width of the barrier has fluctuated and the mouth to the sea has periodically been closed and leading to the shifting of mouth frequently towards the northeast side. The mouth, which was about 1.5 km wide during 1780, was only 0.75 km forty years later. The local fisherfolk regularly had to cut open the mouth to gain access to the sea for fishing activities.

The Chilika Lake is an important wetland body in preserving the genetic diversity because of the multiplicity of its habitat, flora and fauna. The Zoological Survey of India (ZSI) made an intensive survey of the lake between 1985 and 1988 and identified about 800 species of fauna, including many rare, endangered, threatened and vulnerable species, excluding terrestrial insects. Most of these faunal components have significant ecological, social and economical value such as fish, crustaceans, molluscs etc. In addition, about 350 angiosperm plants including mangroves have been recorded from the Lake area. The lake is also an important habitat and breeding ground for both resident and migratory and other aquatic birds. Thousands of migratory birds arrive from Siberia, Iran, Iraq, Afghanistan and the Himalayan range during winter season. Due to this, part of the lake is designated as Chilika Lake Bird Sanctuary. The Nalaban Island within the lagoon is notified as a Bird Sanctuary under the Wildlife Protection Act. The lake is also home to a large number of fish, the Irrawaddy Dolphin (*Orcaella brevirostris*) and the rare endemic limbless lizard *Barkudia insularis*.

On account of its rich biodiversity components of marine, brackish and freshwater biota and presence of several endangered, threatened and vulnerable categories, Chilika Lake was designated as a *Ramsar site* in the year 1981 and identified as a priority site for conservation and management by the Ministry of Environment & Forests, Government of India. The lake is also renowned for its fishery resources. Fisheries wealth of Chilika lagoon comprises of more than 300 species which includes finfish, prawns, crab and molluscan species. About 70% of fish species of the lake are commercially important. Over one lakh fifty thousand fisher-folk living in 130 villages on the shore and islands of the Chilika depending for their survival and contribute significantly to India's local as well as international fish trade. The annual average fish, prawn and crab production together is about 6000 tons from the lake. But in recent times due to dredging of new mouth the average finfish yield during the years 2001-2003 was raised to about 9,170 MT (Data of CDA).

Hydrology of the Lake

The hydrology of the lake is very interesting. The maximum temperature of lake waters are 39.9 °C and minimum of 14 °C at various seasons of the year. The lake experiences South-West and North-East monsoons with an average annual rainfall of 1,200 mm. The wind speed varies from 5.2 to 16 metres/hour and move from south and southwesterly direction due to the influence of the SW monsoon and from North and north easterly direction during the rest of the period. The total annual freshwater input to the lake is estimated to 1.76 cubic kilometres including river systems and direct precipitation over the lake. The land system comprises two of the three southern branches of the River Mahanadi that divided near Cuttack drains over 60% of the total fresh water inflow into lake. The other non-perennial drainage system contributes rest of the percentage. Every year all these inland river branches are carrying over 13 million metric tons of silt into the lake making waters more turbid.

The recent extensive limnological investigations made by The Chilika Development Authority (CDA), Orissa revealed the following physico-chemical characteristics of the lake waters.

- Extreme shallow depths in the northern sector of the lake, with less than 1.5 m and the southern sector with the maximum depth of 3.9 m.
- Waters are highly turbid due to strong mixing of surface water with sediments and the transparency values ranging between 9 cm and 155 cm.
- Waters are alkaline and pH ranging from 7.1 – 9.6 with highest alkalinity near southern part of the lake.
- Salinity levels in the lake show wide temporal and spatial variation due to a mixing of freshwater inflow, evaporation, wind flow and tidal influence of seawater ranging 0 ppt near the Daya River mouth to hyper-

saline level of 42 ppt in the channel confluent withsea during the dry period.

- The Dissolved Oxygen values were between 3.3–18.9 mg/l.
- The values of nutrients like Phosphate phosphorus (0–0.4 ppm), nitrate nitrogen (10–60 ppm) and silicates (1–8 ppm) are high in the north and northwest part of the lake where most of the rivers discharge into the lake.
- Tidal influx of seawater during monsoon is almost reduced by the strong inflow of a large amount of fresh water from the northern and central zones of the lake. Brackish water conditions in the southern zone prevail due to low water exchange even during monsoon period. Salinity in the southern zone decreases during the post-monsoon period and in winter as northern winds facilitate mixing of water with rest of the lake. Due to lowest level of water in the lake during summer intrusion of salt water from the outer channel into the lake increases. A general increase in salinity of the central and northern zones occurs due to wind induced mixing by the predominantly southern winds and the salinity in the southern zone does not rise appreciably.

Threats and Conservation

Over the last few decads, the ecosystem of the lake encountered several problems and threats due to indescriminate and over-exploitation of the biological resources, un controlled tourism and other socio-cultural activities brought the lake to the near extinct. The following are some of the major threats to the existence of lake.

- Siltation due to sediment inflow from the inland river systems
- Shrinkage of water surface area due to dumping of solid waste and bad land usage pattern around the lake
- Inflow of sewage and pollutants due to settlements in and around the lake
- Choking of the inlet channel as well as shifting of the mouth periodically connecting to the sea

- Decrease in salinity of lake waters
- Loss of biodiversity and fishery resources with decline in productivity which inturn affecting the livelihood of the dependent community on it
- Legal problems between fishermen and non-fishermen communities over fishing rights in the lake
- The extensive practices of commercial aquaculture of prawn has contributed drastically to the decline of the lakes fisheries and faunal diversity including the visiting bird population
- Rapid and prolific growth of invasive fresh water aquatic weed and fauna.

Keeping in view of the lake's significance due to its estuarine nature and support of unique assemblage of marine, brackish and freshwater species, several rare and endangered species, over a million migratory waterfowl and shorebirds during winter, great value in preserving genetic diversity, fisheries that are the lifeline of the community and an increase in weeds and aquaculture activities, rapid degradation of its habitats the Chilika Lake was designated as *Ramsar Site* during 1981, the first Indian wetland of international importance under the Ramsar Convention.

Due to rapid degradation of the lake's ecosystem and welfare of the local communities who were dependent upon the lake's resources, the Government of Orissa has set up the Chilika Development Authority (CDA) in 1992 for restoration and overall development of the lake under the administrative jurisdiction of the Department of Environment and Forests with a view to restore and conserve the Lake ecosystem with all its genetic diversity, formulate the management plan for Resource Management and sustainable utilisation of its resources by the dependent communities and implementation of multidisciplinary research and developmental activities by the authority and through various National and the International institutions and Non-Governmental organisations.

Due to constant conservation and monitring afforts and opening of the new lake mouth by the CDA, the Lake is being gradually coming to the stable state and many fish species once considered as threatened like Milk fish (*Chanos chanos*), Indo-Pacific Tarpon (*Megalops cyprinoides*), Tenpounder (*Elops machnata*), ilishi (*Tenuealosa ilisha*), Mullet (*Rhinomugil corsula)etc.* have reappeared in the lake. The catch of fish has also shown significant improvement in the lake. Due to better management practices and significant improvement in the ecological condition of the Chilika lake, onece it was put during 1993 under "*The Montreux Record*" as the lake was considered to have "undergone, to be undergoing, or to be likely to undergo change in it's ecological character brought about by human action" has been removed from the record in November 2002.

Ichthyofaunal Diversity of Chilika Lake

The rich and varied fish composition of the Chilika Lake consists of marine, brackish and freshwater species. The pioneering studies on ichthyofauna of the lake made during early 19th centuary by Chaudhuri (1916a, b, c, 1917&1923), Hora (1923), Koumans (1941), Jones and Sujansinghani (1945), Mitra (1946), Devasundaram (1954), Roy and Sahoo (1967), Menon (1961) and Rajan *et al.*, (1968). Subsequently (Rao, 1995) listed about 217 species comprising 147 genera under 71 families. In several cases one and the same species was found cited by various names in different publications. Moreover, the recent revisionary works on many fish families led to the shifting of many genera and species from one family to another and the synonymisation of several taxa. Since information on the fish species occuring in the Chilika Lake is very much scattered in the literature the researchers, conservationists as well as others concerned with fish biodiversity and resource management are facing difficulty in the correct specific status of the fish species of the lake. Therefore, an attempt has been made to fulfill the lacunae by compiling all the records of lake fishes with their current valid names. An updated list of about 259 species of fishes belongs to 76 families reported from Chilika lake presented in the field guide.

About this Guide

The Chilika Lake is a famous brackishwater lake harbouring large variety of fish. Whether you like to fish for consumption or research purpose or an administrator need to know the biodiversity for conservation and management of the lake or need to comply with the fishing regulations at one time or another and one need to has to identify the fish resources properly. Unfortunately, no such comprehensive field guide is made available to identify all the fish species encountered in the Chilika Lake. Therefore, to fill the gap "*A Field Guide to Fishes of Chilika Lake, Orissa*" is designed.

With a little practice in using this guide, one can easily identify almost all of the common and most uncommon fish species of the Chilika Lake. It is designed to facilitate easy, quick and reliable identification of all fishes by specialists as well as nonspecialists and researchers in this field. All the major groups of fishes are arranged in this guide more or less in the order in which researchers classify them, with few exceptions. The illustrations given before the chapter. Glossary show the general meristic and morphometric characters of a typical fish and serve as a visual glossary for limited anatomical terms one need to acquiant for identification of a fish. An illustrated key with distinctive features of each family are highlighted for segregation of fish groupwise at first instance. To go into detailed identification of species, key to genera and species provided. Many of these key features can be readily observed in fresh-caught specimens. Over 150 colour photographs of fishes are provided for compare and identification. For each species diagnostic features, habitat and their distribution in general and remarks are included. The genera and species are presented alphabetically within families. For quick reference an index to species is also appended.

Since this Field Guide is also meant for nonspecialists in the subject, technical jargon has been kept to a minimum. The technical terms that could not be avoided are defined in the Glosssary. The guide is also supported with selected Bibliography at the end. Above all it is designed for easy use in the field. Hope it will find its place in the field kit or in your pocket whenever you go for collection in the field or fish landing centers of the Chilika Lake.

Collection of fish samples: Those who are interested in

fish studies and the researchers can collect the fish samples seasonally or randomly depending on requirement and type of studies. A variety of baits, hooks, traps, nets and similar gear can be used for sampling from the lake. Another way to increase the variety of species sampling is to collect fish from the fishermen at the time of hauling the nets and making periodic visits to fish markets.

Preserving the samples: Immediately after collection the fish samples usually preserved in 10% Formalin solution diluted from full strength Formalin (45 to 50% formaldehyde). After a few weeks, transfer the specimens to alcohol. The specimens can also be preserved permanently in the buffered 5% formalin solution. A slit along the abdomen of the specimens of 8 cm length must be made for proper preservation to avoid spoilage of the samples. Collection labels depicting date of collection, locality, number of examples, name of collector, etc. written on good quality rag paper with water proof ink must be tagged with specimens.

Fish photography: A photograph of each species you collect is useful for identification of fishes. In many cases the colours and pattern are specific to each species. Colours of fishes fade away rapidly after death. The photographs record original colour pattern of the specimens when photographed immediately after capture. Photograph the entire specimen from the side. While taking photograph lay the pectoral fin back against the body, stretch the dorsal, anal and pelvic fins and spread the caudal fin. For sharks a view of head from ventral and dorsal is needed for confirmation of identification of species with specialists. Photography of small fishes needs special lences and lighting. Suitable colour backgrounds must be used while taking photographs to enhance the quality of the picture. While taking picture place a ruler or some object of known dimension next to the fish so that the length of the specimen can be calculated from the print. Before taking photograph, the fish must be prepared in the following way. Lay the fish on its side on wax-bottomed pan or thermocol sheet or cardboard. Stretch the fins and pin them. Using small paint brush, apply full strength formalin on stretched fins. Remove the pins after about five minutes and the fins will remain erect for ever.

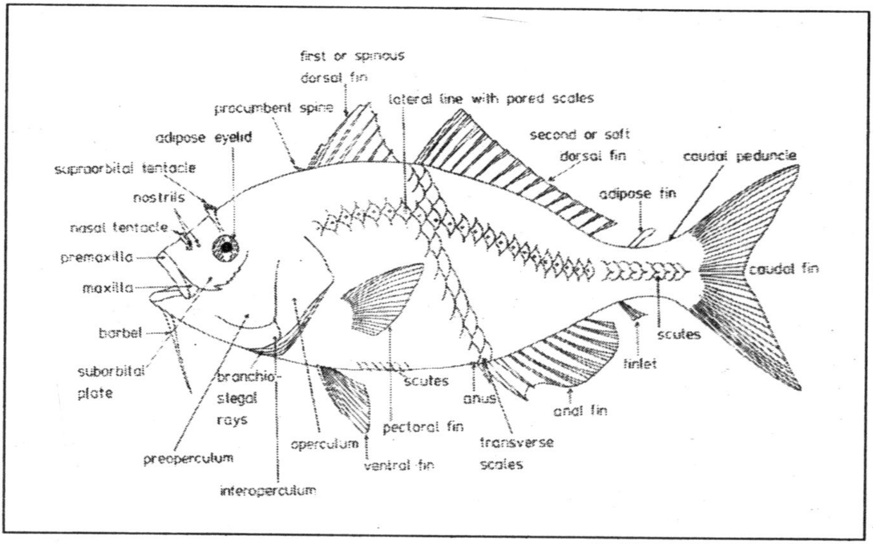

Meristic Characters of a Typical Fish

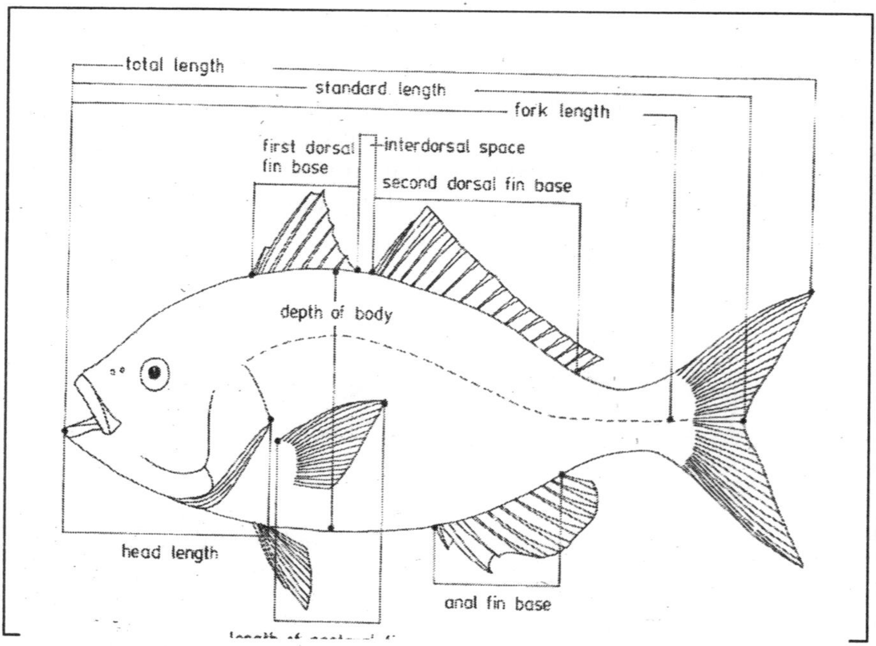

Morphometric Characters of a Typical Fish

Illustrated Key to the Families

The following illustrations are outline drawings of typical members of the families found in this Field Guide with the page reference in parentheses for the detailed species description.

1. Carcharhinidae: Scales absent; dorsal fin without spines; spiracles small or absent; nasal barbels absent; no grooves connecting nostrils and mouth; nictitating eye lids present; last gill slit over pectoral base; 1st dorsal fin anterior to pelvic fins; lower lobe of caudal fin large. (p.)

2. Sphyrnidae: Head much flattened and greatly expanded laterally in hammer form; eyes situated on the ends of the lateral expansion. (p.)

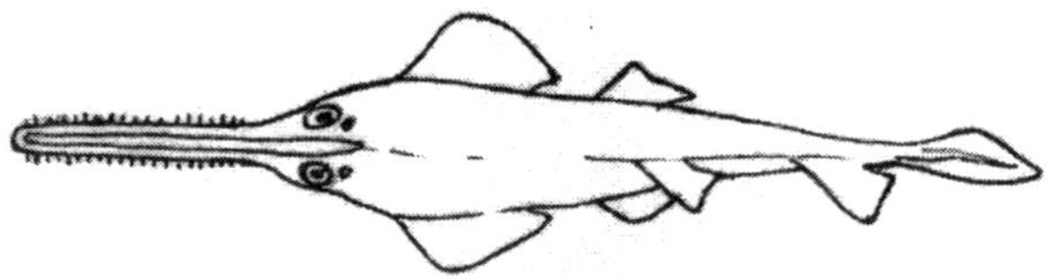

3. Pristidae: Body with shark like appearance; snout flat elongate, bearing narrow sharp teeth on either side like saw; pectoral fins small; gill slits on ventral surface; eyes and spiracles on top of head; nostrils broad with large nasal flaps. (p.)

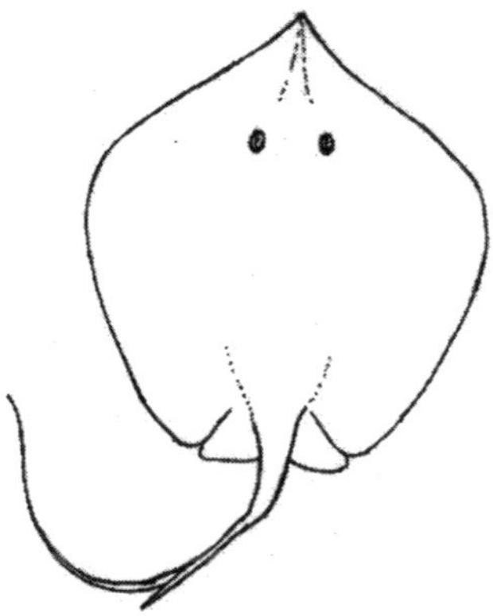

4. Dasyatidae: Head flat merged with body disc; disc rhomboidal to circular; outer margin of pectoral fins continuous along side of head; spiracles large, close behind eyes no dorsal and caudal fins; tail slender and whip-like; one or two stings on tail; dorsal and ventral fin folds present or absent on tail; skin smooth or rough with tubercles or pointed spines. (p.)

5. Myliobatidae: Body flattened and disc-like; head distinct from disc; mouth small, transverse; eyes and spiracles on sides of head; tail whip-like, longer than disc; no caudal fin; gill openings under side of disc; dorsal fin on tail base and sting close behind it; caudal fin absent. (p.)

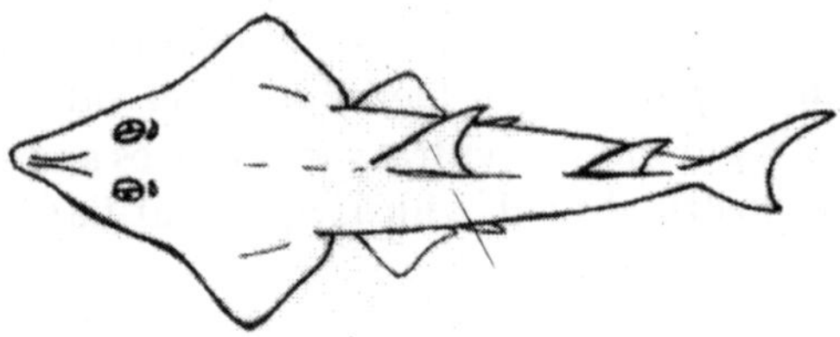

6. Rhynchobatidae: Flattened rays with two large dorsal fins; tail thick; front part of body much depressed and broad; mouth deeply undulated; snout broadly rounded or pointed; tail depressed; nostrils oblique and large; lower caudal fin lobe distinct.. (p.)

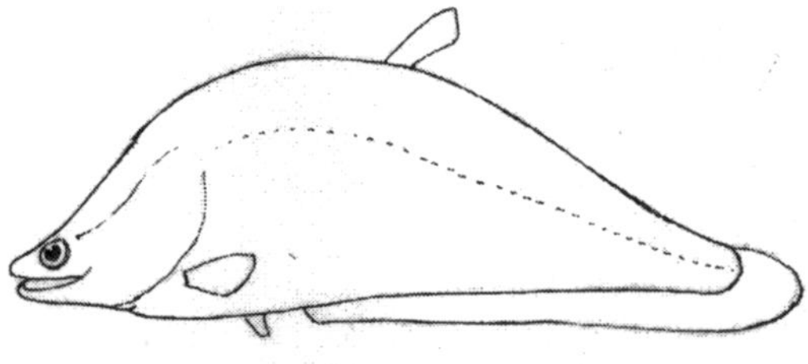

7. Notopteridae: Body elongate, broad and strongly compressed laterally; abdomen serrated before pelvic fins; eyes large and superior; maxilla well toothed and fairly bound together with premaxilla; suboperculum absent; no barbels on chin; single dorsal fin; ventral fins rudimentary or absent. (p.)

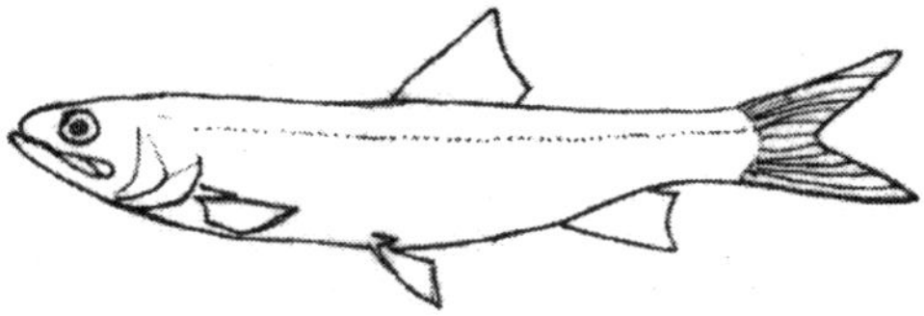

8. Elopidae: Body fusiform; lateral line present; tail long and deeply forked; single dorsal fin placed in the center of body; large bony gular plate under the mouth; lateral line scales 95-120. (p.)

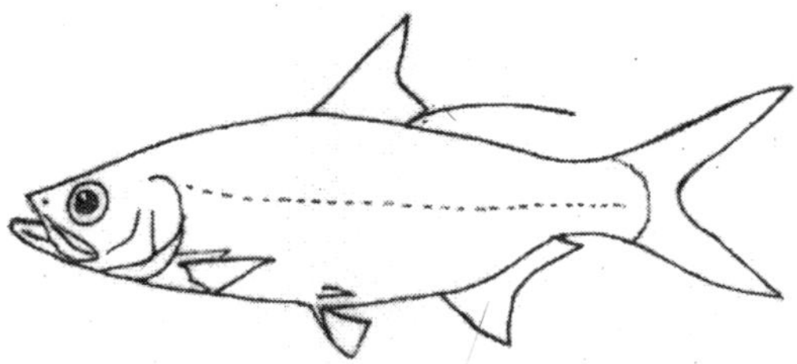

9. Megalopidae: Body somewhat compressed; no scutes along belly; mouth large; the last dorsal ray elongate an filamentous; lateral line distinct, tubes branched, radiating over surface of lateral line scales; anal fin origin slightly behind last dorsal ray. (p.)

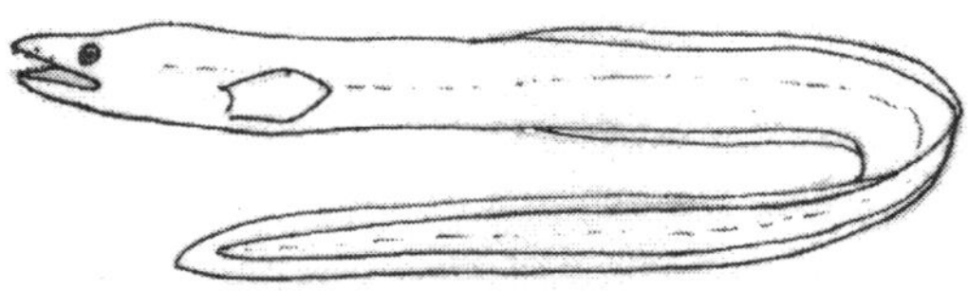

10. Anguillidae: Eel-like fishes; body with minute embedded scales; dorsal fi inserted far behind gill openings; dorsal, anal and caudal fins confluent; pectoralfins well developed; eyes covered by skin; anterior nostrils tubular; tongue free; lateralline distinct. (p.)

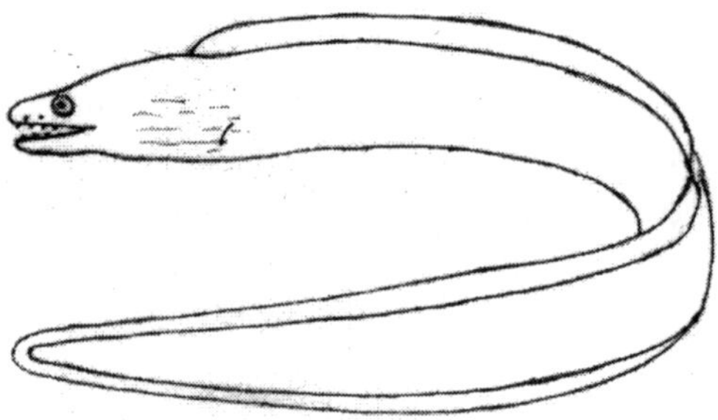

11. Muraenidae: Body robust and slightly compressed; scaleless; canine teeth present; gill openings small and roundish; no pectoral fins; dorsal fin origin before gill openings; dorsal and anal fins continuous with caudal fin; no lateral line, lateral line pores on head only; no scales on body. (p.)

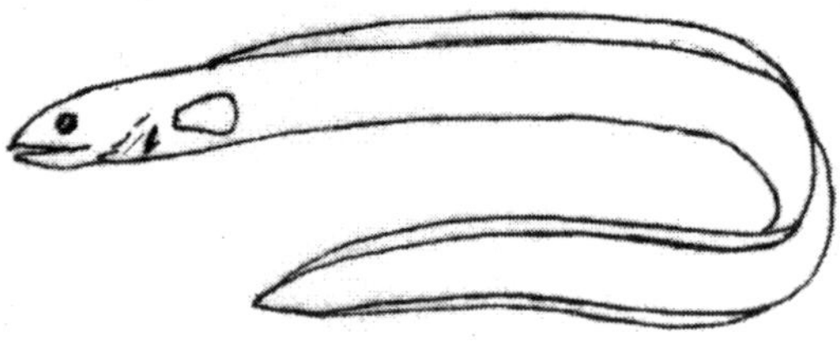

12. Ophichthidae: Body slender and rounded, tail pointed and spike-like; mouth large, cleft behind eye; teeth visible; nostrils widely separated; tongue not free; gill openings are small; lateral line present; pectoral fins present or rudimentary; ventral fins absent; no scales on body; end of tail free. (p.)

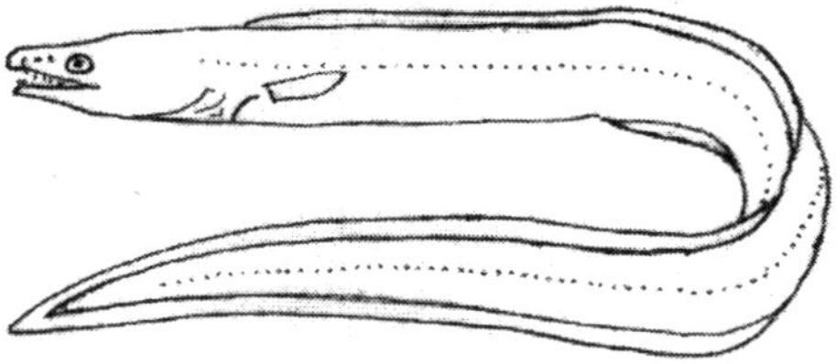

13. Muraenesocidae: Eel-like fishes; anterior part cylindrical, compressed along tail region; tongue not free from floor of mouth; no fleshy lips; gill openings large and placed low on body; dorsal and anal fins confluent with caudal; dorsal origin over pectoral fin bases; anal fin absent; body scaleless. (p.)

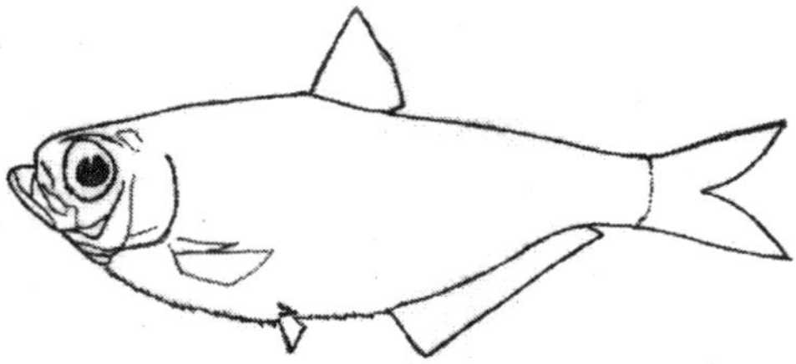

14. Clupeidae: Small fishes with fusiform and compressed bodies, mouth more or less terminal; belly with sharp scutes; teeth small or absent; dorsal fin single; no spines in fins; ventral fins abdominal; caudal fin deeply forked; head scaleless; scales deciduous; no lateral line. (p.)

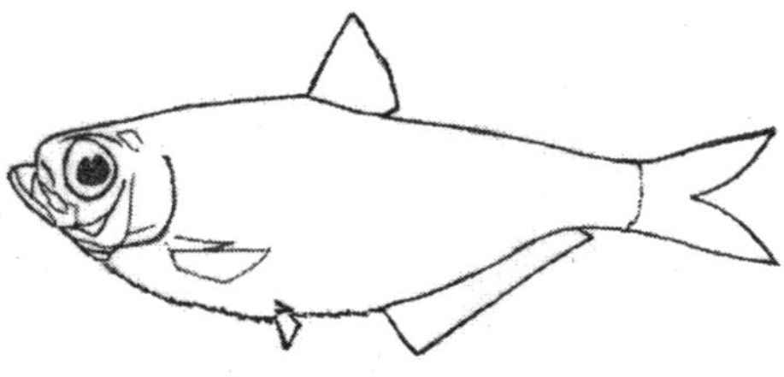

15. Pristigasteridae: Body fairly elongate and compressed; abdomen with sharp keeled scutes; lower jaw projectiong; anal fin with more than 30 rays; ventral fins present or absent; 4-8 branchostegalrays. (p.)

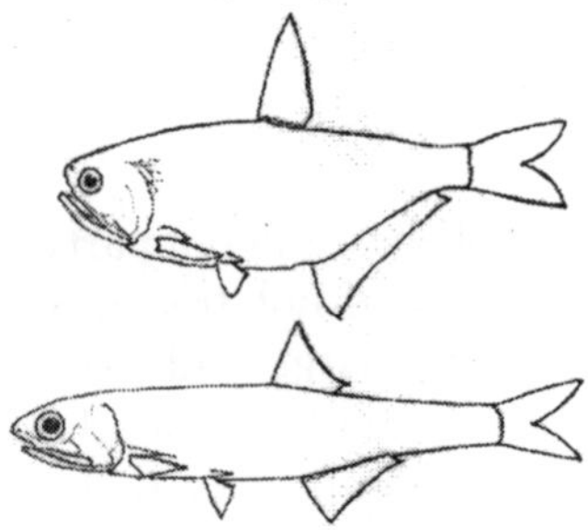

16. Engraulidae: Body fusiform, and subsylindrical; snout prominent; mouth far back on ubderside of head; lower jaw small and inconspicuous; abdomen with keeled scutes; gill rakers long and slender; no spines in fins; dorsalfin at mid oint of body; caudal fin forked; no laterl lne. (p.)

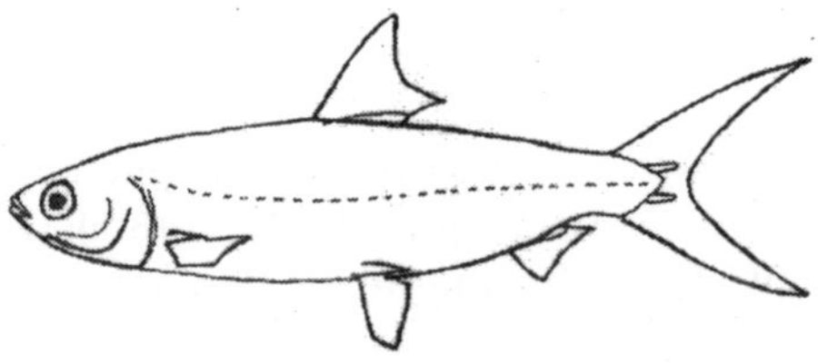

17. Chanidae: Body torpedo-shaped and slightly compressed; mouth terminal; eyes covered with thick transparent skin; head scaleless; dorsal fin origin over middle of the body; dorsal and anal fin bases scaly; no spines in fins. (p.)

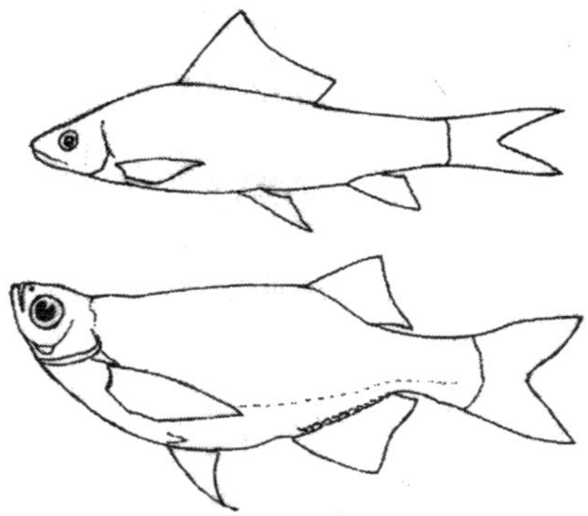

18. Cyprinidae: Body compressed; abdomen rounded or cutting; eyes not covered with skin; mouth transverse, more or less protrusible and toothless; lower jaw sometimes with a knob at symphysis; lips thin; gill openings wide; 1-2 pairs of barbels present or absent; lateral line present or absent. (p.)

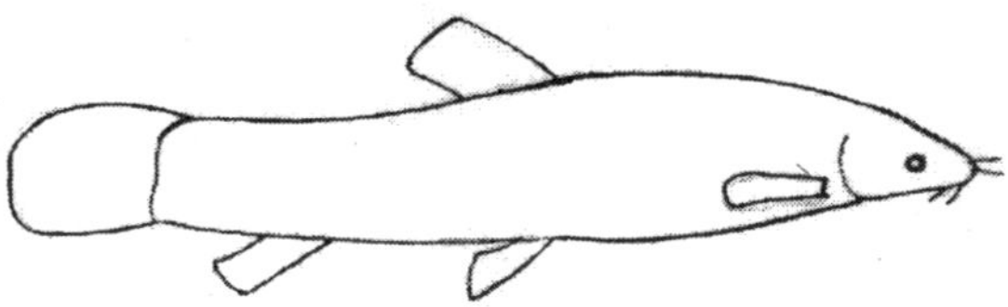

19. Cobitidae: Body small and cylindrical; posteriorly compressed; small scales of body, usually immersed in mucus; mouth subterminal to inferior; lips thick, fleshy and papillated; three pairs of barbels; an erectile spine before or below eye; fins without spines; lateral line present. (p.)

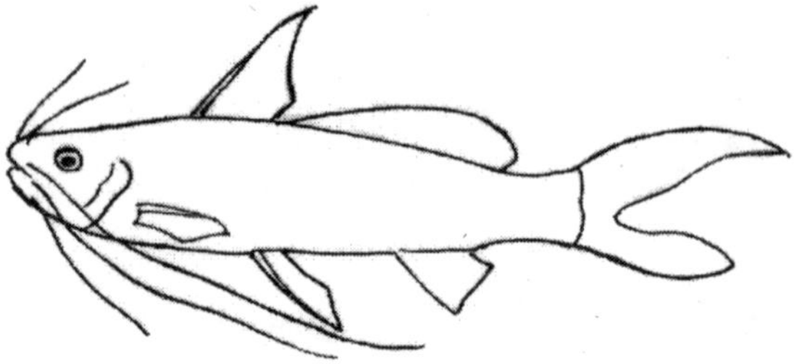

20. Bagridae: Large sized elongate fishes with compressed body; nostrils widely separated; 6-8 barbels; gill openings wide extending to above base of pectoral fins; adipose dorsal present; anal fin not confluent with caudal; caudal fin deeply forked or emarginated; lateral line present. (p.)

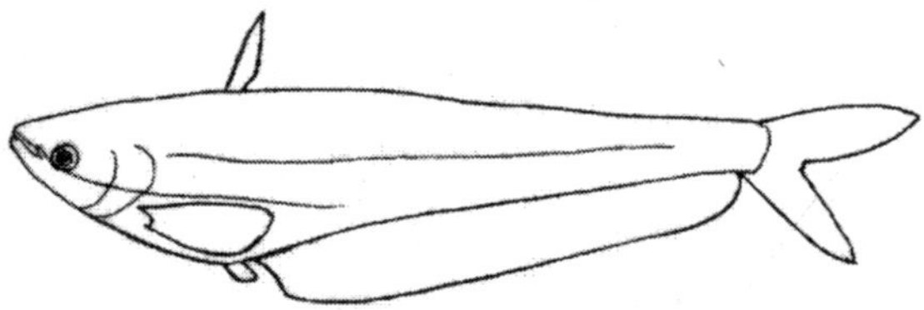

21. Siluridae: Body elongate and compressed; depressible teeth on premaxillaries, mandible and vomers; posterior nostrils valved; 4-6 barbels; nasal barbells absent; dorsal fin short with 4-5 rays; adipose absent; pectoral fin with strong spine; anal fin long, extending to caudal or confluent with it; ventral fin small or absent; caudal rounded. (p.)

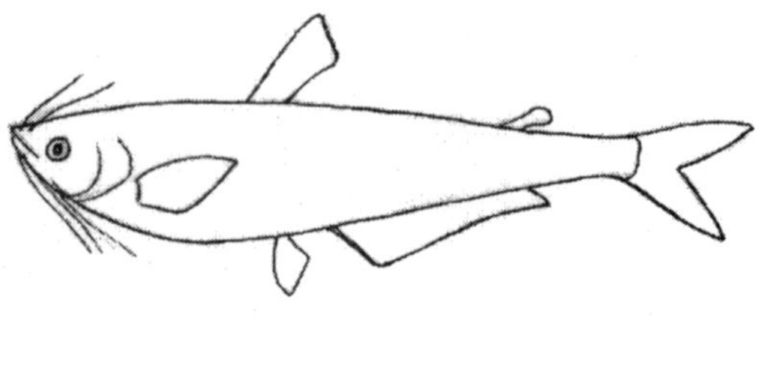

22. Schilbeidae : Body compressed; teeth premaxillaries, mandible and vomer; posterior nostrils slit-like or with flap; barbells 2-8; dorsal fin and adipose fin present or absent; anal fin long, not confluent with caudal; caudal fin forked; lateral line simple and complete. (p.)

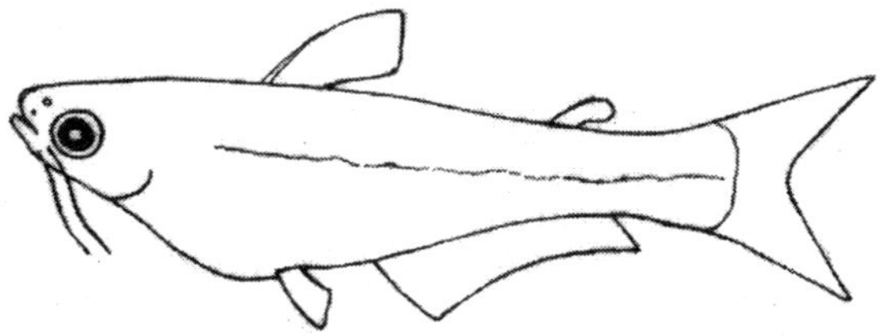

23. Pangasiidae: Large sized fishes with compressed body; abdomen rounded; 4 barbels; no nasal barbels; lips thin; gill membranes united with each other; dorsal and adipose fin present; pectoral with strongly serrated spine; anal fin long; caudal fin forked. (p.)

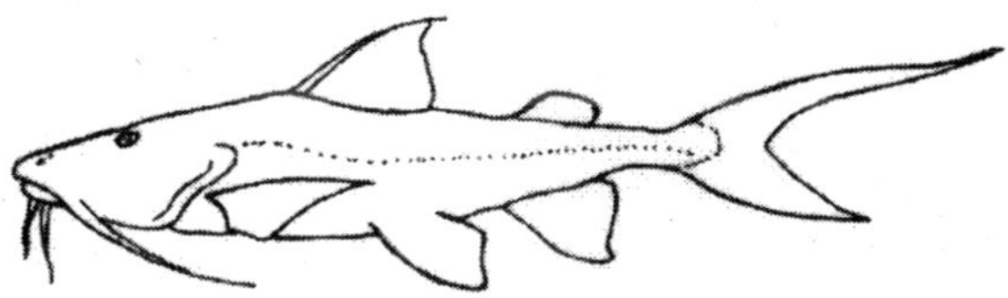

24. Sisoridae: Medium sized fishes; head and anterior part of body depressed; tail compressed; adhesive apparatus on thorax present or absent; nostrils slit like, close together; nasal barbels present; barbels 8; adipose dorsal present; dorsal and anal fins short, not confluent with caudal; caudal fin forked or truncate; lateral line complete. (p.)

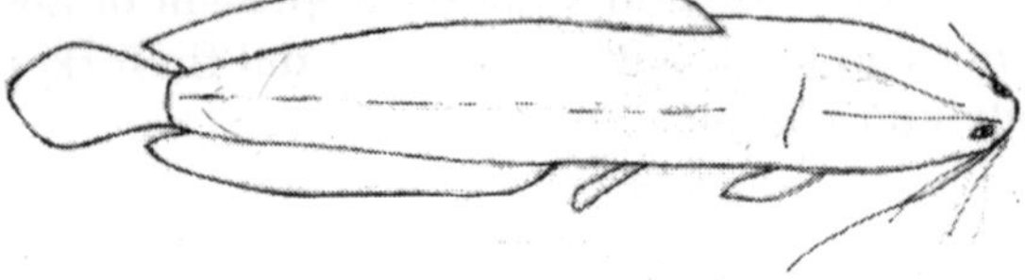

25. Clariidae : Body compressed, nostrils widely separated; posterior nostrils slit-like; nasal barbels present; branchiostegal rays 7-9; dorsal fin long, separate or continuous with caudal fin; no adipose fin; anal fin long not confluent with caudal; caudal fin rounded; lateral line present. (p.)

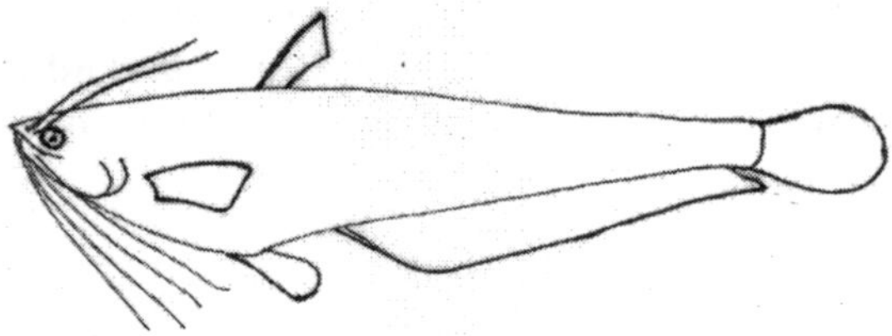

26. Heteropneustidae: Moderately elongate fishes with compressed body; posterior nostrils slit-like; nasal barbells present; branchiostegal rays seven; dorsal fin very short; adipose present or absent; anal fin long reaching or united with caudal; caudal fin rounded. (p.)

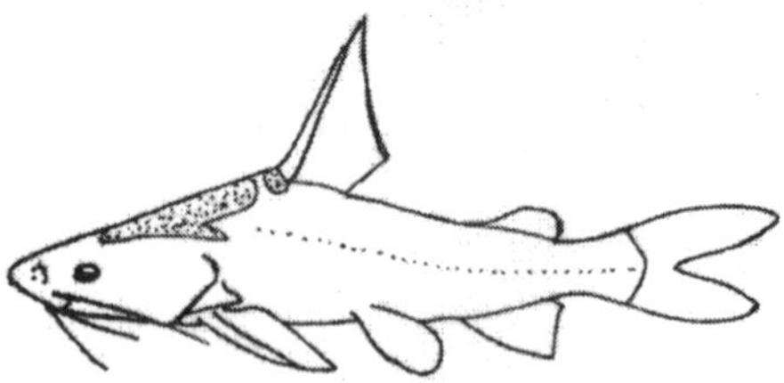

27. Ariidae: Body robust and compressed; posterior nostrils with valve; no nasal barbels; 2-6 barbels; branchiostegal rays 5-6; dorsal fin small with pungent spine; adipose fin present; anal not confluent with caudal; caudal fin forked. (p.)

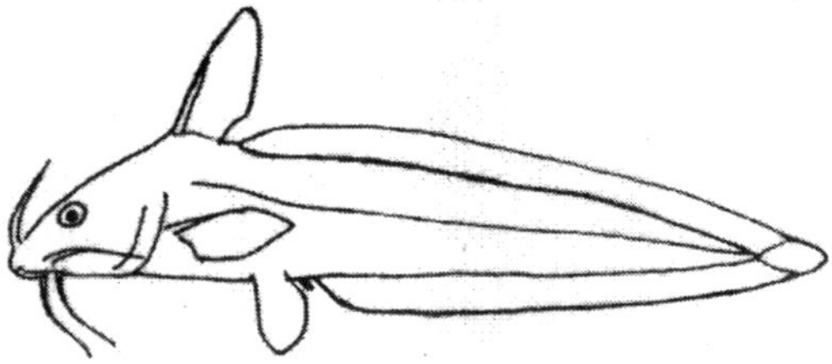

28. Plotosidae: Body elongate and compressed, no scales; posterior nostrils split-like; second dorsal, anal and caudal fins continuous; fins with sharp spines; no adipose fin; ventral fins present; snout with four pairs of fleshy barbels; tail bluntly rounded or tapering; lateral line conspicuous. (p.)

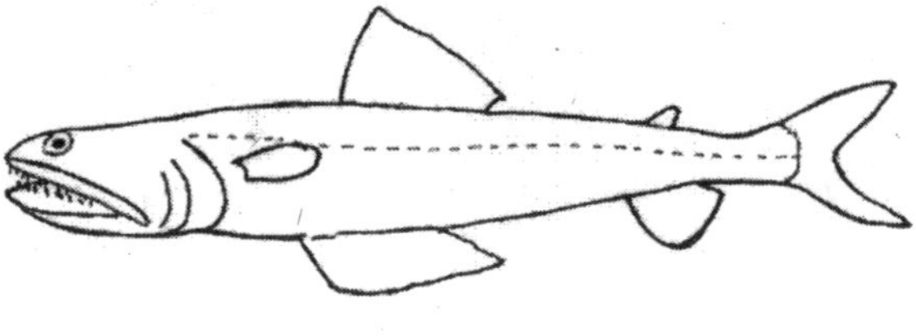

29. Synodontidae: Elongate and cylindrical; head distinctly depressed and lizard-like; mouth large with slender, pointed canine teeth; maxillary absent; body scales large; single dorsal fin; no fin spines; small adipose fin near tail present; most are brownish and blotched. (p.)

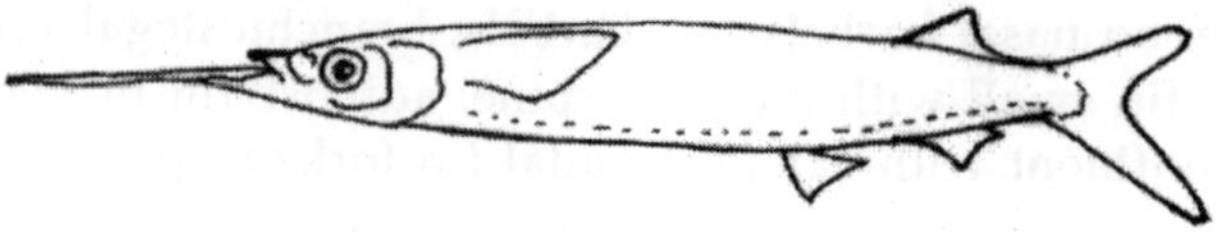

30. Hemiramphidae: Body elongate, laterally compressed or round; lower jaw long, upper jaw much shorter; nostrils in a pit anterior to eyes; dorsal and anal fins far back; no spines in fins; pectoral fins long; lateral line along ventral margin of body; tip of lower jaw bright red in many species. (p.)

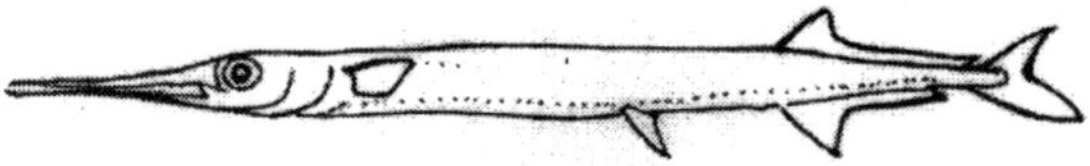

31. Belonidae: Body long, nearly rounded; jaws long and toothed, formed into a pointed beak; no spines in fins; ventral fins abdominal; dorsal and anal fins far behind the body; scales small; caudal fin truncate or emarginated. (p.)

32. Aplocheilidae: Body fusiform and compressed; upper jaw protrusible bordered by premaxilla only; no spines in fins; dorsal inserted on posterior third of body; ventral fin bases close together; scales large; lateral line chiefly on head, not on body. (p.)

33. Syngnathidae: Body slender, elongate and encased in bony rings; snout tubular; dorsal edge of trunk may or may not be continuous with tail; gill openings very small; single dorsalfin; pectorals present or absent; no ventral fins; tail prehensile or not; single dorsal fin; males have a brood pouch on abdomen or tail. (p.)

34. Synbranchidae: Body eel-like; scales small and confined to caudal region if present; teeth on palate and jaws; eyes small or degenerate, covered with dense skin; gill openings restricted to lower half of body; ventral, dorsal and anal fins vestigial in the form of median folds only; caudal fin absent or reduced; pectoral and ventral fins absent. (p.)

35. Scorpaenidae: Body robust; head large, spiny and ridged; eyes moderate to large; single dorsal fin and strongly notched; fns with strong, sharp spines; lateral line present; caudal fin rounded; pectoral fins wedge shaped. Small to medium with venomous spines. Most are camouflaged; some are conspicuous. (p.)

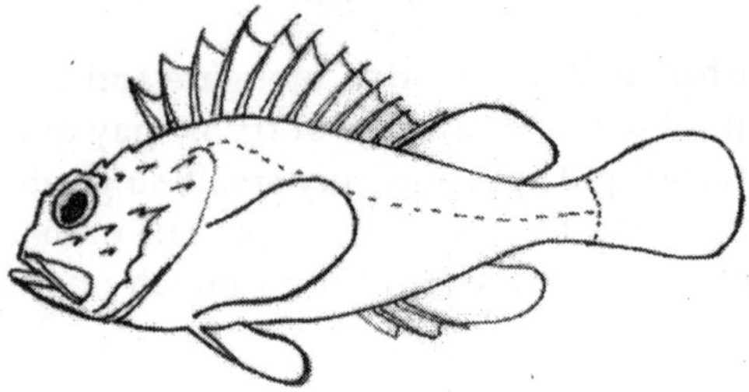

36. **Tetraorogidae**: Moderate-sized fishes; body covered with deeply embedded scales; dorsal fin originates on head before or above eye; sides of head and operculum with spines. Most are camouflaged. (p.   )

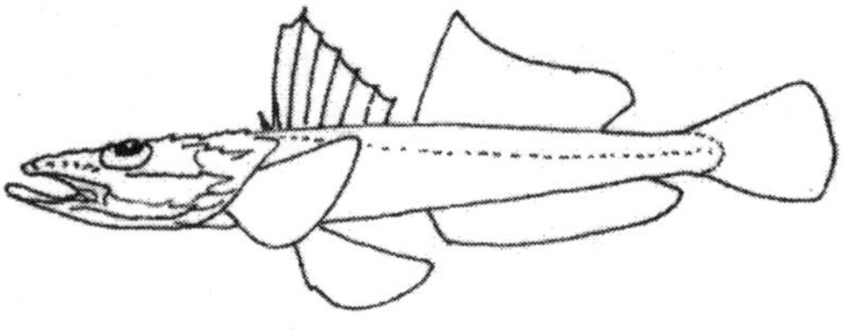

37. Platycephalidae: Body elongate and cylindrical; head depressed; mouth large, lower jaw longer; bony ridges of head with spines and serrations; two separated dorsal fins; ventral fins thoracic; gill openings wide. (p.   )

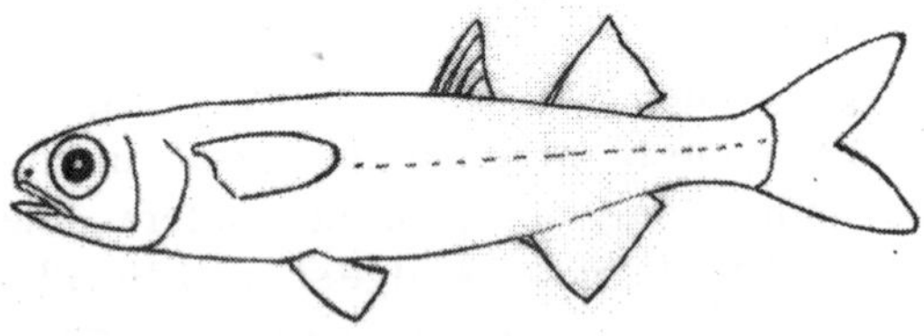

38. Atherinidae: Body slightly elongate, compressed; mouth small and terminal; body scales minute; pre-opercle with or without spines; two widely separated dorsal fins, widely separated; ventral fins abdominal in position; spines in fins; eyes large; no lateral line; ventral fins abdominal; silvery with mid-lateral stripe. (p.)

39. Centropomidae: Body elongate and slightly compressed; mouth small; teeth small; operculum with single well developed spine; preoperculum with spine at angle; scales present on cheek and operculum; soft dorsal and anal with scaly sheath; pored scales of lateral line continued on to caudal fin; caudal fin rounded. (p.)

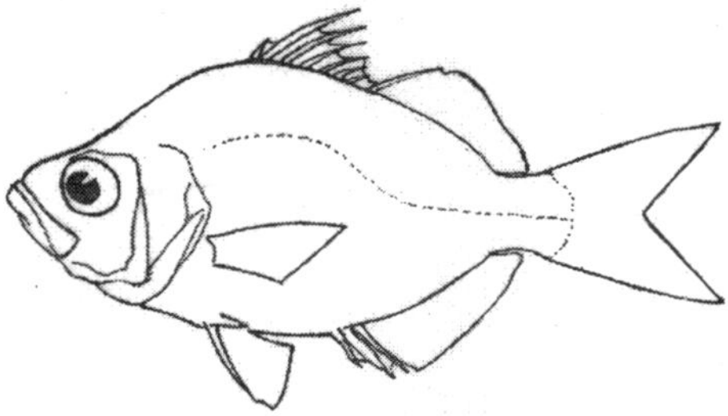

40. Ambassidae: Body laterally compressed and translucent; mouth fairly large; opercle with poorly developed spine; preoperculum double edged; two dorsal fins; ventral fin with one strong spine and axillary scale; caudal fin forked; lateral line complete, distinctly interrupted; dorsal and fins with scaly basal sheath. (p.)

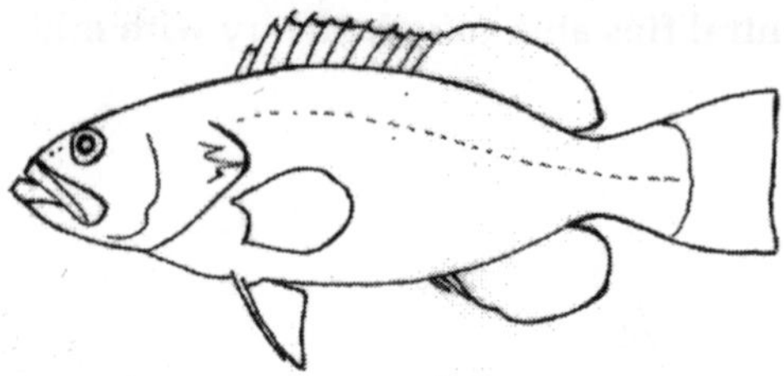

41. Serranidae: Body robust and elongate; scales small or embedded; mouth large with small canines in front of jaws; opercle with three flat spines or with small spines; single dorsal fin, dorsal fin divided or continuous but deeply notched at spinous portion; pectorals rounded; fins scaly; lateral line complete; caudal fin rounded or emarginated. (p.)

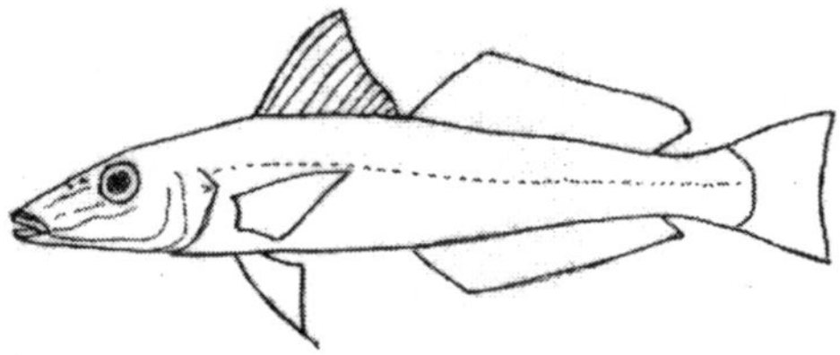

42. Teraponidae: Moderate sized fishes; preopercle serrate; opercle with two strong spines; dorsal fin continuous and deeply notched end of spinous part; no canines in jaws; lateral line complete; caudal fin forked; silvery with black bands. (p.)

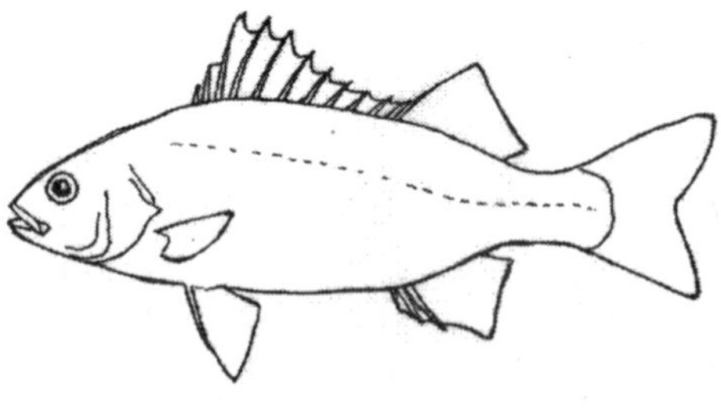

43. Sillaginidae: Body tapering and elongate; scales small and easily shed; operculum with sharp small spine; mouth small and terminal; two dorsal fins; swim bladder absent; caudal fin emarginated. (p.)

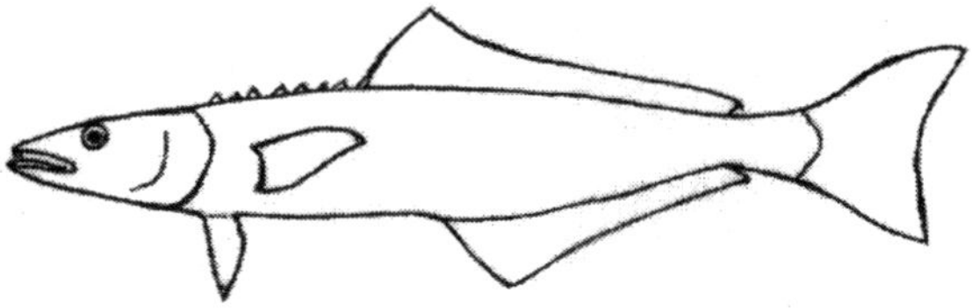

44. Rachycentridae: Body elongate and subcylindrical; head broad and depressed; eyes small, encircled in adipose eyelid; mouth large with fine teeth in jaws, on palate and tongue; spinous dorsal with free spines depressible in grove; scales minute and embedded in skin; caudal fin lunate. (p.)

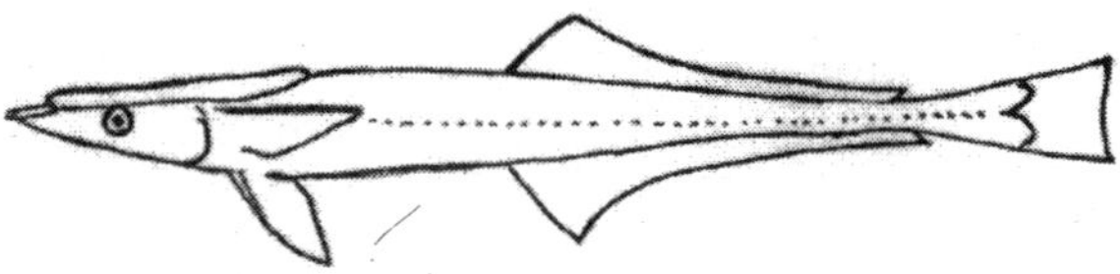

45. Echeneidae: Body elongate and slender; head flattened on top with lamellated adhesive disc; lower jaw slightly projecting; dorsal and anal bases long. (p.)

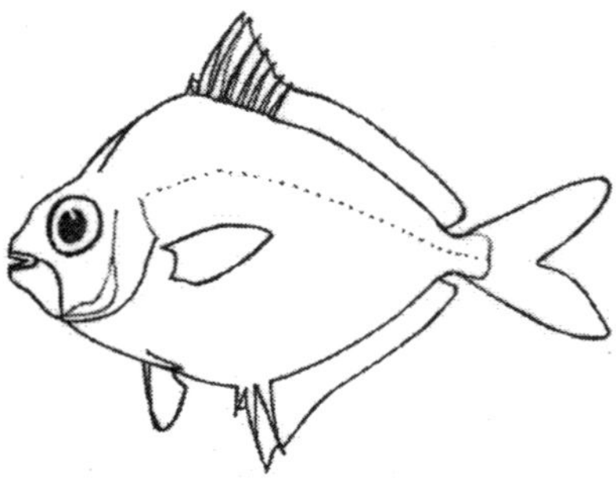

46. Carangidae: Small to large, silvery and very swift predators. Body streamlined, deep and compressed; tail base slender; opercle and preopercle smooth; scales small, cycloid; dorsal fin notched; fin spines embedded in groove; dorsal and anal finlets present or absent; caudal fin deeply forked; posterior part of lateral line scales modified into scutes, may be present or absent in some species. (p.)

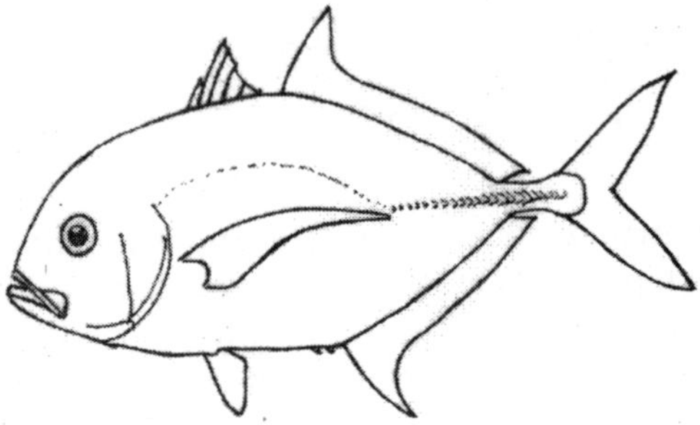

47. Leiognathidae: Body deep, very compressed and slimy; scales small; head naked, upper surface with bony ridges ending in a nuchal spine on nape; mouth small and extremely protrusile and form tube when extended; body silvery. (p.)

48. Lutjanidae: Small to large sized fishes; body slightly deep; jaws with sharp canines (absent in Aphareus); pre-maxilla with a broad based mid-lateral process; opercle with one or two distinct points posteriorly; single dorsal fin; fin spines well developed; dorsal and anal fins scaleless; scales ctenoid; caudal fin forked or truncate. (p.)

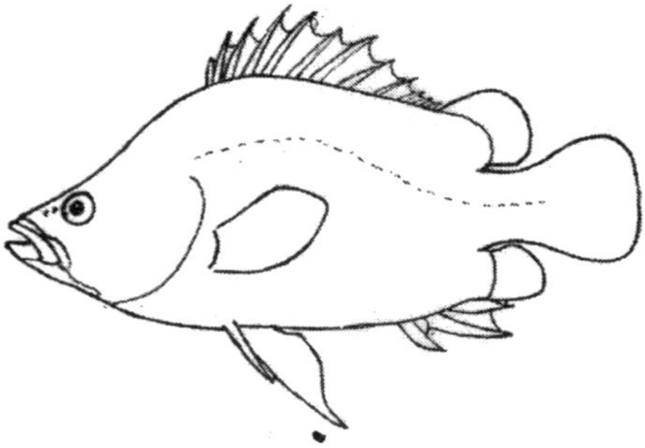

49. Datniodidae: Body deep and strongly compressed; upper jaw slightly longer; no supramaxilla; dorsal fin undivided; dorsal and anal fin spines strong; lateral line complete; scales small and ctenoid; caudalfin rouned. (p.)

50. Gerreidae: Body slender and compressed; mouth very protrusile; eyes large; scales ctenoid, large and deciduous; head scaly and upper surface smooth; single dorsal fin, slightly notched; dorsal and anal fins fold into a scaly sheath; pectoral fins long and pointed; caudal fin forked; silvery. (p.)

51. Haemulidae: Moderate sized fishes; body robust; mouth small, lips thick; no canines; head scaly; body scales moderate; preopercle serrate; opercle with indistinct point posteriorly; lateral line parallel to dorsal profile; 2nd anal spine stout and long; caudal fin emarginated. (p.)

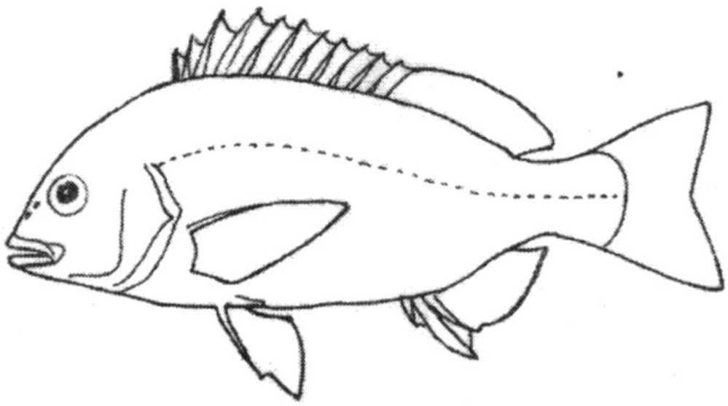

52. Sparidae: Body oblong, deep and compressed; head large with steep upper profile; mouth small; maxilla partly concealed under suborbital bone; snout and suborbital scaleless; no spines or serrations on preopercle; pectoral fins long and pointed; caudal fin emarginated or forked. (p.)

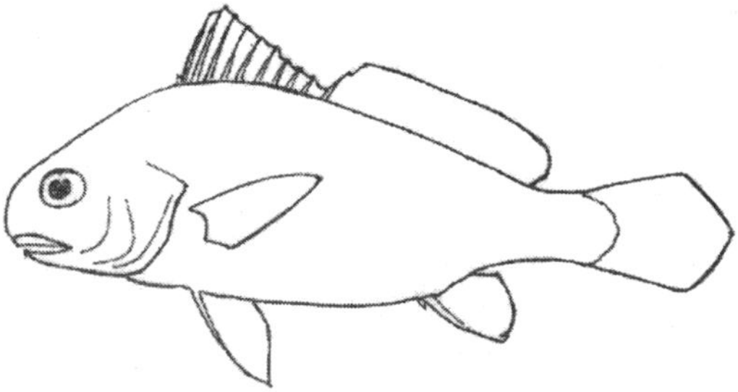

53. Sciaenidae: Body fairly elongate; head and snout scaled; snout rounded or bluntly pointed; mouth terminal or inferior; pores on snout and front of snout; barbells present or absent on chin; dorsal fin long and divided by notch; caudal fin rounded or truncate; lateral line extending to end of caudal fin; gas bladder present. (p.)

54. Monodactylidae: Body deep and compressed; maxilla scaly; mouth small; gill openings continue to under throat; single dorsal fin with long base; ventral fin rudimentary or absent; scales small, ctenoid and deciduous extending onto head and median fins; body usually silvery. (p.)

55. Drepanidae: Body very deep and strongly compressed; mouth small and protractile maxilla distally exposed; spinous dorsal can be differentiated by soft portion by a deep notch; pectoral fin long and falcate; ventral fins present; caudal fin rounded; lateral line strongly arched; body silvery. (p.)

56. Scatophagidae: Body deep, compressed and angular; mouth small; no teeth on reef of mouth; procumbent spine present before dorsal fin; scales extending on to dorsal and anal fins; lateral line complete. (p.)

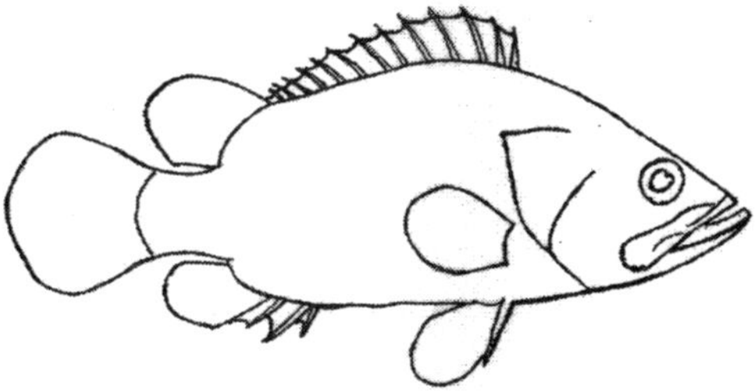

57. Nandidae: Body oblong and laterally compressed; mouth large and protrusible; dorsal fin large, inserted above pectoral fin base, spinous and soft dorsal continuous; pelvic fins thoracic; caudal fin rounded; lateral line; lateral line incomplete or absent. (p.)

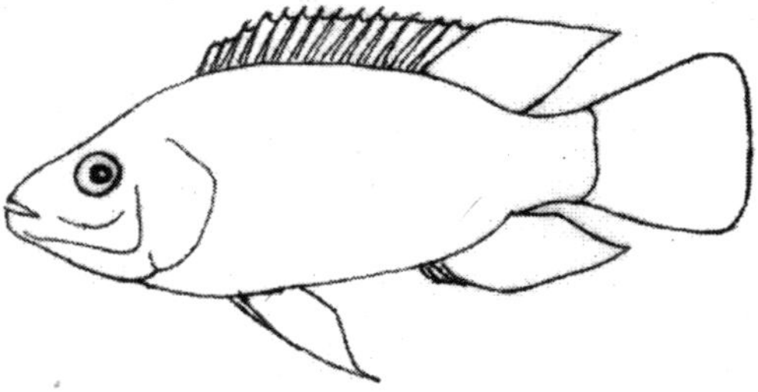

58. Cichlidae: Body moderately deep and compressed; single nostril on each side of snout; dorsal fin with more than 20 spines; anal fin with 3-16 spines; lateral line interrupted or abruptly ceasing; pseudobranchiae absent; air bladder present, large and simple. (p.)

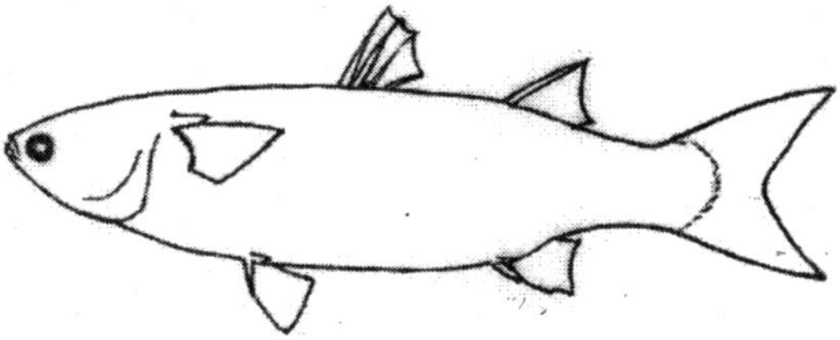

59. Mugilidae: Body slightly elongate; head depressed; mouth small; small teeth present or absent; pre-maxilla protractile; eyes often partly covered by adipose eyelid; scales large, ctenoid; head and body scaled; no lateral line; two separated dorsal fins, axillary scales may be present below 1st dorsal, above pectoral and pelvic fins; caudal fin forked or emarginated; silvery grey. (p.)

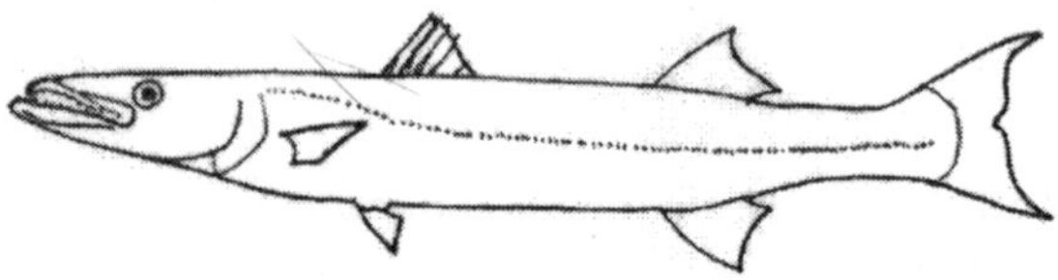

60. Sphyraenidae: Medium very large. Elongate and cylindrical anteriorly; snout pointed, lower jaw projecting; teeth large and sharp; lateral line present; two dorsal fins widely separated; scales small, cycloid; caudal fin forked; body silvery. (p.)

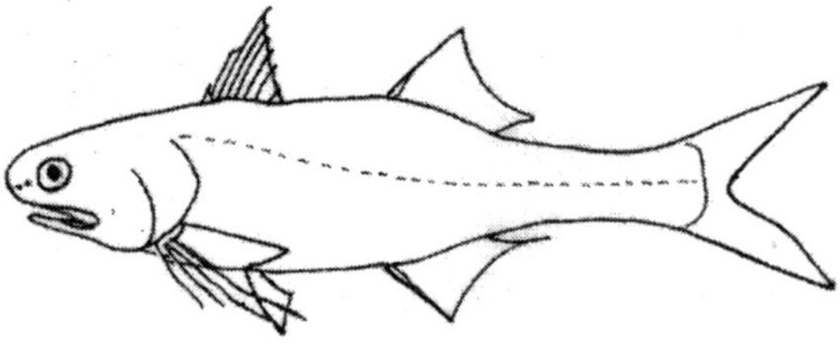

61. Polynemidae: Body moderately elongate; mouth subterminal; snout conical and prominent; two widely separated dorsal fins; lower part of pectoral fin with 3-15 free filamentous; lateral line continuing to end of caudal fin; caudal fin deeply forked. (p.)

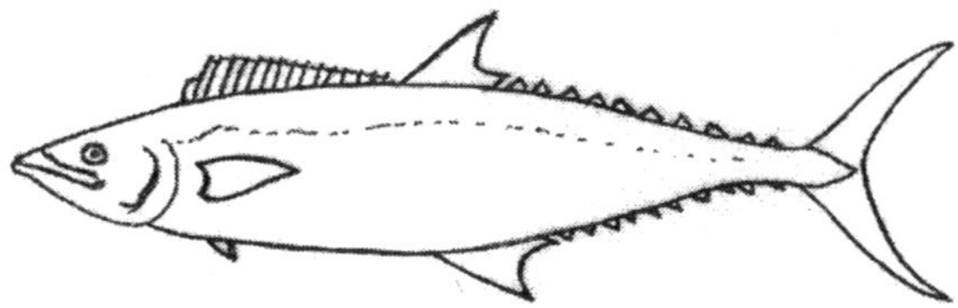

62. Siganidae: Small to moderate, ovate, compressed; caudal peduncle very narrow; mouth small, upper lip broader than lower; scales minute, cycloid, not visible; ventral fin with an inner and outer spine separated by three soft rays; caudal fin truncate to forked. (p.)

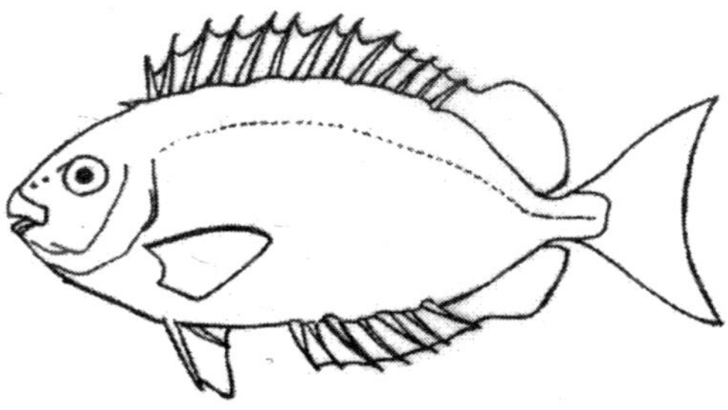

63. Scombridae: Body streamlined and caudal peduncle slender; two keels on each side of caudal peduncle; two dorsal fins, folded into grooves; finlets behind second dorsal and anal fins; scales very small and cycloid; caudal fin forked or lunate. (p.)

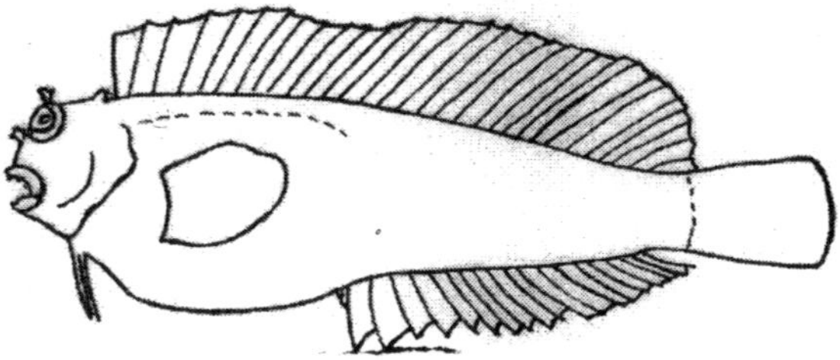

64. Blenniidae: Small to very small; elongated, scaleless; mouth inferior; head blunt with cirri, tentacles or fleshy crest; single dorsal fin, sometimes notched; fin spines flexible; ventral fins much reduced; caudal fin rounded; variable colour pattern with blotches and dashes or spots. (p.)

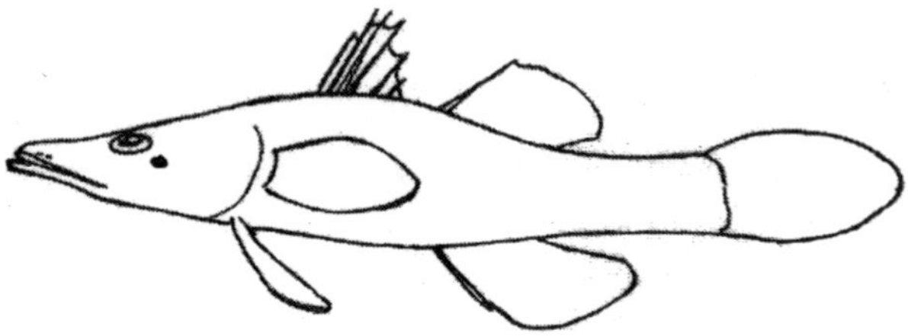

65. Eleotridae: Body oblong to elongate; lower jaw prominent; teeth small and in several rows; gill membranes joined to isthmus; two dorsal fins; anal fin inserted behind dorsal fin origin; ventral fins widely separated, not connected by membrane; body and head scaled; lateral line present; canals and pores present on head. (p.)

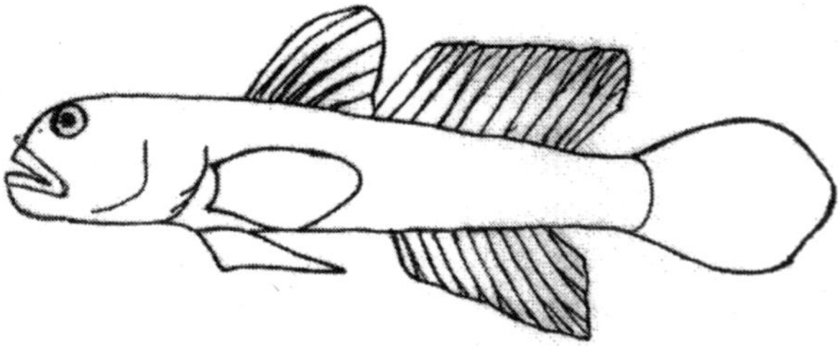

66. Gobiidae: Small to vary small fishes, slightly elongate fishes; head large and blunt with pores and canals or absent; mouth large; lateral line absent; scales cycloid, ctenoid or absent; two dorsal fins, some times single; fin spines flexible; ventral fins separate or united to form a disc; lateral line absent; caudal fin rounded. (p.)

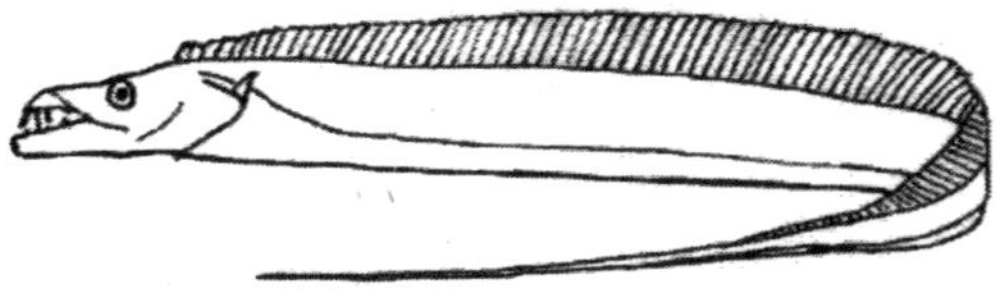

67. Trichiuridae: Body elongate, ribbon-like and strongly compressed; mouth large and lower jaw projecting; teeth strong, those on upper jaw fang-like; dorsal fin extremely long, its origin slightly above head; anal fin with short spinules, may not be visible; ventral fin reduced to a scale like spine and one rudimentary ray or absent; caudal fin small or tapering; body naked. (p.)

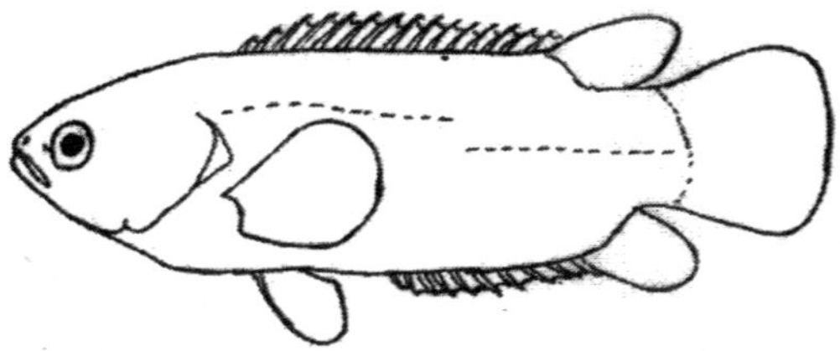

68. Anabantidae: Body oblong and posteriorly compressed; head broad; operculum serrated; jaws with small fixed conical teeth; no teeth on palatines; spinous and soft dorsal not separated; pectoral fins bluntly rounded; two lateral lines; scales on body ctenoid; caudal fin rounded. (p.)

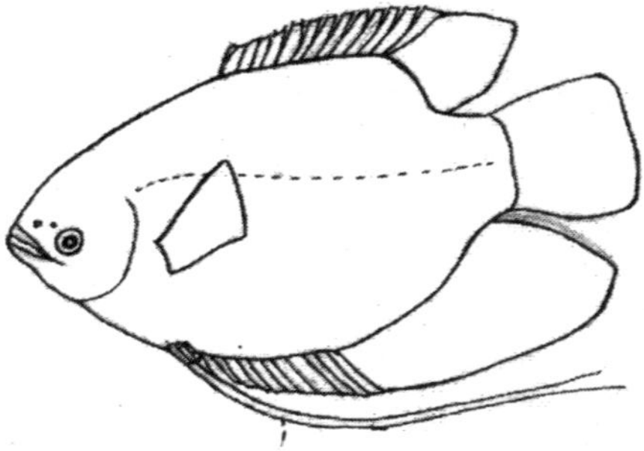

69. Osphronemidae: Body deep and strongly compressed; mouth small slightly protractile; opercular bones serrated; dorsal fin inserted far behind base of pectoral fins; anal fin base shorter than dorsal; lateral line complete. (p.)

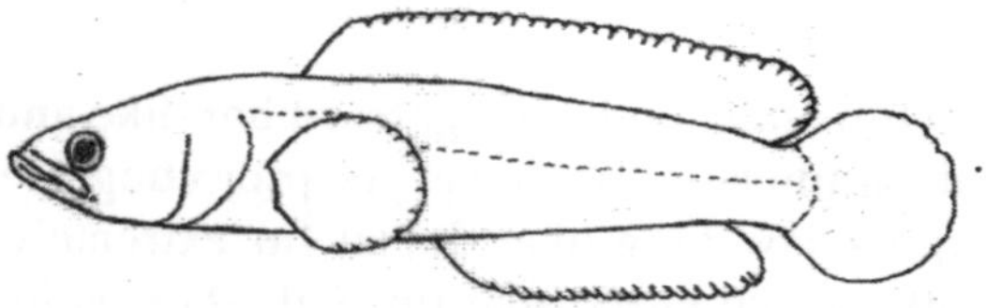

70. Channidae: Body elongate and cylindrical; head looks like a snake head; mouth large; jaws and palate toothed; scales on head larger than on body; caudal fin rounded; dorsal and anal fins entirely soft-rayed; air bladder elongate, extending to caudal peduncle. (p.)

71. Mastacembelidae: Body eel-like, compressed and elongate; covered with minute scales; snout long and supported by a cartilaginous rod and ending in a tubular nostrils; pre-operculum with or without spines; dorsal fin long with 7-40 detached, depressible spines; ventral fins absent; caudal fin short. (p.)

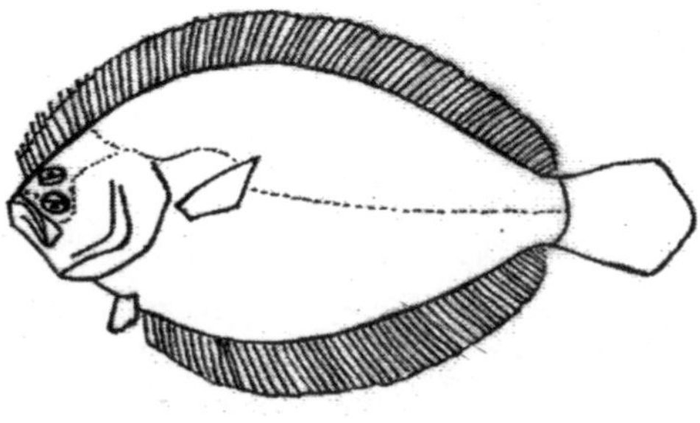

72. Paralichthyidae: Flat fishes; both eyes on left side of head; mouth protractile; asymmetrical; dorsal fin long its origin in front of lower eye; both paired fins present; single lateral line equally developed on both sides. (p.)

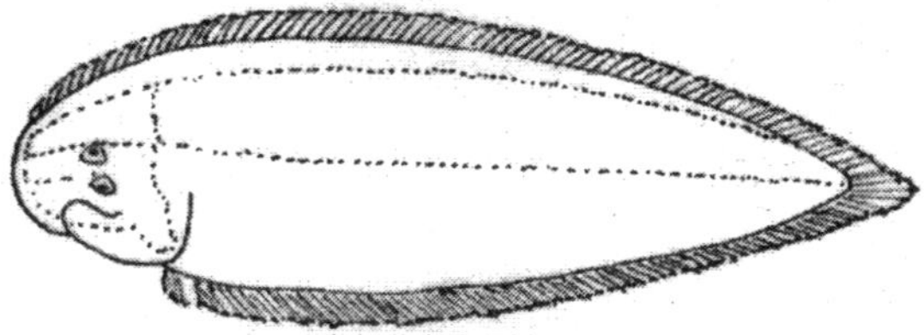

73. Cynoglosidae: Body flat and oval; eyes on left side of head; mouth small, curved and twisted to eye side; snout projects beyond mouth; no lateral line in many species; no pectoral fins; ventral fin present only on eye side; dorsal and caudal fins joined to caudal fin. Brownish with bars, blind side pale. (p.)

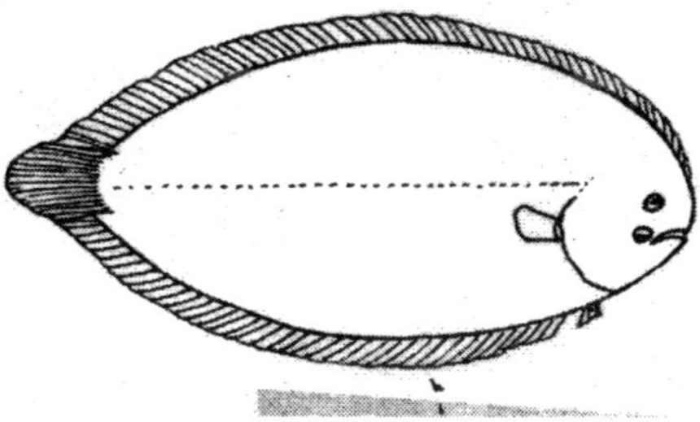

74. Soleidae: Body flat; eyes on right side of head; eyes very small; dorsal fin origin above or before eyes; no fin spines present; pectoral fins present or absent. (p.)

75. Triacanthidae: Small fishes, body strongly compressed; caudal peduncle slender; scales very small and rough; two separate dorsal fins, 1st dorsal spine long and strong; no spines in anal fin; ventral fin reduced to a single stout spine; caudal fin forked. (p.)

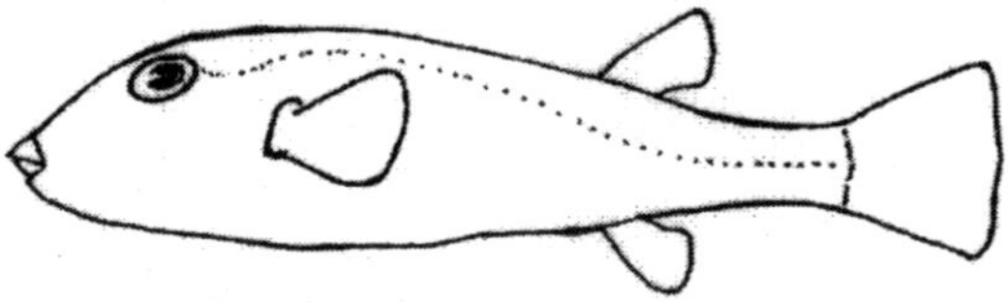

76. Tetraodontidae: Small to medium-sized; body slightly elongate and heavy; skin tough and naked or with spines or prickles; dental plates beak-like with median suture; no spines in fins; dorsal and anal fins posterior in position; no ventral fins; able to inflate body swelling water or air. (p.).

Systematic Account

Class: Elasmobranchii

Order: Carcharhiniformes

Family: **CARCHARHINIDAE**

Key to the species of Family Carcharhinidae

1(a) Teeth with smooth edges; all oblique and without swollen bases ..... *Scoliodon laticaudus*

1(b) Teeth small, some or all serrated both on their bases and on their cusps 2

2(a) Upper anterior teeth with broadly triangular cups, not well delimited from tooth bases; snout very short, posterior portion of caudal rather dark .... *Glyphis gangeticus*

2(b) Upper anterior teeth narrow cups, well delimited from bases; colouration not as in 2a .... 3 (*Carcharhinus*)

3(a) Snout very short and bluntly rounded ; body lemon-brown, all fins distinctly black tipped; entire edge of caudal fin margin black .... *C. melanopterus*

3(b) Snout long; body grey, whitish ventrally; pelvic fin tips black ...... *C. limbatus*

1. *Carcharhinus limbatus* (Valenciennes, 1839)
Black-tip shark

Diagnostic features: Body fusiform and moderately slender; snout long, its tip narrowly rounded; teeth in 14 to 16 rows; first dorsal fin with narrowly rounded apex; pectoral fins falcate; no dermal ridge between dorsal fins. Tip of dorsals, anal, pectorals and lower lobe of caudal fin dusky in juveniles, but fade with growth. Body grey or ashy blue on back, belly white; pelvic fin tips black. Attains 200 to 240 cm.

Habitat: Pelagic; Oceanic but frequently enter Chilika Lake in search of food. Feed on fish and crustaceans. Not aggressive.

Distribution: Widely distributed in all tropical Oceans.

Remarks: Caught with hook & line, gill nets. The liver is reported to be high potency. Commercially important shark.

2. *Carcharhinus melanopterus* (Quoy & Gaimard, 1824)
Black-tip Reef shark

Diagnostic features: Body almost cylindrical; snout moderately short and rounded; labial folds short; 11 to 13 rows of teeth in upper jaw; inter-dorsal ridge absent; gill openings relatively short; first dorsal fin falcate, its origin slightly posterior to inner rear corner of pectoral fin; second dorsal fin origin over the origin of anal fin; upper caudal fin lobe slightly longer. Body lemon-brown above, white below; all fins distinctly black tipped, caudal fin with distinct wide black margin along its entire edge.

Habitat: Amphidromous. Inhabits shallow coastal waters, on coral reefs and in the intertidal zone, also found in mangrove areas, moving in and out with the tide and even in fresh water. Frequently enter Chilika Lake in search of food. Common shark. Feeds on small fish, crustaceans, cephalopods and other mollusks. Usually harmless, can be aggressive. Attains about 200 cm or above.

Distribution: Widespread in Indo-West and Central Pacific.

Remarks: Caught with hook & line, gill nets. Commercially important fish. Liver of fish possess large amount of oil.

3. *Glyphis gangeticus* (Muller & Henle, 1839)
Ganges Shark

Diagnostic features: Body moderately stout; snout short, its length equal to distance between nostrils and less than mouth width; teeth in upper jaw triangular; tail erect and strongly hooked; total teeth 27-30; upper precaudal pit is shallow; longitudinal depression on the dorsal surface of caudal peduncle. Body grey superiorly, white beneath; posterior portion of caudal rather dark.

Habitat: Demersal; amphidromous. Found in shallow coastal waters, rivers and estuaries. The most common shark of the Chilika Lake. Feed on small fish and crustaceans. Attains 200 cm Total Length.

Distribution: India, Pakistan, also reported from Taiwan.

Remarks: Caught with hook and line and gillnets. Subsistence fisheries. Good food fish.

4. *Scoliodon laticaudus* (Muller & Henle, 1839)

Spadenose shark

Diagnostic features: Body slender and fusiform; snout long and depressed; upper labial furrow poorly developed; no interdorsal ridge; lower precaudal pit indistinct. Body pale grayish above, sides dull white; fins darker than body colour; no conspicuous markings on body.

Habitat: Demersal. Found on rocky substrates of coastal waters and lower reaches of rivers. Frequently encountered in Chilika Lake. Forms large schools. Feed on fish and small crustaceans and cuttlefish. Attains 70 to 100 cm Total Length..

Distribution: Widely distributed in Indo-West Pacific region.

Remarks: Constitutes a good fishery in the lake area. Caught

with hook and line and gillnets. Consumed fresh; processed into fishmeal and used as bait for other sharks and bony fishes.

Family: SPHYRNIDAE

Eusphyra blochii (Cuvier, 1817)

Arrow-headed hammerhead

Diagnostic features: Body elongate and laterally compressed; head hammer-shaped and extremely wide; eyes and nostrils are widely separated; first dorsal fin moderately large and erect, the outer posterior margin concave; free rear tip of second dorsal nearly reaching caudal fin; base of second dorsal fin longer than second dorsal fin. Body brownish grey above, shading to white below.

Habitat: Inhabits shallow coastal areas. Enters estuaries and occasionally brackish lagoons. Feeds on small fishes and squids. Viviparous. Attains about 150-180 cm Total Length.

Distribution: Indo-West Pacific.

Remarks: Not aggressive to man unless provoked. Occasionally caught in Chilika Lake. Consumed fresh or salt-dried; liver for oil extraction.

Order: Rajiiformes

Family: **PRISTIDAE**

5. ***Pristis pectinata*** (Latham, 1794)
Smalltooth Sawfish

Diagnostic features: Body elongate, robust and moderately depressed; snout prolonged as a flat firm blade, narrowing evenly towards its tip with 24 to 34 pairs of rostral teeth, the length of saw is 8.0 to 9.0 times in its total length; first dorsal fin large and erect, its origin above pelvic fin origin. Body uniform olive-green above, dirty cream below; disc edges, pectoral and ventral edges buff; hind body keels and caudal lobe. Attains 7.0 to 7.5 m and is the largest of the sawfish.

Habitat: Demersal. Shallow coastal waters, estuaries and lagoons and often enters freshwater in the larger rivers.

Distribution: Indo-West Pacific, Atlantic and Mediterranean.

Remarks: Flesh is good eating. Occasionally entangle in gill nets.

6. Family: **DASYATIDAE**

Key to the species of Family Dasyatidae

1(a) Cutaneous fold on ventral surface of tail only, extends more than halfway to it tip, and is very broad .... *Pastinachus sephen*

1(b) No membranous fold along tail, if present it is very low .... 2 (*Himantura*)

2(a) Cutaneous fold on tail low and on both its upper and lower surfaces; tail short about as long as length of disc, with one caudal spine .... *H. imbricate*

2(b) No cutaneous folds on tail 3

3(a) Two buccal processes on floor of mouth; disc subcircular; 1 or 2 large serrated spines on tail; no large tubercle in center of disc; all tubercles are of uniform size and small .... *H. walga*

3(b) Four buccal processes on floor of mouth; disc rhomboidal; 1 to 3 spines on tail; large median white tubercle in central of disc.................................. *H. uarnak*

7. *Himantura imbricata* (Bloch & Schneider, 1801)

Schnedier's Scaly Stingray

Diagnostic features: Disc as broad as long, snout produced and pointed; mouth undulated with two buccal processes on floor of mouth; spiracles as large as eyes and close behind tail whip-like, as long as disc length, single caudal spine with low longitudinal cutaneous folds on its upper and lower surfaces; small tubercles on nape and back with a row of conical spines on shoulder and back. Dorsal side reddish with yellow spots and ventral whitish. Attains 3.0 to 3.5 m width.

Habitat: Demersal. Shallow coastal waters, estuaries and off river mouths. Occasionally found in Chilika Lake.

Distribution: Wide spread in Indo-West Pacific, from Indian coasts to East Indies and Philippines.

Remarks: Salt dried or consumed fresh. Occasionally entangled in nets.

8. *Himantura uarnak* (Forsskal, 1775)

Hony-comb stingray

Diagnostic features: Disc rhomboidal, slightly wider than long; tail longer than disc length; surface of the disc almost naked; skin smooth, only mid-dorsal row of denticles extending on to tail base, a large median white tubercle in centre of disc; mouth long, undulated, with transverse series of four fleshy papillae on floor of mouth; snout angular with a sharp point; tail 2.6 to 3.0 times longer than disc, no cutaneous folds. Disc brown to black with white to yellow lines forming a reticulated pattern, under side of the disc white. Tail striped brown and white in juveniles.

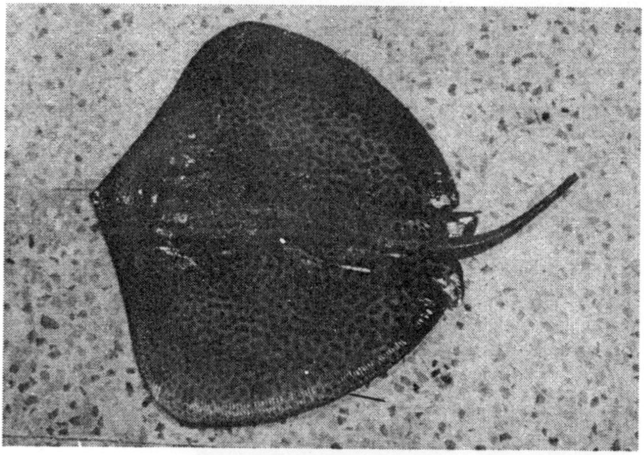

Habitat: Demersal. Found on sandy bottoms near shallow to 25m depth. Feed on small bivalves, crustaceans and worms. Ovoviviparous. Stings cause fatal wounds. Attains 5 m or above.

Distribution: Indo-West Pacific.

Remarks: Salt dried or consumed fresh. Occasionally entangled in fish nets.

9. *Himantura walga* (Muller & Henle, 1841)

Scaly Stingray

Diagnostic features: Disc sub-circular, as broad as long; spiracles nearly equal to eyes, close behind it; eye diameter 3.3

in inter-orbital width; mouth undulated with two buccal processes on floor of mouth; tail whip like, slightly longer than disc length, no cutaneous folds, with one or two large serrate spines; small tubercle on interorbital, interspiracle and mid-dorsal surface of disc; a series of small spines between root of tail and caudal spine. Dull grey or brown above, whitish below.

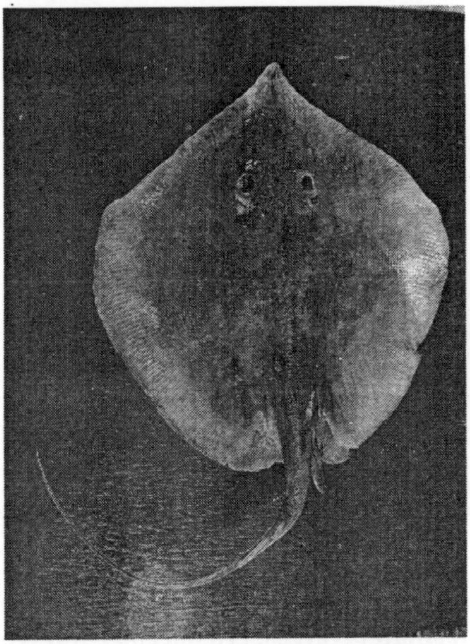

Habitat: Demersal. Shallow coastal areas. Enter estuaries and lakes.

Distribution: Red Sea to China and East Indies.

Remarks: Salt dried or consumed fresh. Occasionally entangled in fish nets.

10. *Pastinachus sephen* (Forsskal, 1775)

Feathertail Stingray

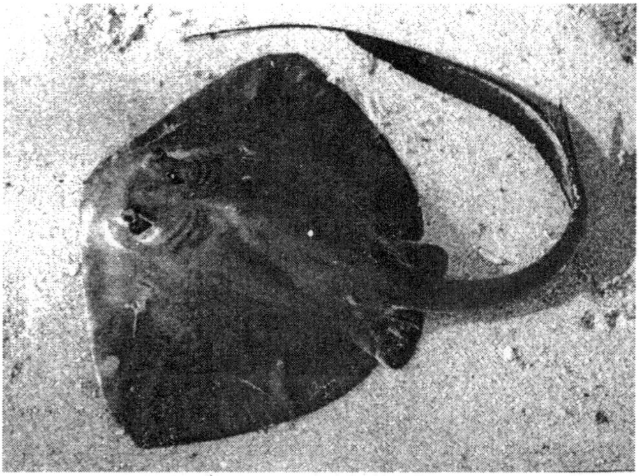

Diagnostic features: Disc somewhat quadrangular; mouth undulated with four papillae; tail depressed with broad feather-like lower cutaneous fold which extends more than half way to its tip; a strong serrated spine on second quarter of the tail; dorsal surface of the disc granular with three flattened tubercles arranged in a vertical row centrally. Disc dark-grey, gradually paler towards sides; ventral side white; caudal fold and filamentous part of tail black.

Habitat: Found in shallow sandy coastal and brakish areas. Feed on crustaceans, molluscs, worms and small fish. Attains over 200 cm. Ovoviviparous. Sting causes dangerous wounds.

Distribution: Widespread in Indo-Pacific region.

Remarks: Salt dried or consumed fresh. Frequently entangle in fishing nets.

Family: **MYLIOBATIDAE**

Key to the species of Family Myliobatidae

1(a) Single series of large teeth in each jaw; caudal spines present; skin smooth .... 2 (*Aetobatus*)

1(b) Three series of teeth in each jaw; no caudal spines; skin tuberculated in adults; 3-5 blue cross bands on disc (disappear with age) .... *Aetomylaeus nichofii*

2(a) Disc with solid white spots or white circular rings .... *A. anrinari*

2(b) Disc dark brown, no spots or rings .... *A. flagellum*

11. Aetobatus flagellum (Bloch & Schneider,1801)

Longheaded eagle ray

Diagnostic features: Disc strongly angular; a fleshy sub-orbital lobe or 'snout' projecting anteriorly from lower surface of the head; one row of tooth plates in each jaw; tail cylindrical, whip-like and long. Disc brownish, ventral side whitish.

Habitat: Benthopelagic. Inhabits inshore waters. Often found in brackish waters. Ovoviviparous. Attains 72.0 cm WD, weight: 13.9 kg.

Distribution: Indo-West Pacific: Red Sea, India, East Indies, and southern China. Possibly in the eastern Atlantic.

Remarks: Minor commercial value. Categorised as endangered.

12. *Aetobatus narinari* (Euphrasen, 1790)

Spotted Eagleray

Diagnostic features: Disc strongly angular; a fleshy sub-orbital lobe or 'snout' projecting anteriorly from lower surface of the head; one row of tooth plates in each jaw; nasal curtain deeply notched; tail cylindrical and whip-like; dorsal fin situated posterior to base of pelvic fins; two serrated spines behind dorsal fin; tip of pectoral fins acutely pointed and falcate; skin smooth. Disc bluish-black with numerous scattered white spots or rings, ventral surface white; tail black.

Habitat: Benthopelagic. Found around inshore reef areas, common, feed on bivalves, crustaceans and worms. Ovoviviparous. Attains up to 400 cm. Extremely agile and powerful fish often leap high into the air.

Distribution: Atlantic, Indian and Pacific Oceans.

Remarks: Salt dried or consumed fresh. Frequently entangle in fishing nets.

13. *Aetomylaeus nichofii* (Bloch & Schneider,1801)

Nichof's Eagleray

Diagnostic features: The disc twice as long; subrostral fin unilobed; eye 3.5 in snout length; mouth straight without any buccal processes on floor of mouth; spiracles large, about twice eye diameter; single dorsal fin at base of tail; tail long, whip-like, no caudal spine; skin finely tuberculated, but smooth in young. Body dark brown dorsally, whitish ventrally; anterior part of body with 3 to 5 blue cross bands on disc, may disappear with age; posterior part with large close set round greyish blotches.

Habitat: Shallow coastal areas. Occasionally enter estuaries and lakes. Attains 300 cm wide.

Distribution: Widespread in Indo-West Pacific region.

Remarks: Salt dried or consumed fresh. Uncommon in Chilika Lake.

Family: **RHYNCHOBATIDAE**

14. *Rhinchobatus djeddensis* (Forsskal, 1775)

White-spotted Guitarfish

Diagnostic features: Disc larger than wide; snout long and pointed; first dorsal fin triangular, situated above base of pelvic fins; eyes larger and immediately anterior to spiracles;

rows of small thorns or denticles over eyes and spiracles, on back and scapular region. Body olive-grey above with numerous white spots extending up to second dorsal fin; dark spots on inter-orbital; pectoral region with a pair of prominent black spots ringed with small white spots, belly white. Juveniles have a conspicuous black blotch on tip of snout.

Habitat: Demersal. Found in coastal waters. Attains 140-160 cm Total Length.

Distribution: Widespread in Indo-West Pacific region.

Remarks: Frequently entangle in fishing nets. Flesh is tasty; salt dried or consumed fresh; liver oil is much esteemed.

Class: Elasmobranchii

Order: Elopiformes

Family: **ELOPIDAE**

15. Elops machnata (Forsskal, 1775)

Ladyfish

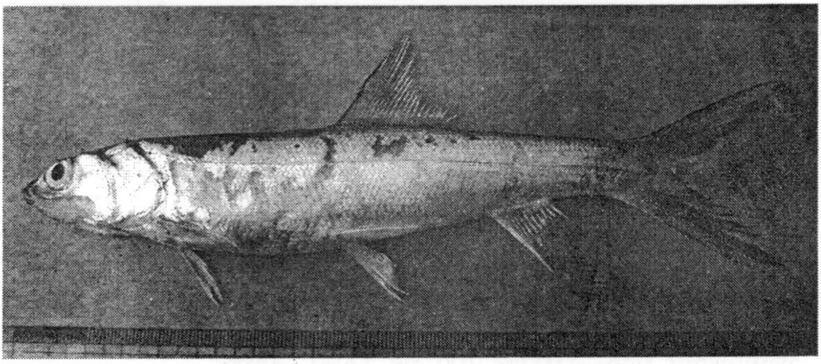

Diagnostic features: D.21-25; A.14-17; P.17-18; V.12-16. Body elongate, oval in cross section; mouth terminal; lower jaw projecting slightly; teeth on jaws villiform; anal fin short, its origin well behind dorsal fin base; pelvic fins a little infront of dorsal fin origin. Body black-blue above, slivery on the flanks while the fins are dusky yellow.

Habitat: Pelagic, found in coastal waters and also enters lagoons and estuaries. It forages for food just after dark and feeds on small fishes and shrimps. Attains 100 cm Total length.

Distribution: Widely distributed in Indo-West Pacific.

Remarks: Flesh is insipid and fully of bones. Consumed fresh.

Family: **MEGALOPIDAE**

16. Megalops cyprnoides (Broussonet, 1782)

Oxeye Tarpoon

Diagnostic features: D. 18-20; A. 26-28; P.15-16 V.10-11; Li. 38-40. Body fusiform; mouth superior; lower jaw projecting; a median gular bone under side of chin; upper jaw extending to hind border of eye: last dorsal ray elongated and filamentous. Body blue-green above, flanks silvery.

Habitat: Pelagoc. Found in creeks, lakes, estuaries and coastal waters. Feed on small fishes and crustaceans. Fast growing carnivorous fish. Attains 100 cm Total length.

Distribution: Wide spread in Indo-West Pacific, from east coast of Africa to China Sea.

Remarks: Flesh is not very esteemed. Caught in large quantities from Chilika Lake.

Order: Anguilliformes

Family: **ANGUILLIDAE**

Key to the species of Family Anguilldae

1(a) Dorsal fin originating nearly above anus; no edentulous groove in teeth bands ... ... *Anguilla bicolor*

1(b) Dorsal fin originating about mid-way between gill opening and anal fin origin; edentulous groove in teeth bands .... *A. bengalensis*

*17. **Anguilla bengalensis*** (Gray & Hardwicke, 1834)

Long-finned Eel

Diagnostic features: Body snake-like, cylindrical anteriorly; mouth slightly oblique, extending beyond eye level; dorsal fin origin midway between gill opening and anal fin origin; edentulous groove in teeth bands; pectoral fins well developed; median fins continuous around tail. Body brownish, mottled with dark brown; belly yellowish.

Habitat: Demersal. A freshwater eel but enters lagoons, creeks, estuaries and coastal waters. Attains 100 to 120 cm Total Length.

Distribution: Pakistan to Burma and East Indies.

Remarks: Fairly abundant in Chilika Lake and common commercial eel. Consumed fresh.

*18. **Anguilla bicolor bicolor*** MacClelland,1844

Short-finned Eel

Diagnostic features: Body snake-like and cylindrical; dorsal fin originating nearly above anus; jaws and vomer with braod bands of closely packed teeth, no edentulous grooves; pectoral fins welldeveloped, median fins continuous around tail. Body dark bluish-brown above, lighter below.

Habitat: Demersal. A freshwater eel but enters lagoons, creeks, estuaries and coastal waters. Attains 100cm Total Length.

Distribution: East coast of Africa to Indian coasts.

Remarks: Fairly abundant in Chilika Lake and common commercial eel. Consumed fresh.

Family: MURAENIDAE

19. *Strophidon sathete* (Hamilton, 1822)

Slender giant moray

Diagnostic features: Body moderately elongate, cylindrical in front, compressed along tail; eyes small; teeth small, biserial, inner series enlarged; head not obviously distinct from trunk; mouth very large, extending to beyond eye; biserial sharp teeth on jaws; dorsal fin inserted on head before gill-opening; no scales on body. Body brownish grey above, lighter below.

Habitat: Demersal. Inhabits freshwater, brackish and marine muddy bottoms; amphidromous. Feed mainly on a variety of small fishes and crustaceans. Longest known eel, attains 360 cm Total Length.

Distribution: Indo-West Pacific

Remarks: Marketed fresh and consumed locally.

Family: OPHICHTHIDAE

Key to the species of Family Ophichthidae

1(a) Dorsal fin origin above middle of pectoral fins; head 9.0, depth 28.0 in total length; edge of dorsal fin black .... *Pisodonophis cancrivorus*

1(b) Dorsal fin origin behind end of pectoral fin; head 9.0-12.0, depth 30.0-36.0 in total length; edge of dorsal fin not black .... *P. boro*

20. *Pisodonophis boro* (Hamilton, 1822)

Estuarine Snake-eel

Diagnostic features: Body slender and snake-like; head 9-12; depth 30-36; teeth multiserial and molariform; dorsal fin origin far behind pectoral fin origin. Body olive brown above, lighter below.

Habitat: Demersal. Found in estuaries, backwaters and lagoons. Attains 100 cm Total Length.

Distribution: Indo-Pacific.

Remarks: Considered as trash fish.

21. *Pisodonophis cancrivorus* (Richardson, 1848)

Longfin Snake-eel

Diagnostic features: Body slender and snake-like; head 9; depth 28; teeth multiserial and molariform; dorsal fin origin above base or middle of pectoral fin. Body olive above, lighter below; edge of dorsal fin black.

Habitat: Demersal. Found in shallow coastal waters, estuaries, backwaters and lagoons. Attains 70 cm Total Length.

Distribution: Indo-West Pacific.

Remarks: Considered as trash fish.

Family: **MURAENESOCIDAE**

Key to the species of Family Muraenesocidae

1(a) Vomerine teeth large, rounded, very acute; each with only minute cups distally; the teeth widely separated; principal teeth on lower jaw of same form, directed almost horizontally outwards; head and body golden yellow .... *Congresox talabonoides*

1(b) Vomerine teeth large, compressed, each with sharp anterior and posterior edges and prominent basal cups; teeth in contact or slightly separated; principal teeth on lower jaw of some from erect or turned slightly inwards; body colour not as in 1a .... 2 (*Muraenesox*)

2(a) Lateral line pores before anus 33-39; eye diameter 3 times snout length; snout long; head and body greenish .... *Muraenesox bagio*

2(b) Lateral line pores before anus 40-47; eye diameter 2.0 to 2.5 in snout length; head and body dull white .... *M. cinereus*

22. *Congresox talabonoides* (Bleeker, 1853)

India Pike-conger

Diagnostic features: Eel like fish, body cylindrical, compressed along tail; mouth large, extends beyond eye; teeth in upper jaw 3 rows, lower jaw in 4 rows; fang-like teeth in front of lower jaw and on vomer; median canines on vomer conical; pectoral fins well developed, its length 4 times in head lemgth; 57-68 dorsal rays before vertical to anus; lateral line pores 35 to 40 before anus. Head and body golden yellow; dorsal anal fins with dusky border.

Habitat: Demersal. Inhabits soft shallow coastal bottoms, also enter estuaries, lagoons and lakes. Attains over 250 cm.

Distribution: Indo-West Pacific, from Red Sea to China.

Remarks: Important food fish; caught by bag-nets, long-lines and trawl nets.

23. *Muraenesox cinereus* (Forsskal, 1775)

Daggertooth pike conger

Diagnostic features: Head broader, interorbital about 8 times in head; interorbital width 8.2 in head; snout long; eye diameter 2-2.5 times in snout length; posterior nostrils much closer to eyes than to anterior nostrils; mouth very large; teeth generally large and conspicuous; lateral-line pores before anus 44-47; dorsal rays before anus 66-78.

Habitat: Demersal. Inhabits soft bottoms; oceanodromous; freshwater; brackish and marine. Feeds on small bottom fishes and crustaceans. Attains 220 cm Total Length.

Distribution: Indo-West Pacific.

Remarks: Marketed mainly fresh. Also used as bait for shark fishing. Caught by bag nets and sceine nets. Culturable fish.

24. *Muraenesox bagio* (Hamilton, 1822)

Pike conger-eel

Diagnostic features: Body snake-like and slightly robust; mouth extends beyond eye; teeth large, those in the middle of vomer very prominent, blade like, with anterior and posterior basal cups; 47-59 dorsal rays before a vertical at anus, 47-59 lateral line pores before anus; head 5.5 to 6.0; depth 16-22 in total length; interorbital width 9-11 in head. Body grayish-brown, lighter below; median fins edged with black.

Habitat: Demersal. Found in shallow coastal waters, estuaries, backwaters and lagoons. Attains 170 cm Total Length. Caught by hook and line and shoreseins.

Distribution: Wide spread in Indo-Pacific.

Remarks: Local people consume. Fairly common in Chilika Lake.

Order: Osteoglossiformes

Family: **NOTOPTERIDAE**

25. *Notopterus notopterus* (Pallas, 1769)

Bronze

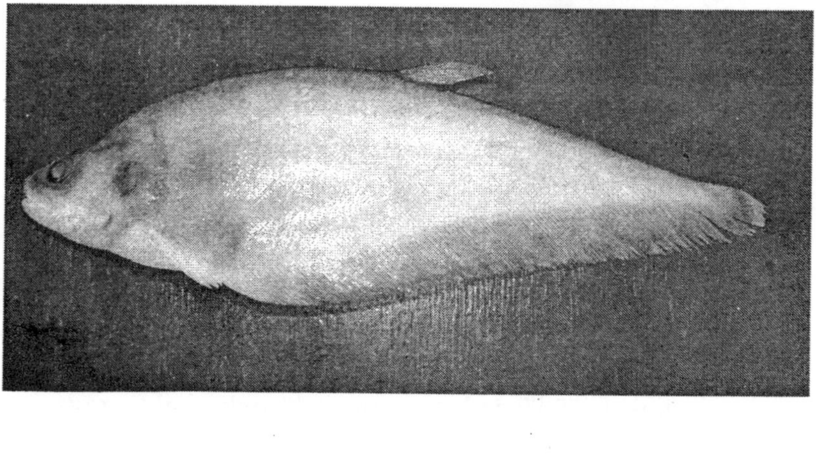

Diagnostic features: D.8-10; A.100-135; P.17. Body oblong and compressed; abdomen with 25-28 pre-pelvic double serrations; craniodorsal profile almost straight head compressed; preopercular scale rows six to eight; dorsal fin small and tuft-like; anal fin ribbon-like and confluent with cauidal; ventral finsrudimentary; caudal fin small. Body silvery-white, dorsal side with plain brown, numerous fine grey spots on body and head.

Habitat: Demersal; potamodromous. Inhabits freshwater and brackish areas. Feeds on insects, fish, crustaceans. Attains 66 cm Total Length.

Distribution: Southern India; Thailand, Malaysia; Sumatra and Java.

Remarks: Commercially important foish; aquaculture species. The fish is consumed both in fresh and dried state.

Order: Clupeiformes

Family: **CLUPEIDAE**

Key to the species of Family Clupeidae

1(a) Mouth inferior, lower jaw flared outwards at corners, last dorsal ray often filamentous; only single supramaxilla present 2

1(b) Mouth terminal, lower jaw not flared outwards at corners; last dorsal ray not filamentous 4

2(a) Last dorsal ray filamentous; more than 200 gillrakers on lower arm of 1st arch .... *Nematalosa nasus*

2(b) Dorsal ray not filamentous; gillrakers less than 200 on lower arm of 1st arch 3

3(a) Maxilla slender, with its tip slightly expanded and curved downward; predorsal scales paired and overlapping in midline; gill rakers on lower arm of 1st arch 90-180; anal fin rays 24-27; lateral sacle series 58-70 .... *Gonialosa manmina*

3(b) Maxilla straight, thin its tip tapering; predorsal scales median; gillrakers 55-95 on lower arm of 1st arch; anal fin rays 15-20; lateral scale series 38-45 ... *Anodontostoma chacunda*

4(a) Upper jaw with distinct notch at centre; two supramaxilla present 5

4(b) Upper jaw without median notch 7

5(a) Scales large; 37-47 in lateral series; lower edge of operculum at 20 degrees to horizontal .... 6 (*Hilsa*)

5(b) Scales small, 77-91 in lateral series; lower edge of operculum at about 45 degrees to horizontal; eyes with broad adipose lid .... *Gudusia chapra*

6(a) Fronto-parietal region with numerous exposed striae; no pectoral fin axillary scale; expanded portion of maxilla with 4-6 longitudinal ridges; 3-7 blotches along flanks .... *H. kelee*

6(b) Fronto-parietal region covered with thick skin; few fronto striae visible; pectoral axillary scale present; expanded portion of maxilla smooth or with fine striae; no such blotches along flanks .... *H. toil*

7(a) Single supramaxilla only present 8

7(b) Two supramaxilla present 9

8(a) Belly keeled with prominent pre and post-pelvic scales; last two anal fin rays separated from rest of the fin .... *Corica soborna*

8(b) Body rounded with 6-9 unkeeled pre and post pelvic scutes......*Ehirava fluviatilis*

9(a) Gill opening smooth, rounded, with no dermal outgrowths; pelvic fin rays 7; silvery stripe on flanks; 2nd supramaxilla large and rectangular ... *Escualosa thoracata*

9(b) Gill openings with two fleshy outgrowths on vertical arm of cleithrum; pelvic rays 8-9; second supramaxillary paddle-shaped; flanks silvery .... 10 (*Sardinella*)

10(a) Pelvic fins with 9 rays; pseudobranch long with distinct ventral ridge; gillrakers on lower arm of arch 145-258 .... *S. longiceps*

10(b) Pelvic fins with 8 rays; pseudobranch short and flat;

gillrakers on lower arm of 1st arch not more than 130 2

11(a) Double row of median predorsal scales; abdominal scutes strongly keeled; 38-74 gillrakers on lower arm of 1st arch; abdominal scutes 16-17+12-13; caudal fin tips jet-black .... *S. melanura*

11(b) Single row of predorsal scales; abdominal scutes barely keeled; belly rounded; gillrakers 43-82 on lower arm of 1st arch 3

12(a) Gillrakers on lower arm of 1st arch 53-82; depth of body 25-39% of standard length .... *S. fimbriata*

12(b) Gillrakers on lower arm of 1st arch 29-42; depth 4.1 to 5.2 times in standard length; 10-20 golden or blue-black spots along flanks .... *S. sirm*

26. *Anodontostoma chacunda* (Hamilton, 1822)

Chacunda

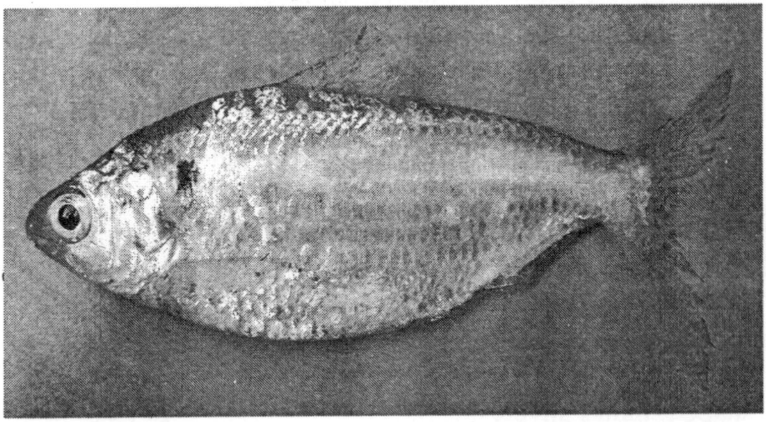

Diagnostic features: D.16; A. 20; P. 16; V.8; Ls. 42-45. Body deep, oval and compressed, ventral profile rounded with 16-18 pre-pelvic and 9-12 post-pelvic scutes; mouth inferior; maxilla straight, thin and tip tapering; lower gillrakers 54-96; teeth on scales thinner than gaps between them; last dorsal ray not prolonged as a filament. Body silvery with indistinct brown longitudinal lines along scale rows; a dark spot on shoulder.

Habitat: Pelagic fish of shallow coastal waters, estuaries, backwaters and lagoons. Feed on plankton, molluscs and crustaceans. Attains 14 to 17 cm in standard length.

Distribution: Widespread in Indian Ocean and western Pacific.

Remarks: Fished throughout the year from Chilika Lake; common commercial fish. Consumed fresh.

27.*Corcia soborna* (Hamilton, 1822).

Hamilton's Corcia

Diagnostic features: D. 12-13; A. 11-12; P.13; V.8; Ls.40-42. Body moderately compressed; head 4 times and body depth 4.2 times in standard length; belly keeled with scutes beginning behind pectoral fin base, prepelvic 10 or 11, post pelvic 6-7; maxilla reaching vertical to eye center; last two anal rays separated from rest of the fin with a gap of three fin ray bases; no lateral line; caudal forked. Body silvery with a light band along sides.

Habitat: Pelgic. Marine, enters estruaries, lagoons and brackish lakes. Attains over 12 cm total length.

Distribution: Bay of Bengal.

Remarks: Of minor fishery value; occasionally caught from Chilika Lake. Consumed fresh and salt-dried.

28. *Escualosa thoracata* (Valenciennes, 1847)

White Sardine

Diagnostic features: D.12-14; A.14-18; V.7. Body strongly deep and compressed, belly keeled from isthmus to vent; pre-pelvic scutes 17-19 and post-pelvic scutes 10-12; mouth terminal, the upper jaw slightly notched; two supra-maxilla, the second large and rectangular. Body dull white, flanks with silvery lateral stripe; fins hychime.

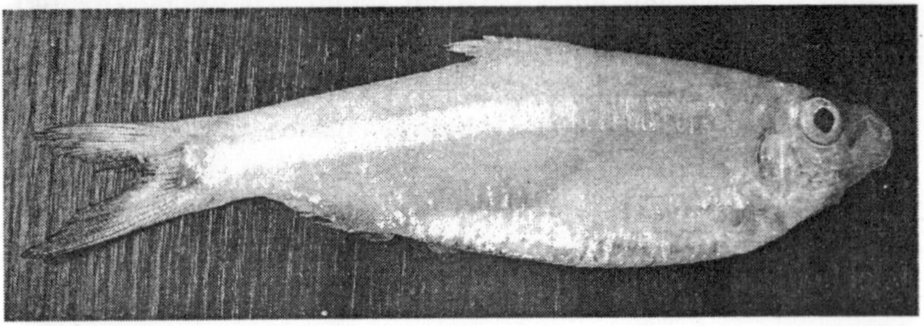

Habitat: Coastal, pelagic and schooling fish, found in shallow waters. Juveniles enter brackish water lakes, rivers but return to the sea while growing. Feed on plankton. Attains 10 cm in standard length.

Distribution: Pakistan, India, Sri Lanka, Indo-Malayan Archipelago.

Remarks: Caught by gillnets and boat seines. Commercially important fish. Consumed fresh and salt-dried.

29. *Ehirava fluviatilis* (Deraniyagala, 1929)

Malabar sprat

Diagnostic features: D. 12-16; A.16. Ls.36-40. Body elongate and compressed; snout blunt; lower jaw a little prominent; 5 to 8 unkeeled pre-pelvic scutes, followed by an equally thin pelvic scute with slender arms; no post-pelvic scutes., second supra-maxilla short, about half length of maxilla blade. Body silvery.

Habitat: Pelagic. Occurs in estuaries, lagoons and up rivers, tolerate a wide range of salinity. Feed exclusively on rotifers. Attains 7.0 cm Total Length.

Distribution: Southern India and Sri Lanka.

Remarks: Minor commercial value. Marketed fresh or dried salted.

30. *Gonialosa manmina* (Hamilton, 1822)

Ganges river gizzard shad

Diagnostic features: D. 13-17; A.24-27; P.14-15; V.8; Ls.58-70. Body deep and compressed; ventral profile more convex than dorsal with 16-20 pre-pelvic and 11-14 post-pelvic scutes; mouth inferior, upper jaw slender at tip and distinctly turned down; scales small; gill rakers fine and numerous, 90 to180 on lower arch. Body silvery, glossed with gold; cheeks purplish; back with bluish green tint, a dark spot behind gill opening.

Habitat: Pelagic. Inhabits rivers, brackish water lakes and creeks. Attains 14 cm Total length.

Distribution: Sri Lanka, India and Bangladesh.

Remarks: Found in small quantities in catches. Consumed fresh.

31. *Gudusia chapra* (Hamilton, 1822)

Indian River shad

Diagnostic features: D.iii.12-13; A.iii,18-22; P.13; V.8; Ls.79-92; GR.100-280. Body fairly deep; 26 to 29 scutes along belly; abdominal profile more convex than dorsal; eyes with broad adipose eyelid; a single triangular pectoral axillary scale; hind margin of scales smooth. Body silvery, back dark; dark blotch behind gill opening, often followed by a series of spots along flank.

Habitat: Pelagic; potamodromous; freshwater. Found in middle and upper reaches of rivers. Also occurs in ponds, beels, ditches and inundated fields. Attains 20.0 cm Total Length.

Distribution: Asia: Rivers of India and Bangladesh affluent to the Bay of Bengal, Nepal and Pakistan.

Remarks: Subsistence fisheries.

32. ***Hilsa kelee*** (Cuvier, 1829)

Kelee shad

Diagnostic features: D.17-18; A.20-22; P.16; V.8. Body fairly deep and compressed, belly with distinct scutes; numerous fronto-parietal striae on top of head; upper jaw with median notch; jaws teethless; gill rakers very fine, about 100-175, those on inner arches distinctly curved outwards; outer row of gill filaments on first arch not more than half length of gill rakers; a series of small triangular scales above axil of pectoral fin. Body dark blue green above, flanks silvery; a dark spot behind operculum, usually followed by about ten spots along flanks; tips of anterior dorsal fin rays dusky; caudal tips grey.

Habitat: Marine, pelagic but enter estuaries, lakes and able to tolerate low salinities. Plankton feeder but also feed on copepods, molluscan and crustacean larvae, prawns, amphipods and polychaetes. Attains about 15-20 cm in Total Length.

Distribution: Indo-West Pacific.

Remarks: Fairly abundant. Consumed fresh.

33. ***Nematalosa nasus*** (Bloch, 1795)

Bloch's gizzard shad

Diagnostic features: D.13-19; A.20-24; P.15; V.8. Body deep and oval with 17-19 pre-pelvic and 11-13 post-pelvic scutes; mouth inferior, lower jaw strongly flared outward; 3rd infra orbital large, its anterior edge just above the anterior arm of pre-operculum, no fleshy gap between them; supra-orbital grooves absent; last dorsal fin ray filamentous; axillary scales in pelvic and pectoral present; pre-dorsal scales from both the sides overlapping in mid-line. Body greenish-gray above, scales silvery with dark longitudinal lines more visible on dorsal row of scales; a black patch on shoulder.

Habitat: Pelagic fish of shallow coastal waters, brackish lakes and creeks. Attains 20 cm in Total Length. Usually caught in set nets and traps.

Distribution: Gulf of Aden, the Persian Gulf, coasts of India, the Andaman Islands, Sri Lanka, Thailand, China, Japan and Philippines.

Remarks: Common in the commercial fish catches. Consumed fresh or salt-dried.

34. *Sardinella melanura* (Cuvier, 1829)

Blackstrip sardine

Diagnostic features: D.12; A.15-16; V.8. Body slightly compressed; belly strongly keeled with pointed scutes; 17 pre-pelvic and 13 post pelvic scutes; 38-74 gill rakers on the lower arm first arch; dorsal fin origin slightly before mid-point of body; anal fin lying far behind dorsal fin; pelvic fin origin below anterior half of dorsal fin; scales thin, cycloid and deciduous; pre-dorsal scales paired and overlapping. Body blue-green above, flanks silvery; tips of caudal fin dark black.

Habitat: Coastal, pelagic and schooling fish, attains about 12 cm in standard length.

Distribution: Widespread in Indo-Pacific.

Remarks: Common in the commercial catches. Consumed fresh or salt-dried.

35. *Sardinella sirm* (Walbaum, 1762)

Spotted sardine

Diagnostic features: D.14-15; A. 15-17; P.16; V.8. Body elongate and sub-cylindrical, belly rounded; scutes with poorly developed keels, prepelvic17 and post-pelvic 13-15; gill rakrers 29-52 on lower arm of first arch; maxilla reaching vertical from anterior part of eye; predorsal median ridge covered by a single longitudinal series of scales. Body blue-green above, silvery flanks; a series of 10-20 golden spots on flanks.

Habitat: Pelagic coastal fish enters estuaries and lagoons. Attains

Distribution: Wide spead in tropical Indo-west Pacific.

Remarks: Common in the commercial fish catches. Consumed fresh or salt-dried.

36. *Sardinella fimbriata* (Valenciennes, 1847)

Fringescale Sardine

Diagnostic features: D.14-16; A.16-19; P. 16; V.8. Body

fusiform, compressed, belly sharp with keeled scutes, 17-18 pre-pelvic and 12-14 post-pelvic scutes; 53-82 gill rakers on lower arm of first arch; dorsal fin origin slightly before mid point of body; anal fin lying far behind dorsal fin; scales thin, cycloid and deciduous, a few perforations posteriorly; posterior scale with four or five vertical striae which are interrupted in the middle; pre-dorsal median ridge covered by adjacent side of two longitudinal series of scales. Body blue green dorsally, sides silvery.

Habitat: Pelagic fish, usually found in shallow coastal waters and lagoons in schools. Attains 11-13 cm in standard length.

Distribution: Coasts of India, Indo-Malayan Archipelago to the Philippines, and New Guinea to Australia.

Remarks: Caught with shore-seines, boat-seines and gill nets. Fairly abundant in fish catches. Consumed fresh or salt-dried.

37. *Sardinella longiceps* (Valenciennes, 1847)

India Oil-sardine

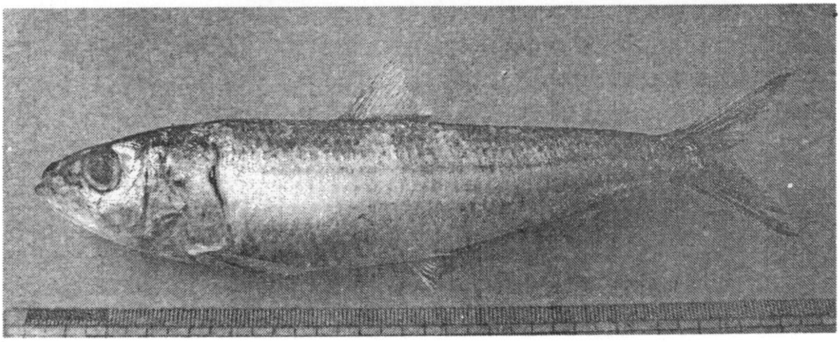

Diagnostic features: D.13-15; A.12-15; V.9. Body elongate and cylindrical; belly rounded with 18-19 pre-pelvic and 14-15 post-pelvic scutes; head long about 29-35% of standard length; 150-250 gill rakers on lower arm of first arch; dorsal fin origin nearer to head than to caudal; origin of anal fin well behind dorsal fin; pre-dorsal median ridge covered by two longitudinal rows of scales. Body dark blue green above, flanks silvery; a distinct dark spot at hind border of gill cover; a faint golden spot behind gill opening followed by a faint golden mid-lateral line.

Habitat: Coastal, pelagic, schooling and migratory fish. Feeds on plankton. Attains 20-23 cm standard length. One of the best known commercially important fish of India.

Distribution: Coasts of India, north Borneo and the Philippines; and westward to east Africa.

Remarks: Important clupeid fish. Commonly known as oil sardines. Its byproducts like oil and guano are useful. It is caught with boat seine, shore seine and gill nets. Consumed fresh or salt-dried.

38. *Tenualosa toli* (Valenciennes, 1847)

Toli Shad

Diagnostic features: D.19; A. 18; P.14; V.8. Body fusiform, deep and compressed; belly with 28-30 scutes; a distinct notch in upper jaw, no fronto-parietal striae; gill rakers fine, 60-100 on lower arm of first arch; pre-operclum with an obtuse rounded angle; no perforations on scales. Body silvery with yellow tinge; a diffuse small dark blotch behind opercle; all fins hyaline.

Habitat: Marine, pelagic and schooling in coastal waters. Euryhaline, perhaps anodromus, often ascending rivers and brackish water lakes to breed. Zooplankton feedr. Attains 55 cm in Total length.

Distribution: India, Sri Lanka to Java Sea and South China Sea.

Remarks: Caught in small quantities. Subsistence fisheries.

39. *Tenualosa ilisha* (Hamilton, 1822)

Ilishi

Diagnostic features: Body compressed, oblong; belly with .... scutes; head large, snout rounded, mouth of cleft not extending to orbit; eye lateral and withadipose lid; lateral line absent; Body silvery, all fins hyaline.

Habitat: Marine, pelagic and schooloing in coastal waters, ascend rivers and brackish water lakes for breeding. Plankton feeder. Attains over 50 cm Total length.

Distribution: India, Sri Lanka to Java Sea and South China Sea.

Remarks: Caught in small quantities. Good food fish.

Family: **PRISTIGASTERIDAE**

Key to the species of Family Pristigasteridae

1(a) Swimbladder with single postcoelomic extension on right side of body; total scutes 34-42; depth 27 to 31% in standard length .... *Ilisha elongata*

1(b) Swimbladder with paired postcoelomic extensions; total scutes 24-33; depth 33 to 42% in standard length .... I. *melastoma*

40. *Ilisha elongata* (Bennett, 1830)

Elongate Ilisha

Diagnostic features: D.14-15; A. 43-53; P.16-17; V.7. Body compressed and slightly slender; head moderately sized, eye large, lower jaw promonent and projecting; belly strongly keeled with 24-26 prepelvic and 10-15 post pelvic scutes. Body slender, belly with 24 to 25 + 10 to 15, total 34 to 42 scutes.,. Dorsal fin origin at about midpoint of body or a little behind; anal fin origin a little behind dorsal fin base; swim bladder with a long tube passing back down right side of body above anal fin base. Body silvery white, dorsal profile dark brown.

Habitat: Marine, pelagic; found in semi-enclosed sea areas, shallow coastal areas, enter estuaries also. Tolerate low salinities. Attains 60 cm in Total length.

Distribution: Indo-Pacific: from Kuwait to East China Sea.

Remarks: Highly commercial fish.

41. *Ilisha melastoma* (Schneider, 1801)

India Ilisha

Diagnostic features: D.16-19; A.35-48; P.16-17; V.7. Body moderately deep, its depth 2.5 to 3.0 times in standard length; belly sharp with 17-21 pre-pelvic and 8 or 9 post-pelvic scutes; eyes large, lower jaw projecting; 21-25 gill rakers on lower arm of first gill arch; dorsal fin origin mid way between snout and caudal; anal fin origin under hind part of dorsal fin base; vertical striae on scales traversing whole scale. Body silvery white, dorsal profile dark brown; dorsal fin with dark pigments; pectoral and anal fins hyaline; caudal fin margin dark.

Habitat: Marine, pelagic and coastal fish but enter estuaries also. Attains 17 cm in Total length.

Distribution: India: Kerala coast to Kolkata and the Andaman Islands; Java Sea, South China Sea and East China Sea.

Remarks: Mostly caught by gill nets and cast nets and boat seines over depth of 10-15 m. Fairly common in catches. Consumed fresh or salt-dried.

Family: **ENGRAULIDAE**

Key to the species of Family Engraulidae

1(a) Abdominal scutes present only before pelvic fin bases; anal fin short with less than 25 rays; gill rakers 18-35 on lower arm of 1st arch .... 2 (*Stolephorus*)

1(b) Abdominal scutes present before and behind pelvic fin base; anal fin longer with more than 30 rays .... 5 (*Thryssa*)

2(a) Predorsal spine present and spine on pelvic scute 3

2(b) Predorsal spine and spine on pelvic scute absent 4

3(a) Gillrakers on lower arm of 1st arch 20-24 .... *S. baganensis*

3(b) Gillrakers on lower arm of 1st arch 25-31 .... *S. dubiosus*

4(a) Maxillary reaching to or beyond anterior border of preoperculum; pelvic fin tips failing to each vertical rim dorsal fin origin .... *S. indicus*

4(b) Maxillary reaching to or beyond posterior border of preoperculum; pelvic fin tips reaching well past vertical from dorsal fin origin .... *S. commersonii*

5(a) Maxillary reaching to pectoral fin base or slightly beyond 6

5(b) Maxillary reaching to or slightly beyond edge of gill cover 7

6(a) Gillrakers on lower arm of 1st arch 14-16; anal fin rays 24-37; a blotch behind gill opening .... *T. mystax*

6(b) Gillrakers on lower arm of 1st arch 17-19; anal fin rays 40-45; no blotch on upper part of gill opening .... *T. stenosoma*

7(a) Gillrakers on lower arm of 1st arch 12-22 8

7(b) Gillrakers on lower arm of 1st arch 24-35 11

8(a) Gill rakers on lower arm of 1st arch 12-14 .... *T. hamiltonii*

8(b) Gillrakers on lower arm of 1st ach16-22 9

9(a) Anal fin rays 38-44 .... *T. purava*

9(b) Anal fin rays below 39 10

10(a) Maxilla reaching slightly beyond edge of gill cover; pair of dark lines on back, from nape to caudal fin .... *T. gautamiensis*

10(b) Maxilla reaching edge of gill cover; small spots on cheek, gill cover and paired fins; inside of gill cover tallow and gold .... *T. malabarica*

11(a) Total scutes on belly 25-27 (15-17+9-10); gillrakers 25-27 on lower arm of 1st arch; anal rays 35-39; dark blotch on upper part of gill opening ...... *T. polybranchialis*

11(b) Total scutes on belly 23-25 (15-16+8-9); gillrakers 26-32 on lower arm of 1st arch; anal fin rays 30-33; a diffuse saddle on nape .... *T. kammalensis*

42. *Stolephorus baganensis* (Hardenberg, 1933)

Bagan anchovy

Diagnostic features: D.14-17; A.20-23; P.13-15; V.7. Body fusiform and slightly compressed; belly with 6-7 needle-like scutes between pectoral and pelvic fins; a distinctive spine on pelvic scute between fin bases; small predorsal spine present; maxilla tip pointed, reaching to gill opening; gill rakers on lower arm of first 18-24; anal fin origin below dorsal fin base. Body white, bright silvery stripe on flankssmall pigment spots on back behind dorsal fin in two rows.

Habitat: Coastal pelagic species, also enters estuaries and lakes. Attains 12 cm Total Length.

Distribution: East coast of India, Indo-Malayan Archipelago.

Remarks: Occasionally caught by gill nets and shore seines. Consumed fresh or salt-dried.

43. *Stolephorus commersonii* (Lacepede, 1803)

Commerson's anchovy

Diagnostic features: D.15-17; A. 21-23; P.13-14; V.7. Body cylindrical, belly rounded with 2-4 sharp scutes between pectoral and ventral fins; maxilla long, tip pointed and extending beyond posterior border of pre-operculum; small teeth present on upper edge of hyoid bones; isthmus continuous; no silvery plate in front of isthmus; ventral fin reaching beyond dorsal fin origin; gill rakers 23-28 on lower arm of first arch; no pre-dorsal spine; anal fin origin below second half of dorsal fin base. Body creamy white with bright silvery stripe along flanks; a double dark line on back before dorsal fin.

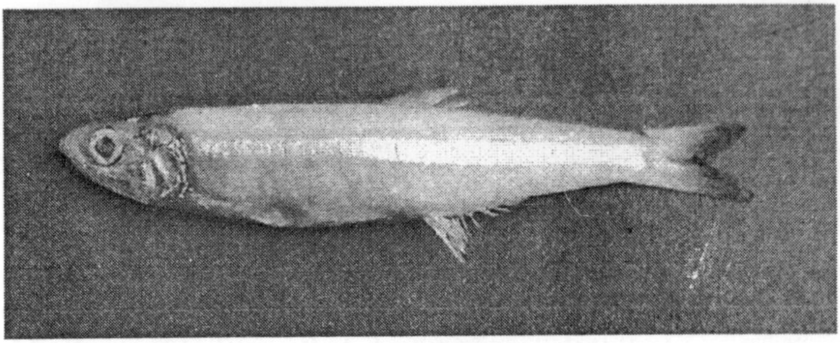

Habitat: Coastal, pelagic and schooling fish. Enters estuaries and creeks. Feed on plankton. Attains 10.5 cm. Total length.

Distribution: Indo-west Pacific, from Tanzania to Thailand and Samoa Islands.

Remarks: Quite common in catches, forms bulk of the anchovy fishery. Used as live bait for tuna fishing.

44. *Stolephorus dubiosus* (Wongratan, 1983)

Thai anchovy

Diagnostic features: D. A.18-19; P.13-14; V.7. Maxilla tip pointed, reaching to or beyond hind border of pre-operculum, belly with 4 to 7 small needle-like pre-pelvic scutes; a small pre-dorsal spine and another on the pelvic scute; anal fin short, with origin below about middle of dorsal fin base. Body creamy white with bright silvery stripe along flanks; a double pigment line on back behind dorsal fin.

Habitat: Coastal, pelagic and schooling fish; amphidromous;

brackish and marine; tolerates low salinities. Attains 7.5 cm Total Length.

Distribution: Eastern Indian Ocean: northern part of Bay of Bengal. Western Pacific: Gulf of Thailand, Java Sea.

Remarks: Subsistence fisheries. Good food fish.

45. *Stolephorus indicus* (Van Hasselt, 1823)

Indian anchovy

Diagnostic features: D.16-17; A.18-21; P.14-15; V.7. Body slender and elongate; belly rounded with 3-5 small, needle-like scutes between pectoral and pelvic fin bases; snout prominent, rather pointed; maxilla tip pointed reaching to just beyond anterior border of pre-opercle; gill rakers 21-28 on lower arm of first arch; no pre-dorsal spine; ventral fin tips not reaching to below dorsal fin origin; anal fin origin below center of dorsal fin base. Body creamy white with silvery stripe along flanks; no dark lines on back between head and dorsal fin.

Habitat: Amphidromous. Coastal, pelagic and schooling fish. Enters estuaries and tidal rivers. Feed on Zooplankton. Attains 15.5 cm Total length.

Distribution: Widespread in Indian and Western Ocean.

Remarks: Taken commercially in small quantities. Consumed fresh or salt dried.

46. *Thryssa hamiltonii* (Gray, 1835)

Hamilton's Thryssa

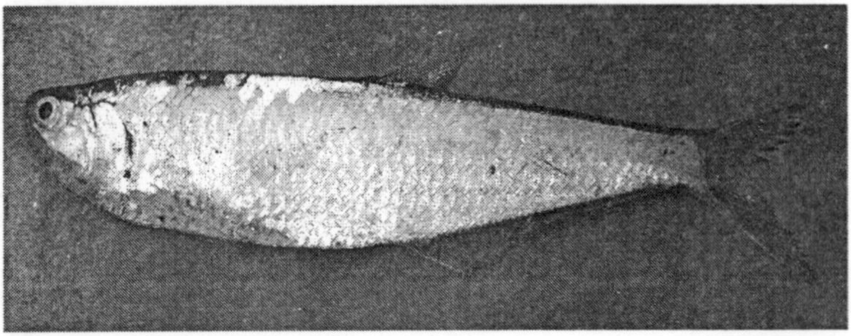

Diagnostic features: D.13-15; A.37; P.12-13; V.7. Body fusiform and strongly compressed, belly with 16-18 pre-pelvic and 10-12 post-pelvic scutes; tip of snout above level of eye center, maxilla extending to gill opening; gill rakers 11-15 on lower arm of first arch. Body silvery, back dark; a dark blotch on shoulder; fins hyaline.

Habitat: Pelagic; amphidromous. Marine and inshore schooling fish, enters estuaries and lagoons. Feeds on zooplankton and crustaceans. Attains 22 cm in Total Length.

Distribution: Indo-West Pacific, from Pakistan, coasts of India, the Andaman Islands, Sri Lanka to East Indies and to China Sea.

Remarks: Consumed fresh or salt dried. Frequently occur in catches.

47. *Thryssa gautamiensis* (Babu Rao, 1971)

Gautama thryssa

Diagnostic features: D.14; A.34-37; P.12-13; V.6. Tip of snout at about level of upper rim of eye; maxilla projecting slightly beyond edge of gill cover; first supra-maxilla minute, oval; jaw teeth slightly enlarged; belly with 25 to 27 (rarely 24) keeled scutes from isthmus to anus.A dark blotch behind upper part of gill opening; a pair of dark lines on back, from nape to caudal fin.

Habitat: Pelagic and schooling fish; amphidromous; inhabits brackish and marine waters, entering estuaries. Attains 22.0 cm Total Length.

Distribution: Indian Ocean: east coast of India, possibly also Myanmar.

Remarks: Subsistence fisheries.

48. *Thryssa stenosoma* (Wongratana, 1983)

Slender thryssa

Diagnostic features: D.15; A.40-45; P.12; V.6. Head length 4.8-5.1 times in standar length; tip of snout at about level of eye center or just a little higher; maxilla long, reaching to pectoral fin base or slightly beyond; first supra-maxilla minute and oval; teeth in lower jaw slightly enlarged; belly with 15 to 17 + 10 to 12 (total 26 to 28) keeled scutes; 16-21 gill rakers on lowe arm of first arch. Back brown, flanks silvery; no dark blotch behind upper part of gill opening; a pair of dark lines along back.

Habitat: Pelagic; amphidromous; brackish. Attains 15.0 cm Standard Length.

Distribution: Eastern Indian Ocean: northern part of Bay of Bengal, in Godavari and Ganges estuaries.

Remarks: Subsistence fisheries. Caught in small quantities.

49. *Thryssa polybranchialis* (Wongratana, 1983)

Humphead thryssa

Diagnostic features: D.13-14; A.35-39; P.13; V.6. A distinct hump at nape; tip of snout above upper rim of eye; maxilla short, just reaching to edge of gill cover; first supra-maxilla minute and oval; belly with 15 to 17 + 9 or 10 (total 25 to 27) keeled scutes. Back brown, flanks silvery; a dark blotch behind upper part of gill opening.

Habitat: Pelagic; inhabits shallow marine waters, estuaries and backwaters. Attains 17.5 cm Total Length.

Distribution: Indian Ocean: eastern and western coasts of India.

Remarks: Subsistence fisheries. Caught in small quantities.

50. *Thryssa kammalensis* (Bleeker, 1849)
Kammal Thryssa

Diagnostic features: D.13-14; A.34-35; P.12; V.7. Body fusiform, strongly compressed; belly keeled with 8 pre-pelvic and 5 post-pelvic scutes; snout bluntly pointed; maxilla reaching slightly beyond gill opening; gill rakers on lower arm of first arch 27-29. Back brown, flanks silvery; dark area on shoulder occasionally present.

Habitat: Coastal, pelagic; enters estuaries and brackish water areas. Attains 16 cm Total Length.

Distribution: India and East Indies.

Remarks: Occasionally caught; subsistence fisheries.

51. *Thryssa malabarica* (Bloch, 1795)
Malabar Thryssa

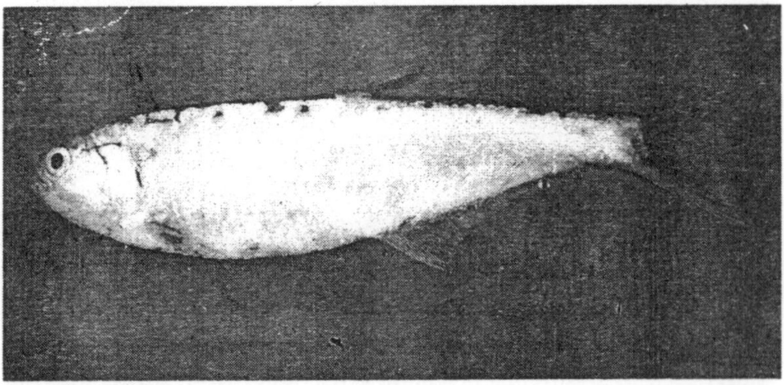

Diagnostic features: D.13-15; A.38-42; P.14; V.7. Body fusiform and compressed; belly keeled, with 14-17 pre-pelvic and 8-10 post-pelvic scutes; mouth oblique; tip of snout at about level of upper rim of eye; maxilla short, reaching up to edge of gill cover; gill rakers 17-19 on lower arm of first arch. Body silvery, back brown; a dark blotch on shoulder; small spots on cheek, gill cover, maxilla and paired fins; inside of gill cover golden yellow; dorsal and caudal fins yellow with narrow dusky margin; inner part of anal fin deep yellow with white margin; pectoral fins black.

Habitat: Marine, pelagic schooling fish, enters creeks and estuaries. Attains 17.5 cm in Total Length.

Distribution: Pakistan, India and Sri Lanka.

Remarks: Common component in fish catches. Consumed fresh or salt-dried.

52. *Thryssa mystax* (Schneider, 1801)
Moustaced thryssa

Diagnostic features: D.13-15; A.35-78; P.12-13; V.7. Body compressed with 16-18 pre-pelvic and 8-12 post-pelvic keeled scutes; snout bluntly rounded, its tip at level of eye center; maxilla long, its tip pointed and reaching to pectoral fin base; mouth nearly horizontal; gill rakers 14-15 on lower arm of first arch. Body silvery, back brown, a dark area on shoulder.

Habitat: Coastal, pelagic schooling fish enter creeks and estuaries. Attains 22 cm in Total length.

Distribution: Indo-west Pacific, from Pakistan, coasts of India, the Andaman Islands, and Sri Lanka to East Indies.

Remarks: Common anchovy of the fish catches, caught by gill nets and boat seines. Consumed fresh or salt-dried.

53. *Thryssa purava* (Hamilton, 1822.)

Gangetic anchovy

Diagnostic features: D.9-12; A. 38-44; P.15; V.6; Ll.46-47. Body fusiform and fairly compressed; head 4.06-4.7 times in standard length; mouth strongly oblique; maxilla long, its tip extending to or beyond pectoral fin base; gill rakers on lower arm of first arch 17-21; a small spine before dorsal fin; belly with 26 or 27 keeled scutes from isthmus to anus. Back brown, flanks silvery; an indistinct dark blotch behind upper part of gill opening and a faint dark line along back.

Habitat: Shallow coastal waters and pelagic. Attains15.8 cm Total Length.

Distribution: East coast of India, also Myanmar.

Remarks: Minor commercial value, tender and oily fish; consumed fresh.

Order: Gonorhynchiformes

Family CHANIDAE

54. *Chanos chanos* (Forsskal, 1775)

Milkfish

Diagnostic features: D. 13-17; A. 9-11; P. 15-17; V. 10-12; Ll. 78-90. Body torpedo-shaped; mouth small without teeth; eyes covered with thick adipose layer; dorsal and anal fins bases with scaly sheath; base of pectoral and ventral fins with axillary scales; no spines in fins; caudal fin deeply forked; dorsal fin falcate. Body bluish green on back silvery on sides; dorsal, anal and caudal fin margins dusky.

Habitat: Often found in small schools in shallow coastal waters, rivers and lagoons. Attains 170-180 cm Total Length.

Distribution: Tropical Indo-west Pacific.

Remarks: Commercially important fish. Esteemed as a food fish. Very ideal species for fish farming. Very common in Chilika Lake.

Order: Cypriniformes

Family: **CYPRINIDAE**

Key to the species of Family Cyprinidae

1(a) Upper lip continuous with skin of snout; mouth conspicuously inferior; pair of rostral and maxillary barbels present lateral line scales 37-39; eye diameter 4.2 to 4.7 in head length; no suctorial disc in lower lip .... *Crossocheilus latius latius*

1(b) Upper lip separated from skin of snout by a deep groove; mouth anterior, subinferior or inferior; lower lip without a suctorial disc 2

2(a) A knob at symphysis or junction of two arms of lower jaw fitting into an incision of upper jaw; dorsal fin with 6-16 rays and without osseous simple ray, inserted behind base of pelvic fins; lateral line running in lower half of caudal peduncle 3

2(b) No knob at symphysis or junction of two arms of lower jaw; dorsal fin with 7-30 rays and with or without osseous ray, inserted before or opposite origin of pelvic fins; lateral line running along middle of caudal fin 10

3(a) A knob at the symphysis of lower jaw absent; predorsal scales do not extend to interorbital space .... 4 (*Chela*)

3(b) A knob at the symphysis of lower jaw present; predorsal scales extend to interorbital space 5

4(a) Lateral line scales 51-68; scales small, numerous on body; body depth 4.0 to 4.25 in total length .... C. *cachius*

4(b) Lateral line scales 34-37; scales large, not many on body; body depth 3.5 to 4.5 in total length .... C. laubuca

5(a) Pectoral fin long with an axillary scale may or may not reach the pelvic fins; abdomen keeled from below pectoral fin to anus; laterl line scales 74-112; gillrakers 17-21 .... Salmostoma bacaila

5(b) Pectoral fin short, without axillary scales, fin not long 6

6(a) Maxillary barbells very long; no symphyseal knob o lower jaw; sides with broad lateral band .... *Esomus danricus*

6(b) Maxillary barbell short or absent; a symphyseal knob present on lower jaw; sides of body with or without lateral band 7

7(a) Upper lip absent; lateral line incomplete with 65-91 scales; no barbells; silvery lateral band present .... *Amblypharyngodon mola*

7(b) Upper lip present, lateral line complete, scales below 45; lateral band black 8

8(a) Dorsal fin inserted opposite interspace between anal and pelvic fins; barbells rudiment or absent; dorsal fin rays 10-19; anal fin rays 9-14 .... *Danio rerio*

8(b) Dorsalfin inserted behind origin of anal fin; no barbells; dorsal fin rays 8; anal fin rays 7-8 .... 9 (Rasbora)

9(a) Lateral line with 32-34 scales; a black lateral stripe along center of body .... R. *daniconius*

9(b) Lateral line with 28-31 scales; caudal fin with well defined black border ....R. *rasbora*

10(a) Dorsal fin inserted posterior to pelvic fins in the interspace between pelvic and anal fin, generally extending to over anal fin .... (11) Osteobrama

10(b) Dorsal fin inserted above pelvic fins or slightly anterior to it 12

11(a) Barbels absent; lateral line scales 50-60; anal fin rays 28-91 .... O. cotio peninsularis

11(b) Barbels absent; lateral line scales 73-85; anal fin rays 21-27 .... O. vigorsii

12(a) Lower jaw with post symphyseal knob or a small tubercle; dorsal fin without a spine; dorsal fin rays 7-8; ; upper and lower lips not continuous; 4 barbels present .... Cirrhinus cirrhosus

12(b) Lower jaw without a symphyseal knob; barbels present or absent; dorsal fin rays 9-26 13

13(a) Head broad; no barbells; upper lip absent; dorsal fin rays 18-19 ...... *Catla catla*

13(b) Head short or fairly large; 2-4 barbels present or absent; dorsal fin rays 9-26... 14

14(a) No horny covering on inner side of lips which are distinct; lateral line scales 20-47 ....15 (*Puntius*)

14(b) A thorny covering on inner side of one or both lips present; a rostral fold present .... 19 (*Labeo*)

15(a) Barbels present 16

15(b) Barbels abent 17

16(a) Lateral line scales 31-32; finger-like marking on caudal peduncle ...... *P. sarana*

16(b) Lateral line scales above 35; no such marking on caudal peduncle; body with two conspicuous dark blotches; a dark mark at base of anterior dorsal fin ray .... *P. chola*

17(a) Dorsal spine week; ; non osseous, articulated; predorsal scales 8-16; dorsal fin with vertical black streak and a black tip with orange markings; lateral line scales 20-22 .... *P. vittatus*

17(b) Dorsal spine strong, osseous, and serrated...... 18

18(a) Tow black blotches on body .... *P. ticto*

18(b) One black blotch on body .... *P. sophore*

19(a) Lateral line scales 65-84; scales darkest at their margins .... *L. gonius*

19(b) Lateral line scales less than 50; no dark markings on scale margins 20

20(a) Lateral line scales less than 40 or 40; dorsal inserted nearer to snout than caudal fin; 5-6 and half between lateral line and pelvic fins 21

20(b) Lateral line scales more than 40; dorsal fin inserted mid way between tip of snout and caudal fin base 22

21(a) Eye diameter 5.5 times in head length; 2.0 in snout length; 5 ½ to 6 ½ scales between lateral line pelvic fins .... *L. ariza*

21(b) Eye diameter 3.75 to 4.5 times in head length; 1.0 to 2.0 in snout length; 5 to 5 ½ scales between lateral line and pelvic fins .... *L boga*

22(a) Dorsal fin rays 15-18; pectoral fins as long as head length; body deep; mouth distinctly inferior and wide .... *L. calbasu*

22(b) Dorsal fin rays 14-16; pectoral fins as long as head excluding snout; body oblong; mouth terminal and narrow .... *L. rohita*

55. *Amblypharyngodon mola* (Hamilton, 1822)

Mola carplet

Diagnostic features: D. 9; A. 7; P. 13-14; V. 9; Ll. 65-91. Body moderately elongate; subcylindrical; depth 4.0 to 4.25 in total length; head compressed; snout obtusely rounded; upper lip absent; no barbles; eight or ten rows of scales between lateral line and base of ventral fin. Body silvery gray with a silbery lateral band; dark markings in dorsal, anal and caudal fins.

Habitat: Benthopelagic. Found in freshwater and occasionally enters brackish areas. Attains 20.0 cm Total Length.

Distribution: Pakistan, India, Bangladesh and Myanmar Reported from Afghanistan.

Remarks: No commercial value.

56. *Catla catla* (Hamilton, 1822)

Diagnostic features: D.18-19; A. 8; P. V. Ll. 40-43. Body short and deep, with depth 2.5 to 3.0 times in standard length; mouth large and upturned, with a prominent protruding lower jaw; pectoral fins long, extending to pelvic fins; scales conspicuously large; no barbles; caudal fin forked. Body grayish above, silveryon sides and beneath; fins dark coloured.

Habitat: Benthopelagic; potamodromous; Inhabits freshwater and brackish areas. Surface and mid-water feeders, omnivorous. Attains 180 cm Total Length.

Distribution: Pakistan, India, Bangladesh, Nepal and Myanmar

Remarks: Highly commercial fish; aquaculture species. Consumed fresh.

57. *Chela cachius* (Hamilton, 1822)

Diagnostic features: D.10-12; A.20-26; P.13; V.7; Ll.51-68. Body long and compressed; abdomen keeled from below ventral origin to anus; depth 4.0-4.25 times in total length. Body silvery; fins light yellow.

Habitat: Benthopelagic. Inhabits freshwater and brackish areas. Attains 6.0 cm Total Length.

Distribution: Pakistan, India, Bangladesh and Myanmar.

Remarks: Aquarium pet also used as larvicidal fish.

58. *Chela laubuca* (Hamilton, 1822.)

Indian glass barb

Diagnostic features: D.10-11; A.20-22; P.13; V.7; Ll.34-37. Body long and compressed; abdomen keeled from below ventral origin to anus; depth 3.5-4.5 times in total length; pectoral fins stout and long; lateral line curved downwards; caudal fin forked. Body silvery with conspicuous black stripe on posterior half of body.

Habitat: Pelagic fish. Inhabits freshwater and brackish areas. Feeds on insects and plants. Attains 17 cm. Total Length.

Distribution: Pakistan, India, Bangladesh, Sri Lanka, Myanmar, Malay Peninsula and Indonesia.

Remarks: Aquarium pet.

59. *Cirrhinus cirrhosus* (Hamilton, 1822)

Mrigal

Diagnostic features: D. 17-19; A. 8; P. 19; v. 9; Ll. 42-44. Body moderately elongate; head short, snout obtusely rounded; two pairs of barbels; caudal lunate or foreked. Body silvery, abdomen dull yellowish; dorso-lateral body scales with red centre; dorsal and caudal fins gray.

Habitat: Benthopelagic; potamodromous. Found in freshwater and occasionally brackish areas. Feeds on plankton, but also grazes on algae. Attains 105.0 cm Total Length.

Distribution: Indian subcontinent.

Remarks: Highly commercial fish, consumed fresh; good aquaculture species.

60. Crossocheilus latius latius (Hamilton, 1822.)

Diagnostic features: D.10-11; A.7; P.15; V.9; Ll. 37-39. Body elongate, ventral profile horizontal; head small, upper surface broad; snout prominent, overhanging the mouth; mouth inferior, lower lip fleshy; upper lip with uniserially papillated margin; eye 4.2-4.7 times in head length; two pairs of barbels; caudal fin forked. Body olive with irregular black spots; dorsal and caudal fins yellowish, other fins light orange.

Habitat: Benthopelagic; potamodromous. Inhabits freshwater and brackish areas. Attains 13.0 cm Total Length.

Distribution: India. Reported from Bangladesh, Myanmar and China.

Remarks: No commercial value. Aquarium pet.

61. Danio rerio (Hamilton, 1822)

Zebra danio

Diagnostic features: D.9; A.15-16; P.13; V.8; Ll. 26-28. Body elongate and subsylindrical; head moderate and blunt; lips thin and simple; a nob at symphysis of lower jaw; two pairs of barbels, the rostral barbels extend to anterior margin of orbit; maxillary barbels to about middle of opercle; lateral line absent; caudal fin deeply forked. Body with five uniformly, pigmented, horizontal stripes on the side, all extending onto the end of caudal fin rays; anal fin distinctively striped with blue.

Habitat: Benthopelagic. Freshwater and occasionally enters brackish areas. Feed on worms, small crustaceans and insect larvae. Attains 4.0 cm Total Length.

Distribution: Pakistan, India, Bangladesh, Nepal and Myanmar. Reported from Bhutan.

Remarks: Often used for mosquito control. Popular aquarium pet.

62. *Esomus danricus* (Hamilton, 1822)

Flying

Diagnostic features: D.8; A.8; P.15; V.9; Ll. 30-34. Body elongate and strongly compressed; head small, mouth obliquely directed upwards; two pairs of barbles, maxillary pair very long; 14 scales round caudal peduncle; caudal fin forked. Body silvery white with broad black lateral band, fins light yellow; no spot on caudal peduncle.

Habitat: Benthopelagic; potamodromous. Found in freshwater and brackish areas. Attains 12.0 cm Total Length.

Distribution: Pakistan, India, Nepal, Bangladesh, Afghanistan, Sri Lanka and Myanmar.

Remarks: Minor commercial value; aquarium pet.

63. *Labeo ariza* (Hamilton, 1807)

Reba

Diagnostic features: D.11; A.7-8; P.18; V.9; Ll.38. Body elongate to deep; head large, snout swollen; eye diameter 5.5 times I head length, 2.0 in snout lrngth; scales between lateral line and ventral fin five anf half to six and half; snout overhanging mouth, without any lateral lobe; one pair of barbles present; caudal fin forked. Color variable, overall dirty white or greyish, silvery or yellow with thin stripes mostly above lateral line; larger fish sometimes with a broad midlateral stripe.

Habitat: Benthopelagic; potamodromous. Inhabits freshwater occasionally enters brackish areas. Feeds on plankton and detritus. Attains 26.0 cm Total Length.

Distribution: India, Nepal, Bangladesh. Reported from Myanmar.

Remarks: Good food fish, consumed fresh. Species for aquaculture.

64. *Labeo boga* (Hamilton, 1822)

Diagnostic features: D.11-13; A. 7; P.16; V. 9; Ll. 37-39. Dorsal profile more convex than abdomen; snout moderately projecting beyond jaw; lips thin; no lateral lobes on snout; one pair of maxillary barbel present; sacles between lateral line and ventral fin five to five and half caudal fin forked. Body light orangish, a dark spot on the shoulder.

Habitat: Benthopelagic; potamodromous; Inhabits rivers and brackish water areas. Attains 28.0 cm Total Length.

Distribution: Pakistan, India, Bangladesh, Nepal and Myanmar.

Remarks: Good food fish, consumed fresh.

65. *Labeo calbasu* (Hamilton, 1822)

Orange-fin labeo

Diagnostic features: D.15-18; A.8; P. 19; V.9; Ll. 40-45. Mouth small, inferior and surrounded by fleshy lips; two pairs of barbels; pectoral fins as long as head; caudal fin deeply lobed. Body blackish; scales with scarlet centers; fins blackish.

Habitta: Demersal; potamodromous. Occurs in rivers, ponds andbrackish waters.Feeds on aquatic plants, filamentous algae and diatoms. Attains 90.0 cm Total Length.

Distribution: Pakistan, India, Bangladesh, Myanmar, Nepal, Thailand and South Western China.

Remarks: Commerciallly important fish. Consumed fresh.

66. *Labeo gonius* (Hmilton, 1822)

Kuria labeo

Diagnostic features: D. 15-18; A. 7; P.17; V.9; Ll. 65-84. Dorsal profile of body more convex than abdomen; two pairs of barbels; numerous pores on snout; caudal fin deeply forked. Body greenish above, lighter below; margin of scales dark.

Habitat: Benthopelagic; potamodromous. Inhabits rivers and estuarine waters. Feeds on plants. Attains 150 cm. Total Length.

Distribution: Pakistan, India, Bangladesh and Myanmar. Recorded from Afghanistan and Nepal.

Remarks: Commercially important fish; aquaculture species. Consumed fresh.

67. *Labeo rohita* (Hamilton, 1822)

Rohu

Diagnostic features: D. 15-16; A. 7; P. 17; V. 7; Ll. 40-42. Body oblong and deep; abdomen rounded; head large and snout swollen; lips thick, fleshy covering both jaws; mouth terminal and narrow lower profile of head conspicuously arched; short dorsal fin with anterior branched rays shorter than head; two pairs of barbels present; 12-16 predorsal scales. Body brownish along back, silvery along sides and abdomen; a red mark on each body scale.

Habitat: Benthopelagic; potamodromous. Found in freshwater; brackish areas. Attains 200 cm Total Length.

Distribution: Throughout India, Bangladesh, Myanmar, Nepal, Pakistan and Sri Lanka.

Remarks: Commercially important fish. Consumed fresh.

68. *Osteobrama cotio peninsularis* (Silas, 1952)

Diagnostic features: D. I, 11-12; A. 29-36; P. 13; V.10; Ll. 55-60. Body compressed, head short; profile over nape concave; barbels absent; predorsal scales 21-24; scales between ventral fin base and lateral line seven and half to nine and half; caudal fin forked, the lower lobe longer. Body silvery, back dark; sometimes silvery lateral band present.

Habitat: Benthopelagic. Occurs in rivers and streams, occasionally brackishwaters. Attains 15 cm Total Length.

Distribution: Asia: Maharashtra, Orissa and Andhra Pradesh in India.

Remarks: Minor commercial value.

69. *Osteobrama vigorsii* (Sykes, 1839)

Indian Minnow

Diagnostic features: D.I,11-12; A.21-27; P.19;V.10;Ll.75-85. Body very compressed, head short, snout bluntly rounded; two rudiment maxillary barbels present; caudal fin deeply forked, lower lobe longer. Body greenish superiorly, silvery below; snout black.

Habitat: Benthopelagic. Inhabits fast flowing clear streams, rivers and brackish waters. Attains 30.0 cm. Total Length.

Distribution: India.

Remarks: Minor commercial value.

70. *Puntius chola* (Hamilton, 1822)

Swamp barb

Diagnostic features: D. III, 8; A.II,5; P.15; V.9; Ll. 24-28.

Body deep and compressed; dorsal profile more convex than abdomen; single maxillary pair of barbels present; last simple dorsal ray moderately strong and smooth; lateral line complete; scales from dorsal fin origin to lateral line 6; lateral line to pelvic fin origin 4; predorsal scales 11, circumpeduncular scales 14, pre-pelvic scales 11, pre-anal scales 19. Body silvery; small dark blotch near caudal peduncle.

Habitat: Benthopelagic; potamodromous. Inhabits streams, rivers, canals, ponds and enters brackish waters. Feed on worms, crustaceans, insects and plant matter. Attains 15.0 cm Total Length.

Distribution: Pakistan, India, Nepal, Bangladesh, Sri Lanka and Myanmar. Reported from Bhutan.

Remarks: Minor commercial value.

71. *Puntius sarana* (Hamilton, 1822)

Olive barb

Diagnostic features: D.III, 8; A. II, 5; P.15; V.9; LL.31-32. Body oblong, head, small, profile of back elevated; two pairs of barbells, the maxillary pair longer than orbit, rostral pair shorter; last dorsal ray osseus and strong. Body silvery; dark superiorly; opercle shot with gold; fins dark.

Habitat: Benthopelagic; potamodromous. Occurs in rivers, streams, lakes and backwaters. Tolerant of salinity. Forms small schools. Feed on aquatic insects, fish, algae and shrimps. Attains 42 cm Total Length.

Distribution: Afghanistan, Pakistan, India, Nepal, Bangladesh, Bhutan and Sri Lanka. Reported from Myanmar and Thailand.

Remarks: Minor commercial value; gamefish and aquarium pet.

72. *Puntius sophore* (Hamilton, 1822)

Pool

Diagnostic features: D.12; A.7; P.15; V.9; Ll. 20-26. Barbels long and thin; dorsal spine smooth; circumpeduncular scales 9-10; lalteral line incomplete. Body silvery with lateral blotch; pectoral, ventral and anal fins yellowish.

Habitat: Benthopelagic; amphidromous. Inhabits rivers, streams and ponds in plains and enters brackish water areas also. Form large shoals. Attains 18.0 cm Total Length.

Distribution: Pakistan, India, Nepal, Bangladesh, Myanmar and Yunnan, China, Bhutan and Afghanistan.

Remarks: Aquarium pet.

73. ***Puntius ticto*** (Hamilton, 1822)

Ticto barb

Diagnostic features: D. 11; A. 7; P.15; V.9; Ll.23-26. Osseous dorsal ray strong and serrated; barbels absent; lateralline incomplete; preanal scales 11-14. Body silvery with two black blotches, one at the beginning of the lateral line and the other at base of caudalfin.

Habitat: Benthopelagic; potamodromous. Found in still, shallow, marginal waters of tanks and rivers, mostly with muddy bottoms of freshwater and brackish areas. Feed on crustaceans, insects and plankton. Attains 10.0 cm Total Length.

Distribution: Pakistan, India, Nepal, Sri Lanka, Bangladesh, Myanmar and Thailand.

Remarks: Aquarium pet.

74. *Puntius vittatus* (Day, 1865)

Greenstripe barb

Diagnostic features: D.10; A.7; P.12; V.9; LL. 20-22. Body short and moderately elongate, deep and compressed; dorsal and ventral profiles equally convex; no tubercles on snout and lips; barbells absent; scales from lateral line to ventral fin two and half to three; predorsalscales 8-10; lateral line complete. Body silvery; dorsal fin with a vertical blackstreak and black tip with orange markings.

Habitta: Benthopelagic; Inhabits freshwater bodies, enters brackish water also. Feeds on filamentous and blue-green algae. Attains 5.0 cm Total Length.

Distribution: Pakistan, India and Sri Lanka.

Remarks: Minor commercial value. Aquarium pet.

75. *Rasbora daniconius* (Hamilton, 1822)

Slender rasbora

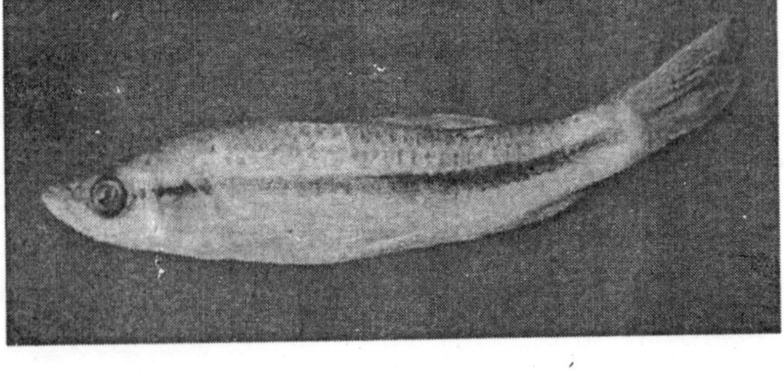

Diagnostic features: D.9; A.7; P.15; V.9; Ll. 32-34. Body elongated, head large and pointed; mouth large; no barbels on chin; abdominal profile more convex than dorsal. Black stripe from eye to caudal fin.

Habitat: Benthopelagic; potamodromous; Inhabits freshwater and brackish areas. Sometimes forms large schools. Feed mainly on aquatic insects and detritus. Attains 15.0 cm Total Length.

Distribution: India, Bangladesh, Malay Peninsula, Myanmar, Nepal, Sri Lanka, Pakistan and Zinzabar.

Remarks: Minor commercial value; aquarium pet.

76. *Rasbora rasbora* (Hamilton, 1822)

Gangetic scissortail

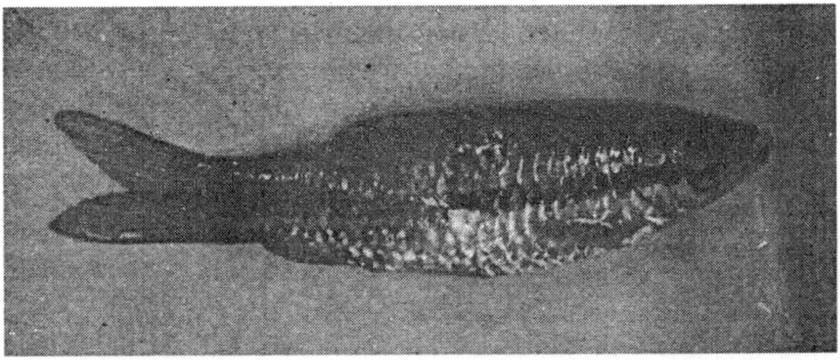

Diagnostic features: D.9; A.7-8; P. 15; V.9; Ll. 28-31. Body elongated, headlarge and pointed; mouth large; no barbels on chin; abdominal profile more convex than dorsal. Body uniform silvery; caudal fin with well defined black border.

Habitat: Benthopelagic. Inhabits freshwater; brackish areas. Attains 13.0 cm Total Length.

Distribution: East coast of India, Bangladesh, Myanmar and Thailand.

Remarks: No commercial importance.

77. *Salmostoma bacaila* (Hamilton, 1822)

Large razorbelly minnow

Diagnostic features: D. 9; A.13-15; P.13; V.9; LL.86-110. Body elongate and compressed; abdomen keeled from pectoral fin to anush; head long and pointed; pectoral fins long with long axillary scale; gill rakers on first arch 17-21; scales between lateral line and ventrl fin base four to six; caudalfin deply forked. Body uniform silvery.

Habitat: Benthopelagic; potamodromous; occurs in fresh and brackish water areas. Feed on larvae and adults of insects. Attains 18.0 cm Total Length.

Distribution: Pakistan, India, Bangladesh and Nepal. Reported from Afghanistan.

Remarks: Minor commercial value. Uncommon in catches.

Family: COBITIDAE

78. *Lepidocephalichthys guntea* (Hamilton, 1822)

Guntea loach

Diagnosstic features: D. 8; A.7 Body elongate, depth less than 6.0 times in standard length; caudal peduncle laterally compressed; head short, snout blunt; mouth inferior; lips thick and fleshy; lower lip interrupted in middle; six barbels; scales absent on head; 25-30 scales from back of body to anal fin; lateral line absent; caudal fin truncate. Pectoral fin with an osseous spine in males. Dark lateral band or dark gray spots on body; dorsal and anal fins spotted; caudal fin with rows of dark spots.

Habitat: Demersal; potamodromous. Inhabits fresh and brackish waters; found in flowing or even clear standing waters. Attains 15.0 cm Total Length.

Distribution: Pakistan toThailand.

Remarks: No commercial value. Aquarium pets.

Order: Siluriformes

Key to the families of Order Siluriformes

1 (a) Adipose dorsal fin absent 2

1(b) Adipose dorsal present as short or low longfin (in Schilbeidae it may absent in adults) 5

2(a) Dorsal fin with spine; ventral fin with 15-16 rays; caudal fin confluent with caudal .... *Plotosidae*

2(b) Dorsal fin without spine; ventral fin six rays; anal fin free 3

3(a) Nasal barbells absent; no accessory respiratory organs .... *Siluridae*

3(b) Nasal barbells present; accessory respiratory organs present on gills or in body cavity 4

4(a) Dorsal fin long with 23-76 rays, accessory respiratory organs on gills .... *Clariidae*

4(b) Dorsal fin short, with 6-7 rays; accessory respiratory organ as tubular air sacs present in body cavity .... *Heteropneustidae*

5(a) Nostrils close together with very little interspace between two 6

5(b) Nostrils wide apart, separated with some interspace between two 7

6(a) No nasal barbels present, 2-6 in number; nostrils separated by a valve .... Ariidae

6(b) A pair of nasal barbels present; barbels eight; nostrils also together, separated by a barbel ....Sisoridae

7(a) Anal fin short with less than 20 rays (8-16) .... Bagridae

7(b) Anal fin long with more than 20 rays (24-90) 8

8(a) Nasal barbels always present; caniniform teeth on jaws; anal fin rays 25-90 .... Schilbeidae

8(b) Nasal barbels present; villiform teeth on jaws; anal fin with 28-34 rays.......... .... Pangasiidae

Family: **BAGRIDAE**

Key to the species of Family Bagridae

1(a) Eyes superior, not visible from below ventral surface; anal fin short with 8-9 rays; dorsal fin spine weakly serrated; interneural shield in between basal bone of dorsal fin and occipital bone present .... *Sperate seenghala*

1(b) Eyes inferior, visible from below ventral surface; anal fin long with 9-16 rays; dorsal fin spine strongly serrated; no such interneural bone present .... 2 (*Mystus*)

2(a) Adipose dorsal fin commencing almost after rayed fin; interspace between two is negligible or shorter than width of rayed dorsal fin; a dark spot at base of dorsal fin; no bands on body .... *M. cavasius*

2(b) Adipose dorsal fin short, commencing after an interspace from rayed dorsal fin, grater than width of rayed dorsal; no dark spot at base of dorsal fin; bands on body present or absent 3

3(a) Body plain without any colour bands; no darl shoulder spot .... *M gulio*

3(b) Body with several longitudinal bands; a dark shoulder spot present .... *M. vittatus*

79. Mystus cavasius (Hamilton, 1822)

Gangetic mystus

Diagnostic features: D, I,7; A.10-11; P. I,8; V. 6. Body elongate and compressed; head conical; occipital process narrow; maxillary barbels extend posteriorly beyond the caudal fin base, but in young specimens, do not extend beyond the anal fin; dorsal spine feebly serrated. Colour is grayish with a more or less well-defined midlateral longitudinal stripe; a dark spot just anterior to the first dorsal spine; dorsal, adipose and caudal fins shaded with black pigments.

Habitat: Demersal; amphidromous. Inhabits fresh and brackish water areas. Attains 40 cm Total Length.

Distribution: Pakistan, Nepal, India, Sri Lanka and Myanmar. Occurs in Thailand.

Remarks: Good food fish. Its pectoral spine can inflict painful wounds

80. *Mystus gulio* (Hamilton, 1822)

Long whiskers catfish

Distribution: D.I,7+adipose; A.12-15; P. I,8-9; V.6. Occipital crest rugose; median longitudinal groove short, extending slightly beyond posterior border of orbit; adipose dorsal fin base shorter than anal fin base; nasal barbel; shorter than head. Bluish brown on back, dull white beneath; outer half of fins black; maxillary barbles black.

Habitat: Demersal; anadromous. Primarily a brackish water fish that enters and lives in fresh water. Form schools of 10 to 25 individuals. Attains 46 cm. Total Length.

Distribution: India to Indonesia and Viet Nam. Reported from Pakistan.

Remarks: Consumed fresh.

81. *Mystus vittatus* (Bloch, 1794)

Striped dwarf catfish

Diagnostic features: D.I,6-7+adipose; A. 12-13; P. I, 9; V.6. Body elongate and slightly compressed; maxillary barbels extending beyond the pelvic fins, often to the end of the anal fin; dorsal spine inner edge finely serrated; adipose fin small, inserted much behind rayed dorsal fin. Colour light gray-silvery to shining golden, with about five pale blue or dark brown to deep black longitudinal bands above and below lateral line; a narrow dusky spot often present on the shoulder; all fins with dark tips.

Habitat: Demersal; inhabit freshwater and brackish water areas. Feed on plants, shrimps, insects, molluscs and fish. Attains 21 cm Total Length.

Distribution: Pakistan, India, Sri Lanka, Nepal, Bangladesh and probably Myanmar. Reported from Malaysia, Laos, Bhutan, Viet Nam and Cambodia.

Remarks: Mnor commercial value; consumed fresh.

82. *Sperata seenghala* (Skyes, 1839)

Giant river-catfish

Diagnostic features: D.I,7+adipose; A. 11-12; P.I,9-10; V.6; C.19-21. Body elongate and compressed; snout broad and spatulate; barbels extend posteriorly to pelvic fins or beyond to anal fin; dorsal spine weakly serrated on its posterior edge; adipose fin base short; caudal fin forked. Colour is brownish-gray on back, silvery on flanks and belly; a dark well-defined spot is on the adipose dorsal fin.

Habitat: Demersal; potamodromous. Found in rivers, canals, beels, ditches, inundated fields and other brackish water areas. Attains 150 cm Total Length.

Distribution: Asia: Afghanistan, Pakistan, India, Nepal and Bangladesh.

Remarks: Commercial and aquaculture fish. Good food fish, copnsumred fresh.

Family: **SILURIDAE**

Key to the species of Family Siluridae

1(a) Gape of mouth very wide; extending beyond eyes posteriorly; dorsal inserted above half of pectoral fin; eyes not visible from below ventral surface; mandibular barbels not rudimentary or small .... *Wallago attu*

1(b) Gape of mouth not wide, not extending beyond eyes posterorly; dorsal fin inserted above last half of pectoral fins; eyes visible from below ventral surface of head; mandibular barbels occasionally rudimentary or small .... 2 (*Ompok*)

2(a) Ventral fins not reaching anal fin origin; anal fin rays 63-69; maxillary barbels extend to slightly beyond ventral fin origin; small black spot on caudal peduncle ... . *Ompok bimaculatus*

2(b) Ventral fins reaching anal fin origin; anal fin rays 48-54; maxillary barbels extend to middle of pectoral fin; no black spot on caudal peduncle ....*O. pabda*

83. Ompok bimaculatus (Bloch,1794)

Buttrer catfish

Diagnostic features: D.4; A. 54-74; P. I,13; V. 8. Body elongated and compressed; head small and depressed; two pairs of barbels; maxillary barbels reaching pelvic fins or anal fins; mandibulary barbels minute; eyes small, covered by skin; dorsal and ventral fins small; ventral fin not reaching anal fin origin; vomerine teeth in two patches; caudal fin forked. Silvery brown, with conspicuous round black blotch above pectoral base.

Habitat: Demersal; potamodromous. Found in streams, rivers and brackish water areas. Feed on vegetable matter, fish, crustaceans and molluscs. Attains 45.0 cm Standard Length.

Distribution: Asia: Afghanistan to China, Thailand and Borneo. Endangered status in the Western Ghats, India

Remarks: Sold fresh or smoked.

84. *Ompok pabda* (Hamilton, 1822)

Pabdah catfish

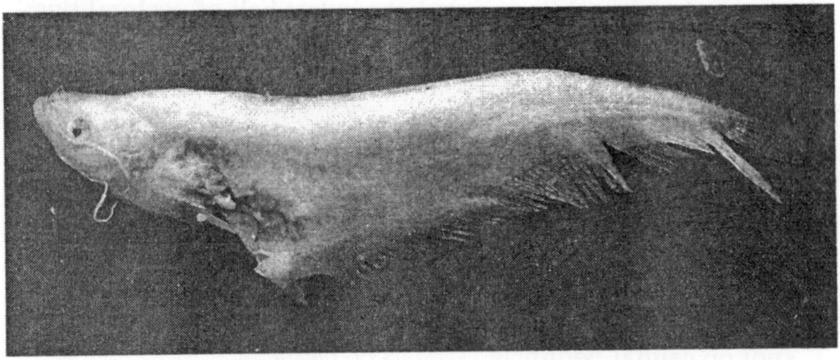

Diagnostic features: D.4-5; A. 66-71; P. 12-14; V.9-10. Body elongated and compressed; head small and depressed; snout bluntly rounded; mouth superior, cleft oblique; no teeth on palatines; two pairs of barbels, mandibular ones rudimentary or small, maxillary barbels shorter than head length; adipose fin absent; ventral fins reaching anal fin origin; caudal fin forked. Body silvery with light shoulder spot.

Habitat: Demersal; potamodromous. Inhabits clear as well as muddy rivers, streams, ponds and brackish water lakes of less saline. Attains 30 cm Total Length.

Distribution: Pakistan, east coast of India, Bangladesh, Myanmar.

Remarks: Commercially important fish. Consumed fresh.

85. *Wallago attu* (Bloch & Schneider, 1801)

Wallago

Diagnostic features: D.5; A.77-97; P.I,13-15; V.8-10. Body elongate, strongly compressed; head broad and depressed; mouth very deeply cleft, its corner reaching far behind eyes. vomerine teeth in two small patches; barbels two pairs; maxillary barbels extending to anal fin origin, dorsal fin small, anal fin very long;

24-30 gill rakers on the first arch; anal fin not confluent with caudal; caudal fin forked with rounded lobes. Body silvery grey.

Habitat: Demersal; potamodromous. Found in large rivers, lakes and brackish waters. Attains 240 cm Total Length. A large voracious and predatory catfish. Sluggish and stays on muddy or silty bottom in search of food. Feed on smaller fish, crustaceans, and molluscs.

Distribution: Asia: Pakistan to Viet Nam and Indonesia.

Remarks: Commercially important; gamefish. Threatened due to over harvesting.

Family: **SCHILBEIDAE**

Key to the species of Family Schilbeidae

1(a) Rayed dorsal fin absent; anal fin long with 58-75 rays; four pairs of barbels, all are in uniform length .... *Ailia coilia*

1(b) Rayed dorsal fin present; anal fin long with less than 55 rays; 4 or 2 pairs of barbels, not in uniform length 2

2(a) Barbels two pairs, maxillary small and mandibular ones vestigial; canine teeth on jaws; lateral line complete and interrupted .... *Silonia silonia*

2(b) Barbels four pairs; villiform teeth on jaws; lateral line complete and single .... *Eutropiichthys vacha*

86. *Ailia coila* (Hamilton, 1822)

Gangetic ailia

Diagnostic features: A.58-75; P.I, 13-16; V. 6. Body short and compressed, head short and greatly compressed; snout over hanging; mouth subterminal, crescentic; dorsal fin absent, adipose fin only present; anal fin long not confluent with caudal; villiform teeth in two patches on palate; four pairs of barbels, longer than head; lateral line complete;ventral profile of body not prominently arched; caudal fin forked. Body uniform silvery to brown. No blotches on body or fins.

Habitat: Pelagic. Found in large rivers and tidal waters. Inhabits surface to mid-waters. Feed on small fish and insects. Attains 30 cm Total Length.

Distribution: Asia: Pakistan, India, Bangladesh and Nepal.

Remarks: An excellent food fish. Uncommon in catches.

87. *Euptropiichthys vacha* (Hamilton, 1822)

Batchwa vacha

Diagnostic features: D. I,7+ adipose; A.38-58; P. I,10-16; V.6. Body elongate and compressed; head conical, snout pointed; four pairs of barbles, lying in deep longitudinal groves in isthmus; nasal barbells reach hind border of head or slightly beyond; dorsal fin inserted above half of pectoral fin; pectoral spine serrated on inner edge; lateral line complete; caudal fin forked. Body silvery, grey along back; pectoral and caudal edged with black.

Habitat: Pelagic; potamodromous. Freshwater and brackish areas. Adults ascend from estuaries into large rivers for breeding during monsoons.Occur in shoals. Attains 45 cm Total Length.

Distribution: Asia: Pakistan, India, Bangladesh, Nepal, Myanmar and Thailand.

Remarks: Commercial fish; gamefish. Good food fish.

88. Silonia silondia (Hamilton, 1822)

Silond catfish

Diagnostic features: D.I,7+ adipose; A.40-45; P. I,11-13; V.6. Body elongate and compressed; head compressed, snout obtusely rounded; enlarged canine teeth on jaws, villiform on palate; jaw teeth project outside mouth opening; two pairs of barbels, maxillary barbels small, not reaching beyond orbit; mandibular barbles vestigial; lateral line complete but indistinct. Bluish along black, silvery on sides; fins grey.

Habitat: Demersal; amphidromous; Freshwater and brackish nature. Attains 180 cm Total Length.

Distribution: Asia: Pakistan, India, Bangladesh, Nepal and probably Myanmar.

Remarks: Commercial and gamefish. Good food fish.

Family: **PANGASIIDAE**

89. Pangasius pangasius (Ham.-Buch.)

Yellowtail catfish

Diagnostic features: D.I,6-7; A.29-32; P. 9-12; V. 6. Body elongate and compressed; snout prominent, bluntly pointed; eyes large, behind corner of mouth; palatine teeth in elongate bands; two pairs of barbles, no nasal barbles; 23-28 gill rakers on first arch. Caudal fin bright yellow in adults.

Habitat: Benthopelagic; potamodromous Standard Length. Found in large rivers and estuaries and brackish water lakes and inshore areas. Atains 300 cm Total Length.

Distribution: Indian subcontinent and Myanmar.

Remarks: Marketed fresh. Good food fish.

Family: SISORIDAE

90. Bagarius bagarius (Hamilton, 1822.)

Dwarf goonch

Diagnostic features: D.I,7; A.13-17; P.9-14; V.6. Body and abdomen elongate; head broad; mouth large, inferior and arciform; body covered by heavily keratinized skin; four pairs of barbels present; pelvic-fin origin in front of the base of the last dorsal ray; adipose-fin origin behind the anal-fin origin; lateral line complete and·simple; caudal fin deeply forked, the upper lobe produced into soft filamentous prolongation. Body gray with large irregular black markings and cross bands; base of all fins black.

Habitat: Benthopelagic; potamodromous. Inhabits rocky pools of large and rivers, enters brackish waters also. Feeds on insects, small fishes and shrimps. Attains 200 cm Total Length.

Distribution: Asia: Ganges. Reported from Salween, Maeklong and Peninsular Thailand.

Remarks: Minor commercial value. Marketed fresh. Important food fish, but the meat spoils rapidly.

Family: CLARIIDAE

91. Clarius batrachus (Linnaeus, 1758)

Walking Catfish

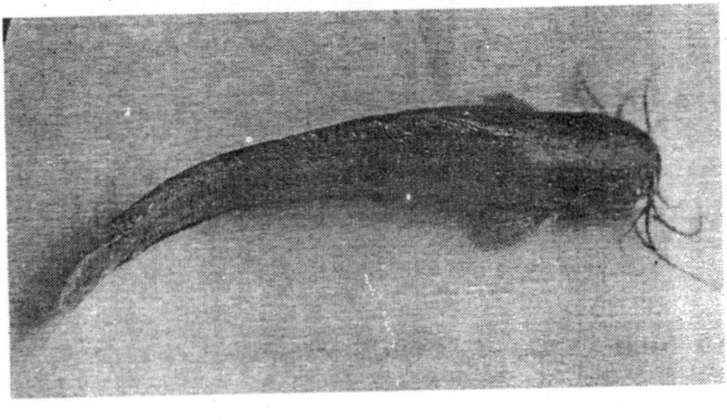

Diagnostic features: D.60-76; A.47-58; P. I,8-11; V.6. Body compressed posteriorly. Upper jaw a slightly projecting. Spine of pectoral fins serrated on its inner edge; occipital process more or less triangular, its length about 2 time in its width; distance between dorsal and occipital process 4 to 5.5 times in distance from tip of snout to end of occipital process. Green or brownish dorsally, becoming lighter beneath; dorsal and anal fins with reddish margins.

Habitat: Demersal; potamodromous. Inhabits lowland streams, swamps, ponds, and low saline brackish waters. Feeds on insect larvae, earthworms, shells, shrimps, small fish and aquatic plants. Attains 47.0 cm Total Length.

Distribution: Asia: India, Sri Lanka, Malay Peninsula, Sumatra, Java and Borneo.

Remarks: An important food fish. Marketed live, fresh and frozen.

Family: **HETEROPNEUSTIDAE**

92. ***Heteroneustes fossilis*** (Boch, 1794)

Stinging catfish

Diagnostic features: D.6-7; A.60-79; P.I,7-8; V.6. Body elongate and compressed; head depressed; snout flat, snout terminal; lips fleshy, four pairs of barbels; no adipose fin; anal fin just reaching caudal; caudal fin rounded. Colour silvery gray, sometimes with two longitudinal yellow bands.

Habita: Demersal. Found mainly in ponds, ditches, swamps and marshes, but sometimes occurs in muddy rivers. Can tolerate slightly brackish water. Attains 30.0 cm Total Length.

Distribution: Asia: Pakistan, coasts of India and Sri Lanka to Myanmar andThailand.

Remarks: Highly commercial; aquaculture fish. Good food fish, consumed fresh. Wounds from the pectoral spine are very painful.

Family: ARIIDAE

Key to the species of Family Ariidae

1(a) One pair of barbels; stiff and semiosseous .... *Osteogeneiosus militaris*

1(b) Three pairs of barbels; not osseous .... 2 (*Arius*)

2(a) Teeth on palate villiform; globular or conical; maxillary barbels long, reaching end of pectoral fins .... *A. caelatus*

2(b) Teeth on palate globular or molar-like; maxillary barbels not long, reaching up to pectoral base or less 3

3(a) Median longitudinal groove on top of head reaching to base of supra-occipital processes; teeth on palate in two pear-shaped large patches; dorsal fin spine not filamentous .... *A. tueneispinis*

3(b) Median longitudinal groove on top of head not reaching to median keel of supraoccipital processes; teeth not pear-shaped patches; dorsal fin spine filamentous 4

4(a) Eyes large, its diameter 1.6-2.5 times in interorbital width; median frontanelle groove on top of head shallow, not reaching base of supraoccipital processes .... *A. arius*

4(b) Eyes smaller, its diameter 2.6 to 4.0 times in interorbital width; median frontanelle groove on top of head deep and long, not reaching base of supraoccipital processes .... *A. maculatus*

93. *Arius arius* (Hamilton, 1822)

Hamilton's Catfish

Diagnostic features: D. I,7+adipose; A. 20-21; P.I,9; V.6. Body elongate and robust; head depressed; eyes large, 1.6 to 2.5 in interorbital space; snout blunt; horn-like conical projection of palatine teeth patch present; median fontanelle groove on head not reaching base of supra-occipital process; three pairs of barbels around mouth; tip of dorsal spine prolonged into a filament; pectoral fin is smaller than dorsal; adipose dorsal fin small. Body silvery steel, sides and below lighter; posterior margins of dorsal and pectoral fins dusky; adipose dorsal with black spot.

Habitat: Demersal. Inhabits Estuaries, lagoons and lakes. Attains 25 cm Total Length.

Distribution: Coasts of India, Bangladesh and Myanmar.

Remarks: Caught by hook & line, gillnets and shore seines. Fairly common in fish catches. Consumed fresh.

94. *Arius caelatus* (Valenciennes, 1840)

Engraved catfish

Diagnostic features: D. I,7+adipose; A.19; P.I,9; V. 6. Body robust, head profile concave at nape; eye diameter 5.5-7.0 in head length and 3-4 times in inter-orbital width; three pairs of strong barbels present, maxillary pair extending to end of pectoral fin median fontanelle groove on head broad, not reaching to median keel of supra-occipital process; head shield strongly rugose and granulated; basal plate before dorsal 'V' shaped; tip of dorsal spine filamentous; adipose fin rather large. Body metallic bluish black, whitish below; tip of dorsal and its filament black; adipose fin black or with a large black blotch on upper half.

Habitat: Demersal. Shallow coastal waters, estuaries and lagoons. Attains 45 cm Total Length.

Distribution: Pakistan to Indo-Australian Archipelago except Philippines or Australia.

Remarks: One of the important commercial catfish. Consumed fresh.

95. *Arius maculatus* (Thunberg, 1792)

Spotted catfish

Diagnostic features: D. I, 7+adipose; A.18-19; P.I,10-11; V.6. Body elongated and head pointed; eyes small, its diameter 2.6 to 4.0 in interorbital width; maxillary barbels reaching to base of pectoral fin base; fontanelle groove on head deep and long; adipose fin small; tip of dorsal spine filamentous. Body bluish brown above, sides grey and belly white; all fins black tipped; adipose fin blackish.

Habitat: Demersal. Shallow coastal waters, estuaries and lagoons. Attains 20-22 cm Total Length.

Distribution: Pakistan to Indo-Australian Archipelago except Philippines or Australia.

Remarks: One of the important commercial catfishes. Consumed fresh.

96. *Arius tenuispinis* (Day, 1877)

Day's catfish

Diagnostic features: D. I, 7+adipose; A.18; P.I,10; V.6. Body robust, snout highly depressed and obtusely rounded; barbels thin not fleshy; teeth patch on palate ovoid or elliptical, placed anteriorly in buccal cavity; basal plate before dorsal fin small and 'V' shaped; dorsal fin spine slender; pectoral fin as long as dorsal spine. Bady dark grey on dorsal surface, merging to silvery grey ventrally; tips of pectoral, dorsal and caudal fins dusky.

Habitat: Demersal, inhabits shallow coastal waters, estuaries and lagoons. Attains 19-25 cm Total Length.

Distribution: Indian Ocean, from east coast of Africa to Sri Lanka.

Remarks: One of the important commercial catfish. Caught in large quantities in all types of gear. Consumed fresh.

97. *Osteogeneiosus militaris* (Linnaeus, 1758)

Soldier catfish

Diagnostic features: D. I, 7+adipose; A.19-22; P.I,10-11; V.6. Body elongate, head depressed; mouth moderate with one pair of stiff bony maxillary barbells, longer than head; head shield rather smooth; fin spines strong and serrated. Body dark blue with silvery reflections, belly silvery white; fins grayish white, minutely spotted with black; tips of dorsal fin and adipose fin dark blue.

Habitat: Demersal. Shallow coastal waters, estuaries and tidal rivers. Attains 22-26 cm Total Length.

Distribution: Pakistan, coasts of India to East Indies.

Remarks: One of the important commercial catfishes. Occur in huge shoals. Caught in large quantities by using all types of gear. Consumed fresh. Coarse isinglass is prepared from air bladder

Family: PLOTOSIDAE

Key to the species of Family Plotosidae

1(a) Body with 2-3 prominent stripes; nasal barbels short, reaching to posterior margin of eye .... *Plotosus lineatus*

1(b) Body withouit stripes; nasal barbells long, reaching well beyond eyes .... *Plotosus canius*

98. *Plotosus canius* (Hamilton, 1822)

Canine eel-catfish

Diagnostic features: D_1. I, 4; D_2 130-140; A. 106-130; P.I, 9-13; V. 10-13. Body eel-like, mouth with thick lips; four pairs of barbels, the nasal barbels extending well beyond eyes; caudal fin pointed confluent with dorsal and anal fins. Dark olive green over head and body, below soiled cream; first dorsal and pectoral fins dark.

Habitat: Demersal. Found in estuaries and lagoons. Feed on a variety of small invertebrates and fish. Attains 28 cm Total Legth.

Distribution: Pakistan to New Guinea.

Remarks: One of the most common and commercially important catfish. Consumed fresh.

99. Plotosus lineatus (Thunberg, 1787)

Striped eel-catfish

Diagnostic features: D_1. I, 4; D_2 90-100; A. 60-80; P.I, 9-13; V. 10-13. Body eel-like, mouth with thick lips; four pairs of barbels, the nasal barbels not extending beyond eyes; first dorsal fin small with pungent spine, caudal fin bluntly pointed and confluent with dorsal and anal. Body brownish black above, whitish below; 2-3 horizontal yellowish white stripes on sides; edges of pelvic fins black.

Habitat: Reef associated. Found in coastal areas estuaries and lagoons. Feed on a variety of small invertebrates and fish. Attains 30 cm Total Length.

Distribution: Indo-West Pacific.

Remarks: Most dangerous fish. Deaths often reported elsewhere due to wounds caused by the venomous spines. Food fish but has less fishery value.

Order Aulopiformes

Family: **SYNODONTIDAE**

100. Trachinocephalus myops (Forster, 1801)

Painted lizardfish

Diagnostic features: D.11-14; A.15-18; P. 11-13; V.8; Ll. 51-61. Body fusiform; head not strongly depressed, but lizard-like, eyes placed near tip of snout; snout shorter than eye diameter; mouth large; no spines in fins, small adipose dorsal present; anal fin base distinctly longer than dorsal base; scales above lateral line three and half and below five and half. Head and back greenish brown; upper flanks with faint blue-green and yellow irregular longitudinal stripes; lower flanks and belly silvery; fins pale yellow.

Habitat: Benthic. Inhabit shallow sandy and mud bottoms of coastal waters and estuaries. Attains 20-22 cm Total Length.

Distribution: Warm waters of all waters.

Remarks: Occasionally caught in Chilika Lake. Consumed fresh.

Order: Cyprinodontiformes

Family: **HEMIRAMPHIDAE**

101. Hyporhamphus limbatus (Valenciennes, 1846)

Valenciennes halfbeak

Diagnostic features: D.12-16; A. 13-16; P.10; V.6. Body narrow, elongate and compressed; upper jaw convex, scaly, much broader than long; origin of pelvic fins mid way between front border of eye and base of caudal fin; gill rakers on lower arm of first arch 23-37; caudal fin emarginated. Back greenish, belly silvery; a brilliant silvery band along sides of body; margin of dorsal and caudal fins dusky.

Habitat: Pelagic. Inhabit estuaries, lagoons and back waters and near by coastal waters. Ascends tidal rivers. Attains 25-34 cm total Length.

Distribution: Persian Gulf to Philippines and China.

Remarks: Minor fishery value. Consumed fresh.

Order Beloniformes

Family: **BELONIDAE**

Key to the species of Family Belonidae

1(a) Dorsal fin inserted opposite anal fin origin; 4-5 blotches on side of body between pectoral and anal fins ....*Xenetodon cancila*

1(b) Dorsal inserted beyond anal fin origin; no blotches on sides of body .... 2 (*Strongylura*)

2(a) A black spot at base of caudal fin; caudal fin rounded; dorsal fin rays 12-15; anal fin rays 15-18 ....*S. strongylura*

2(b) No black spot at base of caudal fin; caudal fin emarginate; dorsal fin rays 17-21; anal fin rays 21-25 .... *S. leiura*

102. Strongylura srongylura (van Hasselt, 1823)

Roundtail needlefish

Diagnostic features: D.12-14; A.15-18; P.11; V.6. Body elongate and rounded in cross section; upper and lower jaws are elongate and with sharp teeth; eyes small, 3 or more times in post-orbital part of head; origin of dorsal fin above 4th ray of anal fin; caudal fin emarginated; no lateral keel on caudal peduncle. Bluish green above, silvery below; a prominent black spot at base of caudal fin; a distinct posterior lateral band bordered with black stripe.

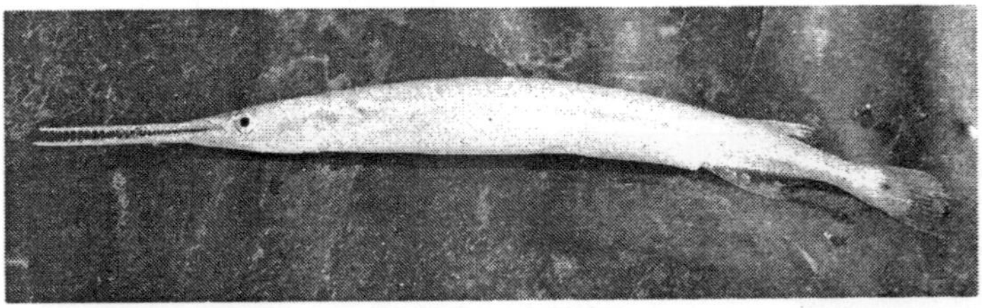

Habitat: Pelagic. Inhabit shallow coastal, estuaries, lagoons, backwaters. Attains 60 cm Total Length.

Distribution: Widespread in tropical Indo-west Pacific.

Remarks: Found in small schools; follow clupeid fishes on which they depend for food. Consumed fresh.

103. *Strongylura leiura* (Bleeker, 1851)

Yellowfin needlefish

Diagnostic features: D.18-21; A. 22-26; P.11; V.7. Body elongate and rounded in cross section; upper and lower jaws are elongate and with sharp teeth directed backwards; eyes small, 2.7 to 3.6 times in post-orbital part of head; dorsal fin origin above 7th to 10th ray of anal fin; caudal fin almost truncate. Back greenish, sides silvery; a prominent black spot at base of caudal fin; a distinct posterior lateral band bordered with black stripe; fins yellow, caudal dusky.

Habitat: Pelagic. Inhabit coastal, estuaries, lagoons and backwaters. Found in small schools, feed on small fish. Attains 45 to 50 cm Total Length.

Distribution: Widespread in tropical Indo-west Pacific.

Remarks: Consumed fresh.

104. ***Xenentodon cancila***
(Hamilton, 1822)

Diagnostic features: D.15-18; A.16-18; P.11; V.6. Body elongate and slightly rounded in cross section; a deep median groove on head; origin of dorsal fin below the level of anal origin. Greenish grey above, lighter below; a dark edged silvery stripe from eye to middle of caudal base; often 4-5 lateral blotches between pectoral and anal bases.

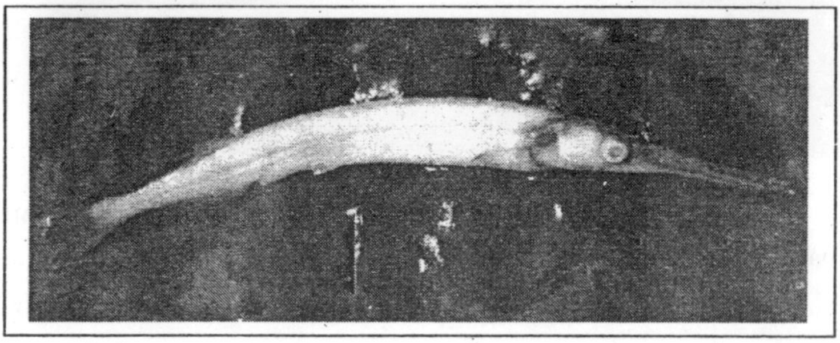

Habitat: Pelagic. Freshwater fish, found in rivers, ponds, lagoons, brackish water lakes. Attains 30 cm Total Length.

Distribution: Pakistan to Indonesia.

Remarks: Caught in small quantities.

Family: **APLOCHEILIDAE**

105. Aplocheilus panchax (Ham.-Buch.)
Blue panchax

Diagnostic features: D.7-11; A. 15-17; P. 15; V. 6; Ll.31-34. Body elongate and compresed; haed and nape broad and depressed; anal fin nearly square, caudal rounded. Upper surface of body greenish, dull white on sides and beneath; fins yellowish, lower third of dorsal fin with large black spot.

Habitat: Benthopelagic; non-migratory; occur in fresh and brackish water, ponds, ditches and mangrove creeks. Sometimes occurring in hypersaline waters. Feed mainly on insects. Attains 9.0 cm Total Length.

Distribution: Pakistan, India, Bangladesh, Myanmar and the Indo-Malaysian Archipelago. Reported from Nepal, Cambodia, Viet Nam and Sri Lanka.

Remarks: Minor commercial value. Utilized for mosquito control. Popular aquarium fish.

Order: Syngnathiformes

Family: **SYNGNATHIDAE**

1(a) Snout short; caudal fin present; all fins present; head normal, no cornet on head; tail not prehensile; body rings osseous, 14-15+38-40 .... *Ichthyocampus carce*

1(b) Snout long; caudal fin absent; ventrals absent; longitudinal axis of head forming a right angle with axis of trunk; prenuchal shield surmounted by a cornet; tail prehensile; rings 11+33-37; spinules on rings .... *Hippocampus fuscus*

106. Hippocampus fuscus Ruppell, 1838

Sea pony

Diagnostic features: D.17-19; A.4; P.13-15. Body compressed, head more or less at right angle to trunk, with an obsolete cornet; no caudal fin, tail prehensile; rings 11+33-37; spinules on rings; dorsal fin inserted opposite vent. Body uniformly dark with light radiating stripes from eye.

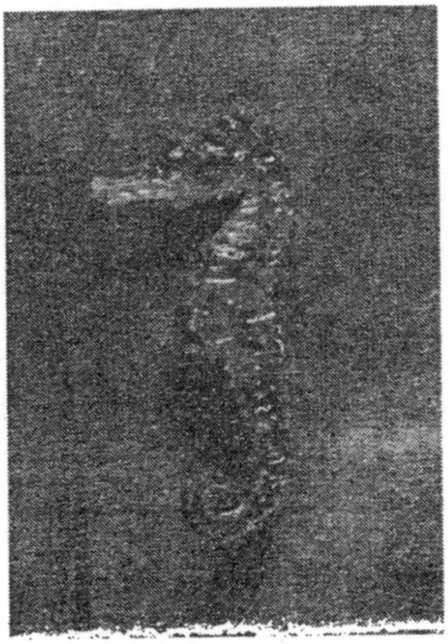

Habitat: Demersal; amphidromous; Found in marine and brackish waters. 14.0 cm Total Length.

Distribution: Indian Ocean: Red Sea, Saudi Arabia, Djibouti, and Sri Lanka.

Remarks: Talwar & Jhinger quoted as *Hippocampus brachyrhynchus* Duncker, 1914 is a junior synonym.

107. Ichthyocampus carce (Hamilton, 1822)

Freshwater pipefish

Diagnostic features: D. 23-26; A.2; P.17; Body rings osseous, 14-15+38-40. Snout slightly elevated on its anterior third; interorbital space slightly concave with a sharp low median ridge passing along snout; a sharp ridge across the opercle; dorsal fin situated in the second to eighth caudal rings. Body deep brown with one or two white spots in the center of each body ring along the infero-lateral ridge; ventral side of snout dotted with black spots; dorsal fin yellow.

Habitat: Demersal; amphidromous; inhabits freshwater, brackish and marine. Most frequently found in rivers, streams and estuaries. Ovoviviparous, male carries the eggs in a brood pouch which is found under the tail. Feed on worms, crustaceans and zooplankton. Attains 15.0 cm. Total Length.

Distribution: Indo-West Pacific: west coast of India to Indonesia.

Remarks: No commercial value.

Order: Synbranchiformes

Family: **SYNBRANCHIDAE**

108. Ophisternon bengalense (McClelland, 1844)

Bengal eel

Diagnostic features: Body much elongated and eel-like; head short, snout rounded; gill opening a single crescentic transverse fold, free from isthmus; scales absent; caudal fin not conspicuous; lateral loine present and conspicuous; all the fins are low. Body dirty brownish red, lighter below.

Habitat: Demersal. Adults inhabit both fresh and brackish waters of rivers and swamps or near the river mouth. Prefers estuarine or tidal areas. Attains 90-100.0 cm Total Length.

Distribution: India and Sri Lanka to south-eastern Asia,

Indonesia, Philippines and New Guinea, also recorded from Australia and Palau.

Remarks: Monior commercial value. Marketed fresh.

Order: Scorpaeniformes

Family: **SCORPAENIDAE**

109. Pterois radiata (Cuvier, 1829)

Radial firefish

Diagnostic features: D. XII, 11; A. III, 6; P. 16; V. I, 6. Scales on the body ctenoid; supra-ocular tentacle smooth without appendages or bars; the dorsal and pectoral fin spines are extremely long. Reddish to brownish and with 5-6 broad dark bars on body separated by pale lines; horizontal dark area on caudal peduncle.

Habitat: Reef associated. Coastal, sometimes in surge zones where in narrow crevices, or along rock-walls in small caves. Also enters brackish lagoons. Feeds exclusively on small crabs and shrimps. Attains 24.0 cm Total Length.

Distribution: Indo-Pacific: Red Sea to Sodwana Bay, South Africa and to the Society Islands, north to the Ryukyu Islands, south to New Caledonia.

Remarks: Very graceful and most beautiful aquarium pet. Capable of inflicting painful wounds with its poisonous dorsal fin spines.

Family **TETRAROGIDAE**

110. Tetraroge niger (Cuvier, 1829)

Blotched Roughfish

Diagnostic characters: D. XIII, 7; A. III, 5; P. 12; V. I, 5. Body small and slender; single dorsal fin, anal fin small; no barbels on lower jaw; anterior post-orbital spine short, the posterior one long; origin of dorsal above posterior part of eye; pectoral thoracic in position; skin covered with small papillae. Colour dark brown with irregular dark blotches; all fins with narrow white border and dark broad sub-marginal band, caudal fin white.

Habitat: Demersal. Found around weedy and silty areas of shallow coastal waters, lagoons and estuaries. Attains 10-12 cm Total Length.

Distribution: Widespread in Indo-Pacific.

Remarks: Uncommon. Fin spines are poisonous.

Family: **PLATYCEPHALIDAE**

111. Platycephalus indicus (Linnaeus, 1758)

Indian flathead or Bartailed flathead

Diagnostic features: D. I+VIII+I, 13; A. 13; P. 18-19; V. I, 5. Large sized fishes. Body very depressed, mouth large; head with bony ridges; a small pre-opercular and two pre-ocular spines present. Body greyish above, whitish below; caudal fin with two horizontal black stripes; first dorsal fin black; pectoral and pelvic fins spotted.

Habitat: Demersal. Found in shallow sandy areas of estuaries, lagoons and backwaters. Attains 100 cm Total Length.

Distribution: Indo-West Pacific.

Remarks: Common fish, frequently encountered. Good food fish.

Order Atheriniformes

Family: **ATHERINIDAE**

Key to the species of Family Atherinidae

1(a) Dentary gently sloping upwards and backwards without tubercle-like elevation at distal end; mid-lateral scales count 39-44 .... *Atherinomorus lacunosus*

1(b) Dentary sloping backwards and upwards and with a distinct tubercle-like elevation at its dorsal end; mid-lateral scale count 33-38 .... *A. duodecimalis*

112. Atherinomorus duodecimalis (Valenciennes, 1835)

Tropical silverside

Diagnostic features: D. IV-VI+I,9-10; A.I,12-13; P.14-17 ; V.I,5; GR. 21-25. Small and robust; snout round and blunt; teeth on jaws small; lateral process of premaxilla broad and flat; dentary sloping backwards and upwards and with a distinct tubercle-like elevation at its distal end; midlateral scale count 33-38. Body blue-green and translucent; head, base of fins and midlateral stripe silvery; rows of spots present below midlateral band.

Habitat: Shallow coastal areas, estuaries and backwaters. Attains 9-10 cm Total Length.

Distribution: Widely distributed in Indo-West Pacific.

Remarks: Caught in small quantities. Consumed fresh or salt dried.

113. *Atherinomorus lacunosus* (Forster, 1801)

Hardyhead silverside

Diagnostic features: D. IV-VII+I, 8-11; A.I,12-17; P.14-16; V.I,5; GR. 18-25. Body sub-cylindrical and laterally compressed; head and eyes moderately large; dentary gently sloping upwards but never elevated posteriorly; posterior edge of preopercle straight; midlateral scale count 39-44. Body blue-green and translucent; silvery parts of abdomen and head highly iridescent; midlateral stripe wider than one scale row; pectoral fin with blackish blotch.

Habitat: Shallow coastal areas. Estuaries and backwaters. Attains 14 cm otal Length.

Distribution: Widely distributed in Indo-West Pacific.

Remarks: Caught in small quantities. Consumed fresh or salt dried.

Order: Perciformes

Family: **CENTROPOMIDAE**

114. Lates calcarifer (Bloch)

Giant seaperch

Diagnostic features: D.VII-IX,10-11; A. III, 7-9; P.17; V.I,5; Ll.52-60. Body elongate and moderately compressed; head pointed with concave dorsal profile becoming convex in front of dorsalfin; operculum with small spine; mouth large, upper jaw extending to beyond eye; two dorsal fins, united at their base, a deep notch dividing both; dorsal fins with scaly sheath; caudal fin rouned.Green blue above and silvery below; eyes bright pink.

Habitat: Demersal. Shallow coastal waters, but ascends estuaries, rivers, lagoons and back waters. Attains 150 cm Total Length.

Distribution: Widespread from Pakistan to Philippines.

Remarks: One of the most important and excellent food fishes of India. Culturabale fish. Consumed fresh. The air bladder is used for making isinglass.

Family: AMBASSIDAE

Key to the species of Family Ambassidae

1(a) Scales large, 25-30 in the longitudinal series; one or two transverse rows of scales on cheek .... 2 (*Ambassis*)

1(b) Scales relatively small; 40 or more in the longitudinal series; 4 or more transverse rows of scales on cheek 3

2(a) Supraorbital ridge smooth with single backwardly directed spine; gill rakers 20-22 on lower arm of arch .... *A. commersoni*

2(b) Supraorbital ridge serrated with 2-4 spines on its posterior edge; gill rakers 23-26 on lower arm of arch .... *A. gymnocephalus*

3(a) Preorbital bone entire, on both ridge and edge; preoperculum entire except for few spines at angle .... *Chanda nama*

3(b) Preorbital bone dentate at least on edge; preoperculum dentate at least on lower edge .... 4 (*Parambasis*)

4(a) Lateral line scales about 90; body orangish-yellow with three longitudinal dusky bands .... *P. lala*

4(b) Lateral line scales 47-65; body transparent with greenish-yellow tinge and a broad silvery lateral stripe .... *P. ranga*

115. *Ambassis commersoni* Cuvier, 1828

Commerson's Glassy perchlet

Diagnostic features: D.VII+I,9-11; A. III, 9-10; P.13 ; V.I,5; Ll. 30-33. Body laterally compressed; mouth large and oblique; supra-orbital ridge smooth, terminated in a single backwardly directed spine; posterior margin of pre-opercular ridge serrated, with a small spine at its angle; one row of scales on cheek; gill rakers 20-22 on lower arm of 1st arch; two dorsal fins separated by a deep notch; lateral line continuous. Body silvery with purplish reflections with bright silvery lateral band; membrane between 2nd and 3rd dorsal spines dusky.

Habitat: Benthopelagic. Inhabits Shallow coastal waters, estuaries, lagoons and rivers. Attains 9-10 cm Total Length.

Distribution: Widespread in Indo-west Pacific.

Remarks: Not commercially important fish, used as a bait fish. Locally consumed.

116. Ambassis gymnocephalus (Lacepede, 1802)

Glassy perchlet

Diagnostic features: D.VII+I,9-10; A. III, 9-10; P.14-15 ; V.I,5; Ll.27-29. Body laterally compressed; mouth large oblique; supra-orbital ridge dentate, terminated in a two or four well developed spine; posterior margin of pre-opercular ridge entire; gill rakers 23-26 on lower arm of 1st arch; lateral line interrupted at middle by 1 or 2 tubeless scales. Body silvery with bright lateral silvery band; membrane between 2nd and 3rd dorsal spines dusky.

Habitat: Demersal. Estuaries, lagoons and rivers. Attains 10 cm Total Length.

Distribution: Widespread in Indo-west Pacific.

Remarks: Not commercially important fish, used as a bait fish. Also eaten locally.

117. Chanda nama Hamilton, 1822

Glass perch

Diagnostic features: D.VII+15-17; A.III+14-17; P.13; V. I,5; Ls.125. Body laterally compressed; mouth large; dorsal and ventral profiles equal with a depression in the orbital region; lower jaw strongly projecting; lower limb of preopercle with double serrated edge; two dorsal fins united at their base; lateral line not interrupted and indistinct. Body yellowish olive, covered with minute black dots; fins orange.

Habitat: Benthopelagic. Inhabits shallow coastal waters, estuaries, lagoons and rivers. Attains 7-8 cm Total Length.

Distribution: Widespread in Indo-west Pacific.

Remarks: Not commercially important fish, used as a bait fish. Consumed locally.

118. Parambassis lala (Hamilton, 1822)

Highfin glassy perchlet

Diagnostic features: D. VII+I,15-16; A. III, 14-15; P. 11; V. I,5; Ls. 60-73. Body elongate and depressed; gill rakers on lower arm of first arch 12-18; second spine of dorsal fin very elongate; caudal fin forked. Body Yellowish olive with three longitudinal dusky bands on sides; black shoulder spot present; fins reddish orange.

Habitat: Demersal; shallow coastal waters, estuaries, lagoons and rivers. Attains 4-5 cm.in Standard Length.

Distribution: Widespread in Indo-West Pacific.

Remarks: Not commercially important fish, used as a bait fish.

119. *Parambassis ranga* (Hamilton, 1822)

Indian glassy fish

Diagnostic features: D. VII+I,15-16; A. III, 14-16; P. 11; V. I,5; Lr. 60-70. Body elongate and compressed; snout pointed; mouth and eyes large; maxilla reaches below the middle of the orbit; depth 2.3-2.4, caudal peduncle depth 8.3 to 9.1 and eye diameter 7.9 to 9.5 in standard length; caudal fin deeply forked. Gill rakers on lower arm of first arch 21-25. Colour olive with a dark spot on the shoulder; margins of dorsal and anal fins dark.

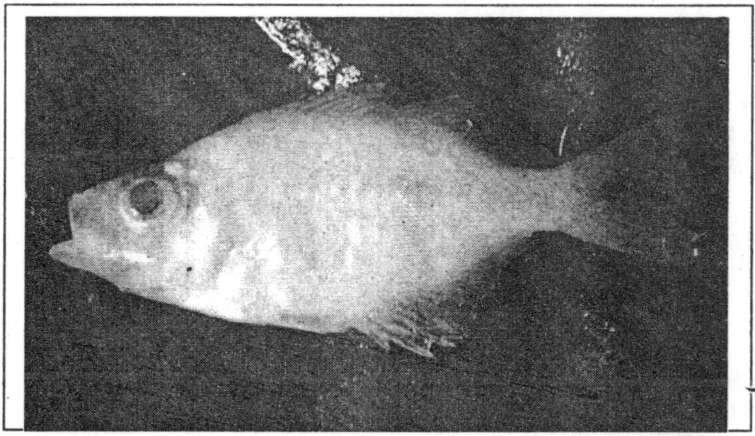

Habitat: Demersal; potamodromous. Shallow coastal waters, estuaries, lagoons and rivers. Feeds on invertebrates, worms and crustaceans. Attains 7-8 cm Total Length.

Distribution: Widespread in Indo-west Pacific. Asia: Pakistan, India, Bangladesh, Myanmar, Thailand, Malaysia and Nepal

Remarks: Not commercially important fish. Subsistence fisheries. Mostly used as a bait fish.Consumed locally. Builds a nest and guards its young. Rare in markets and often found in the aquarium trade.

Family: **SERRANIDAE**

Key to the species of Family Serranidae

1(a) Lateral line scales 63-74; gilrakers 8-10+17-20; head, body and fins with numerous roundish dark spots which vary from dull orange-red to dark brown; a dark blotch at base of last four dorsal pines .... *Epinephelus tauvina*

1(b) Lateral line scales below 65; gillrakers 8-10+14-17; colouration not as in 1a 2

2(a) Adults body vaguely mottled dark brown; fins with numerous small black spots .... *E. lanceolatus*

2(b) Body with numerous orangish or brownish yellow spots of pupil size; five diagonal grayish brown bars on head and body .... *E. coioides*

120. Epinephelus coioides (Hamilton, 1822)

Orangespotted Grouper

Diagnostic features: D. XI, 14-16; A. III, 8; P. 19-20; V. I, 5. Body elongate and not strongly compressed; inter-orbital space slightly convex; caudal fin rounded. Cololur light brown, whitish ventro-laterally, head and body with numerous brownish orange spots; five slightly oblique brown bars.

on head and body which bifurcate ventrally, the first four bars extending basally into the dorsal fin; large brown blotches on head; fins whitish to dusky with brown spots.

Habitat: Reef associated. Found in turbid cool waters, estuaries, lagoons and lakes. Not uncommon. Feeds on small crabs and fish. Attains 100 cm Total Length.

Distribution: Indo-West Pacific.

Remarks: Good food fish. Consumed fresh or salt-dried. Fairly found in fish catches. Caught by hook & line, gill nets and shore seines.

121. Epinephelus lanceolatus (Bloch, 1790)

Giant Grouper

Diagnostic features: D. XI, 15; A. III, 8; P. 19; V. I, 5. Body thick and very deep. Small scales on maxilla and snout; dorsal fin spines short; caudal fin rounded. Colour yellowish brown with vaguely mottled; all fins with black spots and blotches.

Habitat: Reef associated. Found in coastal rocky areas, occasionally in estuaries and lagoons. Very common grouper. Feeds on spiny lobsters, mud crabs and fishes. Attains up to 270 cm Total Length and weighs 400 kg.

Distribution: Widespread in Indo-Pacific.

Remarks: Important commercial food fish. Occasionally attacks divers and swimmers.

122. Epinephelus tauvina (Forsskal, 1775)

Greasy Grouper

Diagnostic features: D. XI, 14-15;, A. III, 8; P. 18-19; V. I, 5. Body elongates; mouth very large; caudal fin rounded. Colour greenish grey dorsally and whitish ventrally; numerous round orange-red to brownish spots on head, body and fins; five faint diagonal dark bars on body.

Habitat: Reef associated. Found in coastal areas, enters estuaries, lagoons. Attains 50-60 cm Total Length.

Distribution: Widespread in Indo-Pacific.

Remarks: Not uncommon. Commercially important fish. Consumed fresh or salt-dried. Large individuals are reported to be aggressive and dangerous.

Family: **TERAPONIDAE**

Key to the species of Family Teraponidae

1(a) Post temporal covered with skin and scales, not expanded posteriorly, not with a serrated edge; gill membranes joined to isthmus; body with five horizontal black stripes; a black blotch on nape .... *Pelates quadrilineatus*

1(b) Post temporal expanded and serrated posteriorly, exposed posteriorly; skin and scale covering reduced; gill membranes free from isthmus .... 2 (*Terapon*)

2(a) Two to four straight longitudinal stripes along side of body; gillrakers 18-24 on lower arm of 1st arch .... *T. puta*

2(b) Three downward curved longitudinal stripes along

body; gillrakers 12-15 on lower arm of 1st arch ....*T. jarbua*

123. *Pelates quadrilineatus* (Bloch, 1790)

Four-lined Terapon

Diagnostic features: D. XII-XIII, 9-11; A. III, 9-10; P. 14-16; V. I, 5. Body moderately deep and compressed; opercular spine small and fairly strong; dorsal fin not deeply incised caudal fin emarginated. Body silvery with five horizontal black stripes on sides; a broad black blotch behind head below dorsal origin present or absent; spinous dorsal fin with black blotch; anal fin light yellow with dark edges; caudal, pectoral and ventral fins light yellow.

Habitat: Pelagic. Found in coastal waters, estuaries, lagoons and lakes. Attains 20 cm Total Length.

Distribution: widespread in Indo-West Pacific.

Remarks: Common component in commercial catches. Good food fish.

124. *Terapon jarbua* (Forsskal,1775)

Crescent-grunter or Jarbua terapon

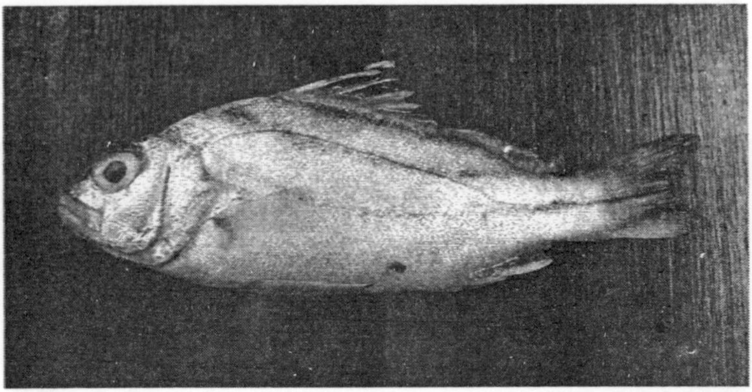

Diagnostic features: D. XI-XII, 9-11; A. III, 8-10; P. 13-14; V. I, 5; Ll. 68-92. Body ovate and slightly compressed; mouth slightly oblique; opercular spines are strong and long; caudal fin emarginated. Body silvery or silvery-grey above, silvery-white below with 3-4 curved dark brown or black bars; spinous dorsal fin with large black blotch; caudal fin with black stripes.

Habitat: Demersal. Found in silty-sand areas of inshore waters, rivers, estuaries, lagoons. Attains 32 cm Total Length.

Distribution: Widespread in Indo-West Pacific.

Remarks: Common component of fish catches. Good food as well as aquarium fish.

125. *Terapon puta* (Cuvier 1829)

Banded grunter

Diagnostic features: D. XI-XII, 9-11; A. III, 8-9; P. 13-14; V. I, 5; Ll. 70-85. Body moderately deep and compressed; maxillary reaching to posterior nostril; no teeth on roof of mouth; gill rakers 18 to 24 on lower arm of first arch; caudal fin emarginated. Body brownish above with three or four straight longitudinal stripes; dorsal fin with blackish blotch between 3rd to 7th spines; caudal fin with an oblique bar on upper lobe and blotch at tip, middle caudal rays with stripe and one or two oblique bars on lower caudal lobe.

Habitat: Benthopelagic. Found in silty-sand areas of inshore waters, rivers, estuaries, lagoons. Attains 30 cm Total Length.

Distribution: Widespread in Indo-West Pacific.

Remarks: Common component of fish catches. Good food as well as aquarium fish.

Family: **SILLAGINIDAE**

Key to the species of Family Sillaginidae

1(a) Snout and head greatly depressed; preopercl smooth; second dorsal spine very elongate, extend to caudal base .... *Sillaginopsis panijius*

1(b) Snout and head not depressed; preopercle serrated; second dorsal spine not elongated .... 2 (*Sillago*)

2(a) Air bladder with two distinct postcoelomic extensions; no black spots on second dorsal fin .... *S. sihama*

2(b) Airbladder with a single postcoelomic extension; second dorsal with 5-7 rows of blackish spots .... *S. vincenti*

126. Sillaginopsis panijus (Hamilton, 1822)

Gangetic whiting

Diagnostic features: D.X+I, 25-27; A. I, 24-26; P.15-16; V. Ll. 84-88. Body elongate, partly cylindrical; head and snout greatly depressed, cheeks swollen; gill rakers on lower arm of 1st arch six; pelvic spine almost hidden by thickened pelvic rays; the second dorsal spine filamentous, very long and extending to caudal base. Body greenish yellow, lower half whitish; fins pale brown.

Habitat: Demersal. Found in silty-sand areas of inshore waters, rivers, estuaries, lagoons. Attains 45 cm Total Length.

Distribution: Coasts of India to Indonesia.

Remarks: Important commercial fish, found abundant in catches. Good food fish.

127. Sillago sihama (Forsskal, 1775)

Silevr sillago

Distribution: D.XI+I, 20-23; A. II, 21-23; P.16-17; V.I,5 Ll. 66-72. Body elongate, snout pointed; head profile sloightly convex; mouth small and terminal. Body light brown, ventral flanks and belly whitish; dorsal and caudal fins dusky.

Habitat: Demersal. Found in silty-sand areas of inshore waters, rivers, estuaries, lagoons. Attains 30 cm Total Length.

Distribution: Wide spread in Indo-Pacific.

Remarks: Important commercial fish, found abundant in catches. Good food fish.

128. Sillago vincenti (Mc Kay, 1980)

Vincent's sillago

Diagnostic features: D. XI+I, 21-23; A. II, 22-24; P.16-17; V.I, 5 Ll. 70-74. Very similar in external morphology to *Sillago sihama*. Swim bladder with a single posterior extension, a short bulbous projection anteriorly with one to three anterolobate or recurved projections; no tubular extensions anteriorly. Body uniform pale tan, with the second dorsal fin spotted.

Habitat: Demersal; amphidromous; inhabits brackish and marine waters in schools on muddy substrates. Attains 25-28 cm Total Length.

Distribution: Indian Ocean: East and west coast of India.

Remarks: Minor commercial value. It is a potential aquaculture species in impoundments and tidal ponds. Growth is reported to be rapid

Family: RACHYCENRIDAE

129. *Rachycentròn canadus* (Linnaeus, 1766)

Cobia or Black Kingfish

Diagnostic features: D.IIV-XI+I,33-36; A.II-III, 22-28; P. 21-22; Ll. 300 above. Body elongate and sub-cylindrical with broad and depressed head, mouth large, lower jaw projecting; spines of 1st dorsal fin short and free not connected by membrane;

caudal fin lunate, upper lobe slightly longer; scales small, embedded in thick skin. Back and sides dark brownish, sides with two silvery bands; outer edge of caudal white.

Habitat: Pelagic. Shallow rocky coastal areas, occasionally enter estuaries, lagoons. Attains over 1.8 m Total Length.

Distribution: Widespread in warm waters of Mediterranean, Atlantic and Indo-Pacific.

Remarks: Excellent game fish of average food value. Caught by hand lines, troll lines and gill-nets.

Family: **ECHENEIDAE**

130. Echeneis naucrates (Linnaeus, 1758)

Shark remora

Diagnostic features: D.34-43; A. 32-38; P. 21-24. Body long and narrow; head flattened on top bearing a laminated adhesive disc containing 21-28 laminae; depth 10-14 in standard length; dorsal and anal fin bases long; lower gill rakers 11-16; caudal fin rounded. Body brown to black with bands on sides.

Habitat: Reef associated. Found in coastal waters. Occasionally enter estuaries and brackish water lakes. Attains over 80 cm Total Length.

Distribution: All warm waters except eastern Pacific.

Remarks: Found attach themselves to shark and other big fish. Occasionally encountered in Chilika Lake.

Family: **CARANGIDAE**

Key to the species of Family Carangidae

1(a) Dorsal fin separated, spines rudimentary ; dorsal fin rays 42-46; ventral fin absent in adults .... *Parastromateus niger*

1(b) Dorsal fin spines not rudimentary; fin rays less than 42; ventral fins present 2

2(a) Posterior part of lateral line with scutes; pectoral fins relatively long, usually falcate 3

2(b No scutes on lateral line; pectoral fin short, not falcate 11

3(a) Eight or nine finlets present behind second dorsal and anal fins; lateral line with 53-58 strong keeled scutes; breast naked .... *Megalaspis cordyla*

3(b) No finlets in dorsal and anal fins; lateral line scutes weak or feeble; breast naked or scaled 4

4(a) Scales minute and embedded in skin; 1st dorsal with six small spines, not connected by membrane; dorsal and anal fin lobes extremely long and filamentous especially in juveniles .... *Alectis indicus*

4(b) Scales small, not embedded in skin; 1st dorsal fin with 7-8 spines, connected by membrane; dorsal and anal fin lobes are not filamentous 5

5(a) Adipose tissue covering the entire eye except central slit .... *Atule mate*

5(b) Adipose tissue bearing anterior half of eye 6

6(a) Eye 2.7 to 3.0 in head length; gill rakers on lower arm of 1st arch 23-27; shoulder girdle margin with a deep cleithral furrow vertically .... *Selar crumenophthalmus*

6(b) Eye 3.5-5.5 times in head length; gill rakers on lower arm of 1st arch 10-30; shoulder girdle margin smooth; no cleithral furrow 7

7(a) Teeth in a single series in each jaw, more enlarged;

scales prominent; breast scaled .... *Alepes djedaba*

7 (b) Jaw teeth fine, villiform, in bands in both jaws; outer rows in both jaws slightly enlarged; scutes weakly developed; breast usually naked ...... *Carangoides praeustus*

7(c) Jaw teeth in band in upper jaw, outer row enlarged; a single series in lower jaw, with 2-4 anterior canines; scutes prominent; breast rarely entirely naked .... 8 (*Caranx*)

8(a) Breast completely naked 9

8(b) Breast naked ventrally, with a small patch of scales immediately in front of pelvic fins 10

9(a) Upper jaw reaching to below front edge of eye; anal fin rays 17-20; dorsal fin rays 20-24 .... *C. melampygus*

9(b) Upper jaw reaching to posterior edge of eye; anal fin rays 14-16; dorsal finrays 18-21 .... *C. sexfasciatus*

10(a) Lateral line with 28-30 scutes; dorsal fin rays 19-20; base of pectoral fin naked .... *C. ignobilis*

10(b) Lateral line with 33-37 scutes; dorsal fin rays 20-22; base of pectoral fin not naked .... *C. carangus*

11(a) Body slender; soft dorsal and anal fins not strongly falcate; scales elongate or needle-like .... 12 (*Scomberoides*)

11(b) Body relatively deep; soft dorsal and anal fins strongly falcate; scales normal, oval shaped ....14 (*Trichonotus*)

12(a) Total gill rakers 8-15; dorsal fin lobe uniformly pigmented; blotches above or intersecting lateral line 13

12(b) Total gill rakers 21-27; distal half of dorsal fin lobe abruptly and heavily pigmented; double series of 6-8 dusky roundish blotches above and below lateral line; scales lanceolate .... *S. lysan*

13(a) Large oval patches above or touching lateral line; upper jaw extending well beyond posterior margin of eye; snout

snout 21-26% of head length ....*S. commersonianus*

13(b) Vertical elongate blotches intersecting lateral line; upper jaw extends slightly beyond posterior margin of eye; snout 26 to 30% of head length .... *S. tala*

14(a) Teeth on tongue absent; anal fin lobe dark......... *T. blochii*

14(b) Teeth on tongue present; anal fin lobe relatively clear .... *T. mookalee*

131. Alectis indicus (Ruppell, 1830)

India Threadfin Trevally

Diagnostic features: D. VI+I, 18-20; A. II+I, 18-19. Body strongly compressed and deep; head profile almost vertical with a distinct hump above eye; pectoral fins are large and falcate; anterior dorsal and anal fin rays are extremely long in young; gill rakers short and stout, 30-35 on first arch; 5-12 weak scutes on caudal peduncle. Body dark blue above, silvery white below; a dusky spot on upper edge of operculum. Juveniles with dark cross bars on sides.

Habitat: Reef associated. Found in coastal waters and adjacent estuaries, lagoons etc., form large schools. Attains 60 cm Total Length.

Distribution: Indo-West Pacific.

Remarks: Frequently found in commercial catches. Good food fish. Consumed fresh or salt-dried.

132. *Alpes djedaba* (Forsskal, 1775)

Shrimp scad

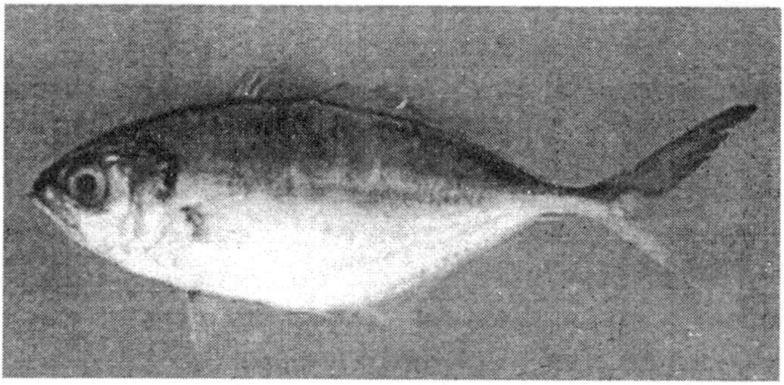

Diagnostic features: D. VIII+I, 23-24; A. II+I, 18-20. Body oblong and compressed; dorsal and ventral profiles equally convex; jaws nearly equal with single row of comb like teeth; eyelids developed on rear half of eye; adipose eyelid well developed on posterior half of eye only; lateral line with 42-48 scutes. Greyish green above, silvery below with distinct black blotch on upper edge of opercle bordered above by a small white spot; fins pale yellow; upper lobe of caudal fin dusky distally.

Habitat: Reef associated. Common in inshore waters, estuaries and lagoons in schools. Feed on crustaceans, cephalopods and small fish. Attains 25 cm Total Length.

Distribution: Indian Ocean.

Remarks: Frequently found in commercial catches. Caught by gill nets, shore seines and hooks.

133. *Atule mate* (Cuvier, 1833)

Yellowtail scad

Diagnostic features: D. VII+I, 23-29; A. II+I, 20; P. 22-23; V. I, 5. Body oblong and compressed; lower jaw prominent; adipose eye lids well developed, covering all the eye except for a small vertical slit; last dorsal and anal fin rays fin let like; 45-50 strong scutes on the lateral line. Body olive green dorsally, shading to white ventrally; 9-19 grey bands wider than pale inter-spaces present dorso-laterally; a black spot on opercle; dorsal and caudal fins yellowish; anal fin pale; pectoral and ventral fins white.

Habitat: Pelagic. Found in shallow coastal waters and estuarine areas in schools. Feed on crustaceans and cephalopods. Attains 25-30 cm Total Length.

Distribution: Wide spread in Indo-west Pacific.

Remarks: Good food fish and very common in commercial fish catches.

134. *Carangoides praeustus* (Bennett, 1830)

Brown-backed Trevally

Diagnostic features: D. VIII+I, 23-24; A. II+I, 19-20. Body oblong and compressed, dorsal profile more convex than ventral; head profile steep; straight part of lateral line conspicuously shorter than curved part with 25-30 scutes. Body brownish above, silvery below; fins yellowish with dusky tips.

Habitat: Demersal. Inhabits coastal waters, estuaries and occasionally lagoons. Attains 50-60 cm Total Length.

Distribution: Coasts of India, Sri Lanka and East Indies.

Remarks: Not frequent in then catches. Consumed fresh.

135. Caranx carangus (Bloch, 1793)

Black-tailed trevally

Diagnostic features: D.VIII+I, 209-22; A. II+I,15-18. Body oblong and compressed; eye diameter 3.5 to 4.0 in head length; pectoral fins falcate; caudal fin forked; triangular lateral area of breast towards pectoral fin partly scaled, ventrally naked except small patch before pelvic fins; lateral line moderately arched with 33-37 scutes. Body silvery, darker above with golden hue; young ones with 4-5 dark cross bars; small opercular spot present; margin of soft dorsal and upper lobe of caudal fin blackish.

Habitat: Reef associated. Inhabits coastal waters and estuaries. Attains 40 cm or more Total Length.

Distribution: Coasts of India to Japan and Philippines and tropical Atlantic.

Remarks: Caught in large quantities. Good food fish.

136. Caranx sexfasciatus Quoy & Gaimad, 1825

Big-eye trevally

Diagnostic features: D. VIII+I, 20-21; A. II+I, 15-16. Body oblong; upper and lower profiles equal, nape elevated; cleft of mouth well below the level of eye; 32-34 strong scutes on lateral line; breast completely scaled; 16-18 gill rakers on lower arm of 1st arch. Body blue green above, silvery below; a small, black spot on upper edge of opercle; tips of soft dorsal and anal fins white; caudal fin yellowish.

Habitat: Reef associated. Found in coastal waters near reefs. Feed on fish and crustaceans. Attains 70-75 cm Total Length.

Distribution: Wide spread in Indo-Pacific.

Remarks: Good food fish and very common in commercial fish catches.

137. ***Caranx ignobilis*** (Forsskal)

Giant Trevally

Diagnostic features:D.VIII+I,18-21;A.II+I,15-17. Body deep and strongly compressed and robust; head profile steep and strongly curved above eyes; ventral profile from lower jaw to anal fin base straight; breast naked ventrally, small patch of scales at pre-pelvic; lateral line with 28-30 scutes. Body silvery grey above, paler below; no dark spot at upper end of opercle; fins dusky.

Habitat: Reef associated. Found around coastal areas. Juveniles and young often enter estuaries and lagoons. Attains 140-160 cm Total Length.

Distribution: Widespread in Indo-west Pacific.

Remarks: Good food fish and very common in commercial fish catches.

138. Caranx melampygus Cuvier

Blue-fin trevally

Diagnostic features: D. VII+I, 23; A, II+I, 19-20. Body oblong, head profile fairly steep; breast completely scaled; 36-39 scutes on lateral line; soft dorsal and anal fin bases are nearly equal; Body greenish blue with small blue-black spots on upper back and sides; silvery white on lower sides; lobes of dorsal and anal fins electric blue; pectoral fins light yellow.

Habitat: Reef associated. Found in coastal and estuarine areas. Feed primarily on fish. Attains 80-90 cm Total Length.

Distribution: Wide spread in Indo-West Pacific.

Remarks Good food fish and very common in commercial fish catches.

139. *Megalaspis cordyla* (Linnaeus, 1758)

Hardtail scad or Torpedo scad

Diagnostic features: D. VIII+I, 10+8-9 finlets; A. II+I, 8+9-10 fin lets; P. 22; V. I, 5. Body torpedo shaped; adipose eyelids well developed; breast naked; lateral line with 54-56 strong and large keeled scutes; caudal peduncle very slender, caudal fin forked. Body green above, silvery below; prominent black spot on upper edge of operculum; all fins light yellow.

Habitat: Pelagic. Found near reef areas in school. Feed on small crustaceans and fish. Attains 80-100 cm Total Length.

Distribution: Wide spread in Indo-Pacific.

Remarks: Good food fish, not common in commercial fish catches.

140. *Scomberoides commersonianus* Lacepede, 1801

Talang queenfish

Diagnostic features: D. VI-VII+I, 20-21; A. II+I, 18-19; P. 18; V. I, 5. Body compressed with blunt snout and depression over

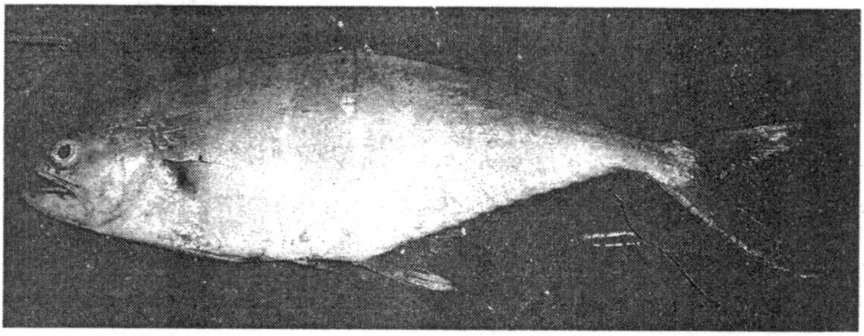

eyes; eyes 4.5 to 6.0 times in head length; upper jaw extending well beyond eye; no scutes on lateral line; gill rakers on first arch 8-15; pectoral fin small, not falcate. Body dusky green above, silvery below with 6-9 large oval blotches intersecting lateral line; pectoral fins pale with a dusky blotch ventrally; ventral fins white.

Habitat: Pelagic.Coastal areas, estuaries and occasionally lagoons. Found in small schools. Feed on fish, cephalopods and pelagic organisms. Attains 100-110 cm Total Length.

Distribution: Widespread in Indo-west Pacific.

Remarks: Good food fish. Common in commercial fish catches.

141. Parastromateus niger (Bloch, 1795)

Black pomfret

Diagnostic features: D.IV-V+I, 41-44; A. II+I, 35-39. Body ovate, deep and compressed; mouth small, teeth small, in a single row in jaws; dorsal and anal fins long, identical, with elevated broadly rounded anterior lobes; ventral fins absent, but minute in young; pectoral fins long and falcate; caudal fin forked; lateral line with 9-19 scutes. Body silvery grey to bluish brown; lower portion light; fins with dark edges; young with three dark cross bands.

Habitat: Coastal, pelagic fish often enter estuaries and lakes. Attains 50-55 cm Total Length.

Distribution: Wide spread in Indo-west Pacific.

Remarks: Occur in large schools. Excellent food fish. Consumed fresh or salt-dried.

142. Scomberoides lysan (Forsskal, 1775)

Double spotted queenfish

Diagnostic features: D. VI-VII+I, 21; A. II+I, 19-21; P. 20; V. I, 5. Body compressed and elongate; eye 4.1-5.7 in head length; upper jaw long; no scutes on lateral line pectoral fin short and not falcate; gill rakers on first arch 21-27. Body grey green above; silvery white below; double series of 6-8 dusky roundish blotches above and below lateral line; distal half of dorsal fin lobe dark; anal fin with a small dusky

blotch on anterior part.

Habitat: Reef associated. Found in coastal waters, enters estuaries and brackish lakes. Feed on small fish. Attains 50-60 cm Total Length.

Distribution: Widespread in Indo-west Pacific.

Remarks: Good food fish and very common in commercial fish catches. Consumed fresh or salt-dried.

143. ***Scomberoides tala*** (Cuvier, 1831)

Deep queenfish

Diagnostic features: D. VI-VII+I, 20-21; A. II+I, 17-19; P. 17; V. I, 5. Body elongate and compressed; frontal profile concave; eye 4.5-5.0 in head; gill rakers on first arch 11-15; lateral line indistinct; pectoral fins short, not falcate. Body silvery, sides with 4-8 vertical elongate blotches, most of them intersecting lateral line; dorsal and anal fins uniformly pigmented.

Habitat: Pelagic. Marine, occasionally enters estuaries and brackish lakes. Attains 50-55 cm Total Length.

Distribution: Widely distributed in Bay of Bengal and Indo-Australian Archipelago.

Remarks: Good food fish. Consumed fresh or salt-dried or cured. Caught in small quantities from Chilika Lake.

144. ***Selar crumenophthalmus*** (Bloch, 1793)

Big-eye scad

Diagnostic features: D. VIII+I, 25-26; A. II+I, 21-22; P. 19; V. I, 5. Body oblong and moderately compressed; eyes large, adipose eyelids well developed covering entire eye except a centered slit; lateral line becoming straight below middle of soft dorsal with 33-34 scutes. Body metallic blue above, shading to white below; operculum with a large black spot; fins pale green; caudal fin lobes dusky.

Habitat: Pelagic. Found in shallow coastal areas and estuaries. Feed on benthic invertebrates. Attains 20-25 cm Total Length

Distribution: All tropical and subtropical waters.

Remarks: Good food fish and very common in commercial fish catches.

145. *Trachinotus blochii* (Lacepede, 1801)

Snubnose pompano

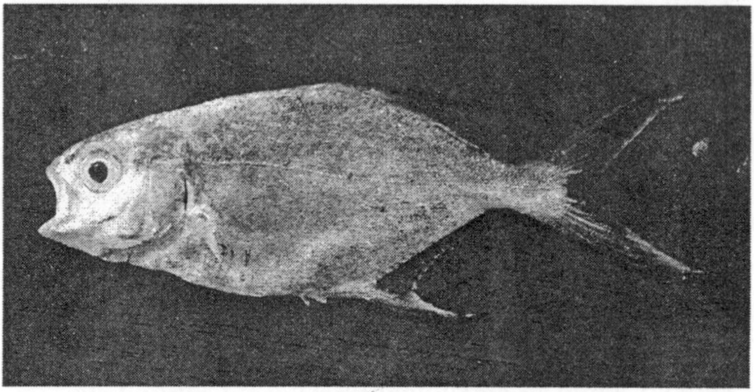

Diagnostic features: D.VI+I,19; A. II+I, 16; P.18; V. I,5. Body deep and compressed, depth 2.2 to 2.7 in standard length; head profile smoothly rounded, snout blunt; eye 3.4 to 4.2 in head; dorsal, anal and caudal fins falcate; pectoral fins short; gill rakers on lower arm of first arch 15-19. Body silvery, paler below; dorsal and anal fins yellow, the lobes dark.

Habitat: Demersal. Found in coastal waters and enter estuaries. Feed on molluscs and fish. Attains 80-90 cm Total Length.

Distribution: Wide spread in Indo-Pacific.

Remarks: Good food fish and common in commercial fish catches.

146. *Trachinotus mookalee* (Cuvier, 1832)

Indian pompano

Diagnostic features: D.VI-VII+I, 18-21; A.II+I,16-19; P.17; V.I,5; C.17. Body compressed with slightly elevated frontal region; snout obtuse, mouth oblique; no fin lets; lateralline unarmed; caudal fin with deep lobes. Body more or less golden; upper half of first five dorsal raysipped with black.

Habitat: Demersal. Inhabits shallow coastal and brackish. Waters. Attains 90.0 cm Total Length.

Distribution: Indo-west Pacific.

Remarks: Minor commercial fish; consumed fresh or salt dried.

Family: LEIOGNATHIDAE

Key to the species of Family Leiognathidae

1(a) Mouth pointing forward when protracted; mouth horizontal; lateral line extending up to caudal end 2

1(b) Mouth pointing upwards when protracted, mouth oblique; lateral line ending slightly before end of dorsal fin .... *Secutor insidiator*

2(a) Distinct canine teeth in jaws; protruded mouth points forward; pectoral axil black ....*Gazza minuta*

2(b) No canine teeth in jaws; protracted mouth pointed downward ...... 3 (*Leiognathus*)

3(a) Cleft of mouth opposite lower third of eye 4

3(b) Cleft of mouth at or below lower edge of eye 5

4(a) Breast naked; yellow band along lateral line; pectoral axil black .... *L. daura*

4(b) Beast scaled; saddle-shaped blotch on nape; vertical zig-zag yellow stripes on back and sides of body . . . . *L. blochii*

5(a) Dorsal and ventral profile of body equally convex; no blotch on caudal peduncle; faint wavy vertical lines on back .... *L. dussumieri*

5(b) Dorsal profile of body strongly arched; small blotch usually present on caudal peduncle; narrow vertical stripes on back .... *L. equulus*

147. ***Gazza minuta*** (Bloch, 1797)

Toothed poonyfish

Diagnostic features: D.VII-VIII, 15-17; A. III, 13-14; P.16-17; V. I, 5; Ll. 58-60. Body oval and compressed, dorsal and ventral profiles equally convex; mouth small, protracted forward; forehead with small spine; eye diameter equal to inter-orbital width; scales on body, no scales on head and breast. Body silvery with brownish wavy lines on upper half; red and blue marks on above pectoral fin; pectoral axil black.

Habitat: Demersal. Coastal areas, estuaries and lakes are nursery grounds. Found in small schools. Attains 14-18 cm Total Length.

Distribution: Wide spread in tropical Indo-Pacific.

Remarks: Contributes substantially to the fishery. Consumed fresh or salt-dried.

148. ***Leiognathus blochii*** (Valenciennes, 1835)

Bloch's ponuyfish

Diagnostic featutres: D.VIII, 16; A. III, 14; P. 18-19; V. I,5; Ll. 60. Body oval and compresed, dorsal and ventral profiles almost convex; snout pointed, protrudes downward; mandibular profile strongly concave; head naked, body and breast scaly. Body silvery with dark saddle shaped blotch on nape; vertical zig-zag yellow stripes on back and sides; upper half of spinous dorsal with black blotch.

Habitat: Demersal. Inhabits very shallow waters, bottom dwelling. Attains13-16 cm Total Length.

Distribution: Coasts of India to Philippines.

Remarks: Fairly common in catches. Consumed fresh or salt-dried.

149. *Leiognathus daura* (Cuvier, 1829)

Gold-striped ponyfish

Diagnostic features: D.VIII, 16; A. III, 14; P. 17-18; V. I,5. Body rhomboid and compressed; mouth small, pointing downwards; head naked; no scales on breast. Body silvery, back greenish with irregular gray streaks; yellow band along lateral line; upper half of spinous dorsal with black blotch; pectoral axil black; lower caudal fin lobe yellow.

Habitat: Demersal. Inhibits shallow muddy coastal waters, estuaries and lagoons. Attains 12-15 cm Total Length.

Distribution; Wide spread in tropical Indo-west Pacific.

Remarks: Not common in the catches.

150. *Leiognathus dussumieri* (Valenciennes, 1835).

Dussumier's ponyfish

Diagnostic features: D.VIII, 16; A. III, 14; P. 17-19; V. I, 5. Body oblong and compressed; dorsal and ventral profiles equally convex; mouth projects slightly downwards when protracted; scales on body, head and breast. Body silvery with wavy vertical lines on back; fins yellowish; dorsal fin hyaline.

Habitat: Demersal. Shallow coastal sandy bottom areas and estuaries. Attains 12-15 cm Total Length.

Distribution: Indo-west Pacific.

Remarks: Fairly common in catches. Consumed fresh or salt-dried.

151. *Leiognathus equulus* (Forsskal, 1775)

Common ponyfish

Diagnostic features: D.VIII, 15-16; A. III, 14-15; P. 18-20; V. I, 5. Body deep and compressed; dorsal profile of body strongly arched; mouth pointing downwards when protracted; mandibular profile strongly concave; head without scales, breast with thin scales. Body silvery with faint, narrow vertical stripes on back; small black blotch on caudal peduncle; pectoral axil dusky; anal fin yellowish.

Habitat: Benthopelagic. Coastal waters, enters brackish waters also, bottom dwelling fish. Attains 25 cm Total Length.

Distribution: Wide spread in tropical Indo-west Pacific.

Remarks: Most common silver belly of the fish catches. Consumed fresh or salt-dried.

152. *Secutor insidiator* (Bloch, 1787)

Pugnose ponyfish

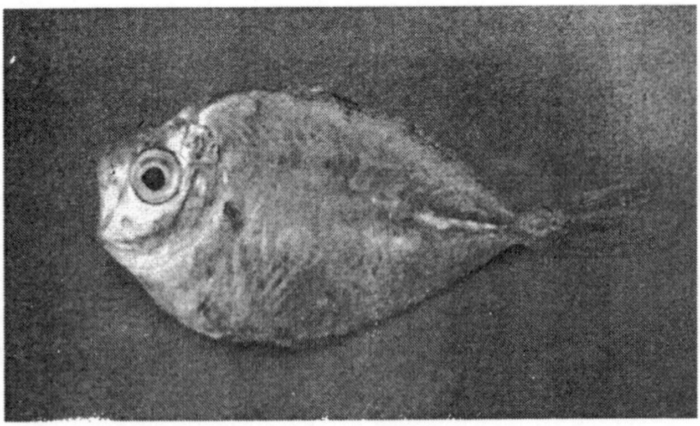

Diagnostic features: D.VIII-IX, 15-17; A. III, 14; P. 17-18; V. I, 5. Body oval and compressed; mouth small, oblique and pointing upwards; two minute spines above each eye. Body silvery with blue spots on back forming vertical bands; lower flanks silvery with minute black dots; tip of dorsal black; pectoral axil yellowish or black.

Habitat: Demersal. Inhabits shallow coastal waters near bottom. Attains 10 cm Total Length.

Distribution: Widespread in Indo-West Pacific.

Remarks: Fairly common in catches. Consumed fresh or salt-dried.

Family: **LUJANIDAE**

Key to the species of Family Lutjanidae

1(a) A large black spot on upper back present 2

1(b) Black spot absent on upper back 3

2(a) Vomarine tooth patch crescentic, without a median posterior extension; scale rows on back parallel to lateral line; no stripes on sides of body .... *Lutjanus johnii*

2(b) Vomarine tooth patch triangular, with a median posterior extension; scale rows on back rising obliquely above lateral line; sides of body with 7-8 golden brown stripes .... *L. russelli*

3(a) Preopercular notch and knob well developed; total gill rakers on 1st arch 20-22; posterior profile of dorsal and anal fins somewhat angular; back and sides bright yellow with four bright blue stripes on sides .... *L. kasmira*

3(b) Preopercular notch and knob poorly developed; total gill rakers on1st arch 16-20; posterior profile of dorsal and anal fins rounded; back and sides greenish-brown or reddish; no stripes on sides of body ....*L. argentimaculatus*

153. *Lutjanus argentimaculatus* (Forsskal, 1775)

Mangrove Red-snapper

Diagnostic features: D. X, 13-14; A. III, 8; P. 16-17; V. I, 5; Ll. 46. Body moderately deep; snout pointed; caudal fin emarginated. Body greenish-brown, belly silvery; scales with a dark centers and white margin; median fins with reddish hue; pectoral and ventral fins dark brown; anterior margin of ventral fin red with narrow white margin. Juveniles are with eight whitish bars on sides and 1 or 2 blue lines across cheek.

Habitat: Reef associated. Found in shallow coastal areas to 30 m depth. Juveniles and young are found in mangroves, estuaries and lagoons. Attains 80-90 cm Total Length.

Distribution: Widespread in Indo-west Pacific.

Remarks: Taken commercially in small quantities. Not uncommon. Good food fish. Consumed fresh.

154. *Lutjanus johnii* (Bloch, 1792)

John's snapper

Diagnostic features: D. X, 14; A. III, 8; P. 16; V. I, 5. Dorsal profile of head deeply sloped; no inter-opercular nob; longitudinal scale rows above lateral line parallel to it and those below lateral line horizontal; caudal fin truncate. Body yellow with silvery sheen, silvery white on belly; center of each scale with reddish brown spots giving an appearance of series of horizontal lines; a round black spot longer than eye above lateral line situated below the anterior soft dorsal rays.

Habitat: Reef associated. Found in shallow coastal waters, juveniles in mangrove and estuarine areas. Attains 60-70 cm.

Distribution: Widely distributed in Indo-west Pacific.

Remarks: Occasionally caught from Chilika Lake. Good food fish.

155. ***Lutjanus kasmira*** (Forsskal, 1775)

Blue-banded snapper

Diagnostic features: D. X, 14-15; A. III, 7-8; P. 15-16; V. I, 5; Ll. 49-50. Body moderately deep; dorsal profile of head steeply sloped; preopercular notch deep and prominent; longitudinal rows of scales above lateral line obliquely ascending to dorsal profile, below lateral line parallel to axis of body; caudal fin emarginated. Body yellow, under side and belly white; four bright black edged blue stripes along side of head and body; all fins yellow; a large black spot on lateral line below anterior soft dorsal rays.

Habitat: Reef associated. Found around shallow coastal waters, lagoons and estuaries. Attains 25-35 cm Total Length.

Distribution: Widespread in tropical Indo-Pacific.

Remarks: Good food fish. Not common in catches.

156. *Lutjanus russelli* (Bleeker, 1849)

Russell's snapper

Diagnostic features: D. X, 14; A. III, 8; P. 16; V. I, 5; Ll. 48-50. Body moderately deep; pre-opercular notch shallow; caudal fin truncate. Body brownish yellow, lower sides and belly yellowish white; 6-7 narrow golden horizontal stripes on sides, the lower ones horizontal and upper ones rising obliquely dorsal profile; a black blotch below anterior dorsal rays; all fins yellowish; caudal fin dusky.

Habitat: Reef associated. Found in inshore marine areas, juveniles in estuaries, tide pools and lagoons. Attains 40 cm Total Length.

Distribution: Tropical Indo-West Pacific.

Remarks: Commercially important species. Frequently found in the catches. Consumed fresh.

Family: **DATNIODIDAE**

157. Datnioides quadrifasciatus (Sevastianov)

Triple tail

Diagnostic features: D.XII+13-14; A. III,8-9; P. 19; V.I,5; Ll.48. Body oblong and compressed; predorsal profile strongly concave; snout pointed, upper jaw protrusible; preopercle serrated; total gill rakers on first arch 20-23; soft dorsal and anal fins rounded; caudal fin rounded. Body brownish with 7 full vertical bars, sometimes with 1 to 4 partial bars between full bars.

Habitat: Benthopelagic. Occurs in brackish water at the mouths of rivers and coastal lagoons, as well as in freshwater lakes and rivers. Feeds on fishes, prawns, crabs and some insect larvae. Attains 30.0 cm Standard Length.

Distribution: India to Indonesia and New Guinea.

Remarks: Good food fish, marketed fresh.

Family: **GERREIDAE**

Key to the species of Family Gerreidae

1(a) Second dorsal spine greatly enlarged, longer than head 2

1(b) Second dorsal spine not forming a filament, much les than head length 3

2(a) Predosal distance equal to or less than body depth; series of vertical or horizontal rows of dusky blotches on back and sides of body .... *G. filamentosus*

2(b) Predorsal distance distinctly greater than body depth; a series of vertical bars on back and sides of body .... *G. macracanthus*

3(a) Scale rows between lateral line and dorsal fin origin .... *G. limbatus*

3(b) Scale rows 5-7 between lateral line and dorsal fin origin 4

4(a) Body oblong, its depth 2.5 to 3.0 times in standard length; pectoral fin long, extending beyond anal fin origin; dorsal and fin spines rather slender .... *G. oyena*

4(b) Body deep, its depth below 2.5 times in standard length, forming a sharp angle at dorsal fin origin 5

5(a) Dorsal fin spines 10; a brown spot at middle of each dorsal ray .... *G. setifer*

5(b) Dorsal fin spines 9; no such colouration in rayed dorsal fin 6

6(a) Body with indistinct longitudinal lines along scale rows on dorsal part of body; dorsal fin with black margin .... *G. abbreviatus*

6(b) Body with prominent dark stripes along scale rows above lateral line; 4-9 oblique dusky bars below lateral line; snout region blackish dorsally .... *G. longirostris*

158. Gerres abbreviatus (Bleeker, 1850)

Deepbody mojarra

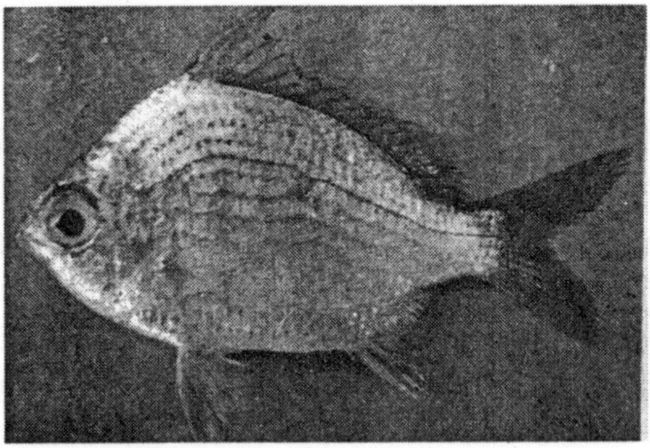

Diagnostic features: D. IX, 10; A. III, 7; P. 6-7; V. I, 5; Ll. 38-41. Body deep, depth 2.0-2.3 in standard length; mouth strong and strongly protractile; pectoral fins long, reaching to anal fin. Body silvery with indistinct longitudinal lines along the scale rows on dorsal part; tip of anal fin and lower caudal fin lobe white.

Habitat: Demersal. Inhabits coastal waters, estuaries and lagoons. Found in small schools. Attains 25-30 cm Total Length.

Distribution: Widespread in Indo-Pacific.

Remarks: Caught throughout the year. Fairly common. Consumed fresh or salt-dried.

159. *Gerres Filamentosus* (Cuvier, 1829)
Whipfin majarra

Diagnostic features: D. IX, 10; A. III, 7; P. 16; V. I, 5; Ll. 44-47. Body oblong, moderately compressed and deep, depth 2.0-2.5 in standard length; mouth small; 2nd dorsal spine long and filamentous. Body silvery, sides with 8-10 vertical series of ovoid bluish spots.

Habitat: Demersal. Inhabits shallow coastal waters. Found in large numbers in tidal creeks, estuaries and lagoons. Attains 30-35 cm Total Length.

Distribution: Indo-west Pacific.

Remarks: Good food fish. Fairly abundant in fish catches.

Gerres limbatus (Cuvier, 1830)

Black-tipped majarra

Diagnostic features: D. IX, 10; A. III, 7; P. 15; V. I, 5; Ll. 33-39. Body oblong, depth 2.3-2.7 in standard length; dorsal fin spines not strong; caudal fin deeply forked. Body silvery with three faint grey vertical bands below dorsal fin; dorsal and anal fins margin dusky.

Habitat: Demersal. Coastal waters, estruaries and lagoons. Attains: 20-25 cm Total Length.

Distribution: India Ocean: Coasts of India.

Remarks: Occasionally found in catches.

160. Gerres longirostris (Lacepede, 1801)

Longtail silverbiddy

Diagnostic features: D. IX, 10; A. III, 7; P. 15; V. I, 5; Ll.34-40. Head and trunk olive-green above, becoming silvery below; snout region blackish dorsally; dorsal fin membrane with faint black blotches or small spots at each spine and ray, just above edge of scaly basal sheath, pectoral and anal fins hyaline; caudal fin dusky with broad darker margin posteriorly; generally, body with prominent dark stripes along scale rows above lateral line.

Habitat: Demersal. Inhabits freshwater; brackish and marine waters. Amphidromous. Feed on small bottom invertebrates. Attains 37.0 cm Total Length.

Distribution: Indo-Pacific: Red Sea to north to the Ryukyu Islands, south to Australia.

Remarks: Sold fresh in markets; processed into fishmeal.

161. Gerres macracanthus (Bleeker, 1830)

Long-rayed mojarra

Diagnostic features: D. IX, 10; A. III, 7; P. 15-16; V. I, 5; Ll. 42-44. Body oblong, depth 2.3 to 2.4 in standard length; mouth small and protractile; head and body fully covered with scales. Body silvery with 5-10 brown diffuse vertical bands on flanks; fins hyaline with yellowish tinge.

Habitat: Demersal. Coastal waters, enters estuaries and brackish water lakes. Attains 25-35 cm Total Length.

Distribution: Coasts of India to Philippines.

Remarks: C aught in small quantities. Good food fish.

162. Gerres oyena (Forsskal, 1775)

Slender spine mojarra

Diagnostic features: D. X,10; A. III, 7; P.15-16; V. I, 5; Ll. 35-41. Body oblong and slightly compressed; depth 2.5 to 3.0 in standard length; anterior part of dorsal fin elevated. Body olive above, silvery grey below with a series of faint paired spots arranged in rows on sides; margin of dorsal and caudal fins dusky.

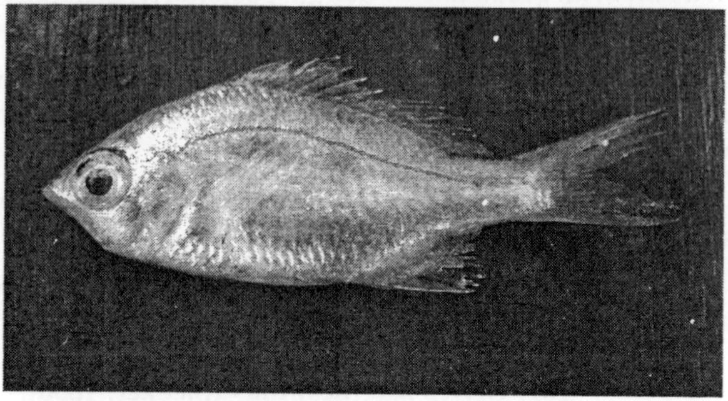

Habitat: Demersal. Found in shallow coastal waters, estuaries and lagoons in small schools. Bottom dweller. Attains 30-35 cm Total Length

Distribution: Indo-west Pacific.

Remarks: Good food fish. Caught in small quantities.

163. Gerres setifer (Hamilton, 1822)

Black-tipped mojarra

Diagnostic features: X,10; A. III, 7; P.15; V. I, 5; Ll. 32-38. Body oblong and slightly compressed; head 4.0-4.2 and depth 3.0 in total length; dorsal and anal fins with scaly sheath. Upper half of flanks greenish, silvery below; spinous dorsal fin dark edged, a brown spot on each dorsal soft ray just about scaly sheath; pectoral, pelvic and anal fins yellowish.

Habitat: Benthopelagic. Coastal but usually found in estuaries and lagoons. Attains 10-12 cm Total Length.

Distribution: Coasts of India and Sri Lanka.

Remarks: Found in large numbers in fish catches. Good food fish.

Family: **HAEMULIDAE**

Key to the species of Family Haemulidae

1(a) Chin with two pores and a longitudinal median groove at lower jaw symphysis; fin spines strong; lips rather thick .... 2 (*Pomadasys*)

1(b) Chin with six pores and no median groove or pit; fin spines weak; lips enormously thick; body uniformly dark, no cross bars .... *Plectorhinchus nigrus*

2(a) Five scale rows between lateral line and origin of dorsal fin; sides of body and spinous dorsal fin with dark brown spots; juveniles with longitudinal stripes on body .... *P. argenteus*

2(b) Seven scale rows between lateral line and origin of dorsal fin; sides of body with rows of spots, disappear with age .... *P. kaakan*

164. Plectorhinchus nigrus (Cuvier, 1830)

Black sweetlip

Diagnostic features: D.XII-XIV, 15-16; A. III, 7-8; P.17; V. I, 5. Body oblong and compressed, depth 2.0 in standard length; upper lip swollen; six pores under chin; caudal fin rounded. Body uniform brown, often with reddish tinge and with a few coppery spots on body; pectoral fins white; pelvic fin dark brown or blackish.

Habitat: Reef associated. Inhabits coastal waters and estuaries. Attains 50-60 cm Total Length.

Distribution: Wide spread in tropical Indo-Pacific.

Remarks: Good food fish. Not common in catches.

165. Pomadasys argenteus (Forsskal, 1775)

Silver grunt

Diagnostic features: D.XII,13-14; A. III,7; P.215; V. I,5; C.

17; Ll.50. Body ovate; head profile almost straight. Mouth small; lips not thickened; two pores and a central groove under the chin; no antrorse spine before the dorsal fin origin; notch between the spinous and soft-rayed portion of the dorsal fin shallow. Body generally silver-mauve to fawn above, white below. Small specimens with numerous spots aligned horizontally or fused into horizontal lines; large specimens plain or with scattered charcoal scale spots on back and upper sides; the snout is dark brown; the upper operculum charcoal or purplish.

Habitat: Demersal. Found in coastal and brackish waters, enters freshwaters. Attains 70 cm Total Length.

Distribution: Indo-West Pacific: Red Sea to the Philippines, north to southern Japan, and south to northern Australia and also reported from New Caledonia.

Remarks: Commercial fish. Marketed fresh, may be salted.

166. Pomadasys kaakan (Cuvier, 1830)

Javelin grunter

Diagnostic features: D.XII, 13-15; A. III, 7-8; P.17-18; V. I, 5; Ll. 43-47 Body oblong and compressed; lips fairly thick; fin spines very strong; caudal fin emarginated. Body silvery; juveniles with bars, the bars break up with growth and become obsolete; round spots on basal half of dorsal membrane.

Habitat: Demersal. Inhabits sand or mud bottoms of coastal waters but prefers estuaries and lagoons and even tolerate freshwater. Attains 40-45 cm Total Length.

Distribution: Widespread in Indo-Pacific.

Remarks: Excellent food fish. Caught in large quantities.

Family: SPARIDAE

Key to the species of Family Sparidae

1(a) Second anal spine much longer than third .... 3 (*Acanthopagrus*)

1(b) Second anal spine not markedly longer than third 2

2(a) A distinct separate group of 4 to 6 enlarged, subequal incisiform teeth anteriorly in upper jaws; dorsal fin rays 12-13; scales with a golden which form yellow longitudinal lines along body .... *Rhabdosargus sarba*

2(b) No anterior group of enlarged teeth; dorsal fin rays 10-11; scales on head and anterior portion of body with black edges; dark lines along rows on body; dorsal and anal fins black, outer portion of ventral fin black .... *Crenidens crenidens*

3(a) Six rows of scales on preoperculum; anal and caudal fins blackish-gray; no silvery edges to body scales .... *A. berda*

3(b) Four or five rows of scales on preoperculum; anal and lower caudal fin yellow; body scales with dark bases and silvery edges .... *A. latus*

167. Acanthopagrus berda

Diagnostic features: D. XI-XII,11-12; A. III, 8-9; P.15; V. I, 5. Dorsal profile of head is more convex than abdomen; snout compressed and pointed; maxilla reaches to front edge of orbit; opercle with a distinct spine; caudal fin emarginated. Body silvery grey, scales dark at bases; black spot on shoulder; dorsal, anal and caudal fins wity black edges; a dark band along the anal fin.

Habitat: Demersal; oceanodromous. Found in freshwater; brackish and marine waters. Feeds on invertebrates, including worms, molluscs, crustaceans echinoderms and small fish. Attains 90.0 cm Total Length.

Distribution: Widespread in Indo-west Pacific. South Africa to India extending to Japan and northern Australia.

Remarks: Important commercial fish; a popular angling species, often caught with hook and line. Excellent food fish, consumed fresh.

168. Acanthopagrus latus (Houttuyn, 1782)

Yellowfin seabream

Diagnostic features: D. XI-XII,10-12; A. III, 8-10; P.14; V. I, 5; Ll.44-46. Body fairly deep and slightly compressed; depth more than 2.4 times in standard length; head large, snout profile oblique with a bulge above eyes; 4-6 canine teeth in front of both jaws; pre-opercular scales 4-5 series. Body dusky grey, belly yellowish; scales with dark bases and silvery edges; a drak band between eyes and a dark spot at origin of lateral line; pelvic fins yellow; pectoral and anal fins dusky at base, yellow at margin; lower caudal fin lobe yellow.

Habitat: Demersal. Inhabits shallow coastal waters, enters estuaries and lagoons. Attains 60-65 cm Total Length.

Distribution: Widespread in Indo-west Pacific

Remarks: Flesh is excellent. Found in moderate numbers in fish catch, caught by gill nets and shore seines.

169. Crenidens crenidens (Forsskal, 1775)

Karanteen

Diagnostic features: D. XI, 11; A. III, 10: P.13-14; V. I, 5; Ll. 55-60. Body slightly oblong; depth 2.5 in standard length; edges of outer teeth wavy; no scales between eyes; cheeks scaly; dorsal and anal fins with basal scaly sheath. Body silvery brown.

Habitat: Benthopelagic. Coastal, occasionally enters estuaries and lagoons. Attains 30 cm Total Length.

Distribution: Indian Ocean.

Remarks: Occasionally caught in Chilika Lake. Good food fish.

170. Rhabdosargus sarba (Forsskal, 1775)

Goldlined seabream

Diagnostic features: D. XI, 12-132; A. III, 11; P.14-15; V. I, 5; Ll. 56-59. Body deep, depth 2.0-2.3; head large, about 4.0 in standard length; inter-orbital and pre-opercle flange naked or with few scales; caudal fin deeply emarginated. Body silvery grey; each scale with a golden centre form longitudinal lines along body; belly yellowish.

Habitat: Bottom living coastal fish, enters estuaries, rivers and lagoons. Attains 55-60 cm Total Length.

Distribution: Wide spread in Indo-Pacific

Remarks: Excellent food fish. Not uncommon.

Family: **SCIAENIDAE**

Key to the species of Family Sciaenidae

1(a) Gasbladder with one pair of simple appendages

v.................. 2 (*Otolithoides*)

1(b) Gasbladder with two or more pairs of arborescent appendages 3

2(a) Soft doesal with 46-48 rays .... *O. pama*

2(b) Soft dorsal with 27-32 rays .... *O. biauritus*

3(a) Gasbladder hammer shaped .... 4 (*Johnius*)

3(b) Gasbladder carrot-shaped 6

4(a) A barbell on chin; 1st pair of gasbladder appendage branching in head 5

4(b) No barbell on chin; 1st pair not branching in head ...... *J. belangerii*

5(a) Body scales ctenoid; soft dorsal fin with 27-33 rays .... *J. macropterus*

5(b) Body scales cycloid; soft dorsal fin with 23 to 26 rays; gill rakers 6-9 on lower arm of 1st arch ....*J. amblycephalus*

6(a) First pair of gasbladder appendages branching on posterior surface of transverse septum and not entering had; upper part of body, dorsal and caudal fins with black spots .... *Protonibea diacanthus*

6(b) First pair of gasbladder appendages cephalic, extending into head and branching between skull and upper gill arches 7

7(a) Teeth on lower jaw uniform, small or rather strong; barbels present or absent on chin 8

7(b) Teeth on lower jaw differentiated in size; pair of minute barbels present on chin .... *Daysciaena albida*

8(a) Single tapering mental barbell present; no stripes along scale rows .... *Dendrophysa russelli*

8(b) No barbels on chin; narrow dark stripes along the scale rows .... *Paranibea semiluctuosa*

171. *Daysciaena albida* (Cuvier, 1830)

Two-bearded croaker

Diagnostic features: D.IX-X+I,23-36; A.II,7; P.17-18; V. I,5. Ll.48-51. Body oblong; snout rounded, slightly projecting beyond upper jaw; mouth slightly inferior; a pair of small tapering barbels on chin; caudal fin rhomboid in adults; scales on head cycloid; gas bladder carrot-shaped with 17-19 pairs of arborescent appendages, the anterior pair twig-lets enter into head. Back grey, shading to silvery on belly, occasionally dark spots in oblique rows along scale rows; pectoral, pelvis and anal fins yellow; axil of pectoral fin black.

Habitat: Benthopelagic. Inhabitat shallow coastal waters and estuaries. Attains 85-90 cm Total Length.

Distribution: Coasts of India to Borneo.

Remarks: Good food fish. Found in large numbers in catches.Consumed fresh or dried salted.

172. *Dendrophysa russelli* (Cuvier, 1830)

Goatee-croacker

Diagnostic features: D.X+I,25-28; A.II,7; P.16; V.I,5; Ll.46-49. Snout rounded; mouth inferior; a single barbel on chin; gill rakers 8-9 on lower arm of first arch; caudal fin rhomboid; scales cycloid on front part of head and lower parts of dorsal and anal fins; gasbladder carrot-shaped with 15-17 pairs of arborescent appendages, the first entering head. Body grey shading to white on belly; spinous dorsal dark, other fins pale.

Habitat: Demersal. Found in coastal waters and estuaries. Attains 25cm Total Length.

Distribution: Coasts of India, Sri Lanka and to East Indies.

Remarks: Fairly common in fish catches of Chilika Lake. Good food fish.

173. *Johnius amblycephalus* (Bleeker, 1855)

Bearded-croaker

Diagnostic features: D.X+I, 23-26; A.II,7; P.18-19; V. I,5. Ll. 48-53. Snout rounded and projecting, mouth inferior; body depth 3.0-3.7, head 3.1-3.4 in standard length; a blunt barbel on chin with median mental pore at front of its base; caudal fin rhomboid; gasbladder hammer-shaped with 14-15 pairs of arborescent appendages, the first branching head.

Habitat: Demersal. Inhabit coastal waters and estuaries. Attains 20-25 cm total Length.

Distribution: Widespread in Indo-west Pacific.

Remarks: Fairly common in fish catches. Good food fish.

174. *Johnius belangerii* (Cuvier, 1830)

Belanger's croaker

Diagnostic features: .IX+I, 27-31; A.II,7-8; P.15-16; V. I,5. Ll. 48-52. Snout steeply rounded, mouth small and inferior; no barbels on chin; interorbital region broadly concave; gill rakers on lower arm of first arch 8-9; caudal fin rhomboid; gasbladder hammer-shaped with 11-14 pairs of arborescent appendages, the first entering in head. Caudal fin rhomboid. Body bronzy, darkly pigmented; sometimes dark bars on back or on dosal fin; ventral surface deep grey; spinous dorsal black; a dark blotch on gill cover.

Habitat: Demersal. Inhabit coastal waters and estuaries. Attains 23-30 cm Total Length.

Distribution: Indo-west Pacific: Pakistan to China and Japan and to eastern coast of Australia.

Remarks: Good food fish. Fairly common in catches.

175. Johnius macropterus (Bleeker,1853)

Long-finned croaker

Diagnostic features: D. X+I, 27-33; A.II, 7-8; P.14-16; V. I, 5. Ll. 44-50. Snout slightly projecting; mental pores five; a short blunt barbel behind the median pore; 10-12 gill rakers on lower arm of first arch; scales cycloid on snout below eyes and on breast; gasbladder hammer-shaped with 13-16 pairs of arborescent appendages, the first branching in head. Body dark grey on back, whitish on flanks and belly with silvery reflections; spinous dorsal darkish.

Habitat: Demersal. Inhabitat shallow coastal waters and estuaries. Attains 20-25cm Total Length.

Distribution: Indo-west Pacific.

Remarks: Fairly common in catches. Good food fish.

176. Otolithoides biauritus (Cantor, 1850)

Bronze croaker

Diagnostic features: D.VIII-IX+I, 27-29; A.II, 7-8; P.17-18; V. I, 5. Ll. 50-60. Snout acute, mouth terminal; operculum with two flat weak spines; gill rakers 11-12 on lower arm of first arch; gass bladder carrot shaped, wity a single pair of long tubular appendages; caudal fin lanceolate or acutely pointed. Head and back grayish, flanks silvery with golden tinge; lateral line golden; dorsal, anal and caudal fins yellowish; pectoral fin brownish with a black spot at axil.

Habitat: Demersal. Marine enters estuaries and lagoons. Attains 120 cm Total Length.

Distribution: Coasts of India to Indo-Australian Archipelago.

Remarks: Not common. Good food fish.

177. Otolithoides pama (Hamilton, 1822)

Pama croaker

Duiagnostic features: D.IX-X+I, 40-45; A.II, 7-8; P.16-17; V. I, 5. Ll. 44-48. Body slender with conical snout; mouth large and terminal; no rostral pores; post-temporal covered with minute scales; caudal fin rhomboid; gass bladder carrot shaped with a tubules. Body brownish along back, silvery-white on belly with indistinct markings; head with golden and purple hue; fins yellowish, upper half of dorsal fin gray.

Habitat: Benthopelagic; amphidromous. Found in coastal waters, estuaries and rivers. Attains 160 cm Total Length.

Distribution: Coasts of India to Guinea.

Remarks: Commercial fish. Good food fish, consumed fresh or dried salt.

178. Paranibea semiluctuosa (Cuvier, 1830)

Half-mourning croaker

Diagnostic features: D.IX-X+I, 27-31; A.II, 7; P.17-18; V. I, 5. Ll. 49-53. Dorsal profile of body more arched than ventral profile, snout slightly projecting; lips thick and papillose; gill rakers 5-8 on lower arm of first arch; caudal fin rhomboid or rounded; gasbladder carrot-shaped with 15-21 arborescent appendages, the first appendage entering head. Body dark with series of narrow dark stripes along the scale rows covering the body except a narrow stripe on belly; anal and pelvic fins very dark; other fins slightly dark.

Habitat: Demersal. Inhabit shallow coastal and brackish waters. Attains 40-45 cm Total Length.

Distribution: Widespread in Indian Ocean.

Remarks: Fairly common in fish catches. Good food fish.

179. Protonibea diacanthus (Lacepede, 1971)

Spotted croaker

Diagnostic features: D.IX-X+I, 22-25; A.II, 7; P.17-18; V. I, 5. Ll. 51-52. Body slender; snout acute and large; three pairs of pores on chin; gill rakers 8-9 on lower arm of first arch; caudal fin rhomboid; gasbladder carrot-shaped with 16-26 pairs of arborescent appendages, the first behind transverse septum. Body silvery with dark blotches on back, many small dots on head, upper half of body, dorsal and caudal fins; anal, pectoral, pelvic and lower part of caudal fins black.

Habitat: Demersal. Inhabit coastal and estuarine muddy waters. Attains 120 cm Total Length.

Distribution: Gulf of Oman to Australia and northwards China and Japan..

Remarks: Commercially important fish. Caught in abundant.

Family: **MONODACTYLIDAE**

180. Monodactylus argenteus (Linnaeus)

Silver-batfish

Diagnostic features: D. VII-VIII, 28; A. III, 28-30; P. 16; Ll. 54-56. Body deep and compressed, depth 1.2-1.5 in standard length; mouth terminal; scales on the body deciduous and extending onto head and median fins; lobes of dorsal and anal fins prolonged; ventral fins rudimentary, reduced to a small spine. Juveniles silvery with two curved dark stripes across head, the first through eye and the second from nape through base.of pectoral to before anal fin; anterior lobes of dorsal and anal fins dusky; all fins pale. Adults silvery, the anterior lobes of dorsal and anal fin dusky.

Habitat: Pelagic. Inhabit sandy coastal waters, estuaries and lagoons. Attains 25 cm Total Length. ***Distribution***: Widespread in tropical Indo-Pacific.

Remarks: Flesh is very soft and good food fish. Favourite aquarium pets.

Family: **DREPANIDAE**

*181. **Drepane punctata*** (Linnaeus, 1758)

Spotted drepane

Diagnostic features: D.IX, 19-22; A.III, 17-19; P.17; V. I, 5; Ll.50-55. Body very deep and strongly compressed; head short, mouth small and protractile; deep notch between spinous and soft dorsal; fourth dorsal spine longest; pectoral fins long and pointed. Body silvery with grayish tinge on upper half; a large orange spot above base of pectoral fin; 4-11 vertical bands of small black spots on upper half of body.

Habitat: Reef associated. Coastal waters and estuaries and lagoons. Attains 30 cm Total Length.

Distribution: Wide spread in Indo-west Pacific.

Remarks: Most common fish of fish catches. Good food fish. Consumed fresh or salt-dried.

Family: SCATOPHAGIDAE

182. *Scatophagus argus* (Linnaeus, 1766)

Spotted butterfish

Diagnostic features: D.XI, 16-18; A. IV, 16-18; P.20; V. I, 5. Body squarish, head triangular, rostro-dorsal profile strongly ascending and followed by a deep concavity; mouth small, not protractile. Body greenish-grey to dusky with numerous irregular large round brown spots, belly silvery.

Habitat: Demersal. Shallow coastal waters, estuaries, lagoons and enters rivers. Attains 30 cm Total Length.

Distribution: Coasts of India to Australia.

Remarks: Good food fish. Consumed fresh or salt-dried. Good aquarium pets.

Family NANDIDAE

183. *Nandus nandus* (Hamilton, 1822)

Gangetic leaffish

Diagnostic features: D.XII-XIV,11-13; A. III,7-9; P. 16; V.I,5; Ll. 46-57. Body oblong and compressed; head large, snout pointed; mouth terminal and strongly protractile; cleft of mouth extending to below posterior border of eye; opercle with one spine, lateral line interruptred; Caudal fin rounded. Bodygreenish brown with black bands and blotches; narroiw dark bands radiate from eye; soft portions of anal, dorsal and caudal fins with bands of spots.

Habitat: Benthopelagic. Found in freshwater and brackish areas. Feed on aquatic insects and fishes 20.0 cm Total Length.

Distribution: Widely distributed from Pakistan to Thailand.

Remarks: Good food fish. Consumed fresh.

Family: **CICHLIDAE**

184. Etroplus suratensis (Bloch, 1790)

Green chromide

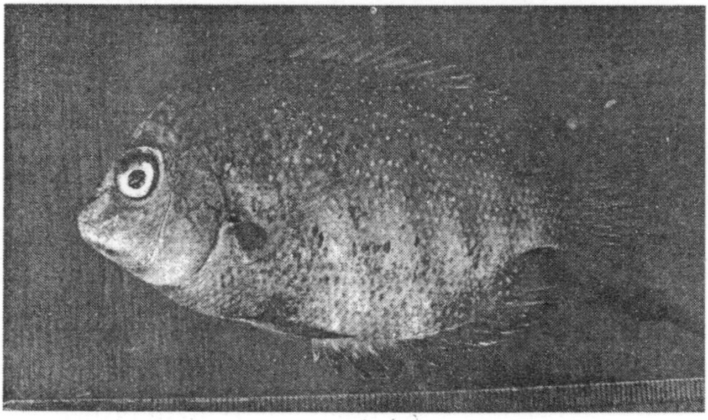

Diagnostic features: D.XVIII-XIX, 9-14; A. XII-XIII, 11-12; P.17; V. I, 5; Ll.35-40. Body elevated and compressed, abdomen rounded snout spout-like, mouth terminal; dorsal fin inserted above level of base of pectoral fin; caudal fin lunate or emarginated.Body light green with eight vertical bands; scales above the lateral line with pearly white spot; pectoral fins yellowish with jet black base.

Habitta: Benthopelagic; brackish water but tolerate fresh or marine waters for short periods. Found in large rivers, reservoirs, lagoons and estuaries. Feed on filamentous algae, plant material and insects. Attains 40 cm Total Length.

Distribution: Western Indian Ocean: India and Sri Lanka.

Remarks: Commercially important fish, consumed fresh; good aquaculture fish.

*185. **Oreochromis mossambicus*** (Peters, 1852)

Mozambique tilapia

Diagnostic features: D. XV-XVII,10-12; A. III-IV,7-12; Ll.30-32. Body elongate, abdomen rounded; head profile concave; snout long; caudal fin slightly rounded; body scales cycloid lateral line incomplete; caudal fin not densely scaled. Females and non-breeding males silvery gery with 2-5 mid-lateral blotches; spiny part of dorsal fin light with dark mottling; soft dorsal, anal, caudal and pelvic fins blackish; indistinct dark opercular spot present

Habitat: Benthopelagic; amphidromous. Inhabits reservoirs, rivers, creeks, drains, swamps and tidal creeks, often enter brackish waters. Attains 38.0 cm Standard Length.

Distribution: Africa. Widely introduced for aquaculture, but escaped and established itself in the wild in many countries, often outcompeting local species.

Remarks: Highly commercial; good aquaculture fish. Consumed fresh.

Family: **MUGILIDAE**

Key to the species of Family Mugilidae

1(a) Head concave between eyes; eyes projecting above head level; upper lip does not form tip of snout or part of dorsal profile .... *Rhinomugil corsula*

1(b) Head flattened dorsally; eye not projecting above head level; upper lip not as in 1a. 2

2(a) Lips with enlarged papillae or crenulations .... *Cenimugil crenilabis*

2(b) Lips without papillae or crenulations 3

3(a) Hind tip of maxilla not curved below tip of maxilla; adipose eye lids well developed .... *Mugil cephalus*

3(b) Hind tip of maxilla curved below tip of maxilla; adipose eye lids developed, feeble or absent 4

4(a) Scales with membranous digitated hind margin; pectoral axillary scale very large ....5 (*Valmugil*)

4(b) Scales without membranous digitated hind margin; pectoral axillary scale rudimentary or absent .... 7 (*Liza*)

5(a) Adipose tissue only a rim around eye; pectoral fin with blue axillary spot .... *V. seheli*

5(b) Adipose tisue tissue covers half to most of eye; pectoral fin axil with black spot 6

6(a) Lateral scale series 37-40; second dorsal and anal fins densely scaled; margin of 1st dorsal fin black .... *V. speigleri*

6(b) Lateral scale series 30-35; second dorsal and anal fins moderately scaled; margin of 1st dorsal not black .... *V. cunnesius*

7(a) Anal fin rays 8 .... *L. vaigiensis*

7(b) Anal fin rays 9 8

8(a) Transverse scale rows 13; ventral fin reaching behind base of fourth spine of 1st dorsal .... *L. macrolepis*

8(b) Transverse scale rows less than 13; ventral fin reaching vertical in front of 4th spine of 1st dorsal 9

9(a) Second dorsal fin origin on vertical more than half of along anal fin base .... *L. tade*

9(b) Second dorsal fin origin over 1st half of anal fin base 10

10(a) Preorbital not filling space between lip and eye; corner of mouth reaches to vertical from anterior nostrils .... *L. subviridis*

10(b) Preorbital fills the space between lip and eye; corner of mouth reaches to vertical from posterior nostrils 11

11(a) Lateral scale series 26-31; 9-10 transverse scale rows .... *L. melinoptera*

11(b) Lateral scale series 31-36; 11 transverse scale rows .... *L. parsia*

186. *Mugil cephalus* (Linnaeus)

Flathead grey mullet

Diagnostic features: D.IV+I,6-8; A.III,8; P.16-17; V. I,5; Ls.38-42. Body robust, head broad and flattened on top; adipose eye lid well developed and covering entire eye; pectoral fin short, not reaching dorsal fin origin; caudal fin forked. Body olive-brown above, silvery on sides, shading to white below; 6-7 indistinct longitudinal brown bars down flanks.

Habitat: Benthopelgaic. Shallow coastal waters, enters estuaries, lagoons and rivers. Attains 60 cm.

Distribution: In all worm and temperate seas.

Remarks: Good food fish. Caught in large quantities.

187. *Liza macrolepis* (Smih,1849)

Borneo mullet

Diagnostic features: D.IV+I, 8; A.III, 9; P.16; V. I, 5; Ll. 31-34. Body moderately robust, head wide, 26-28% in standard length, no adipose eye lids; pectoral folded forward reaches about to front of eye; caudal fin slightly forked. Body dark greenish above, silvery on sides and belly; fins dusky along margins.

Habitat: Demersal. Occur in seas, brackish and freshwater areas. Attains 35 cm.

Distribution: Widespread in the tropical Indo-west Pacific.

Remarks: Caught in large quantities throughout the year. Good food fish.

188. Liza melinoptera (Valenciennes, 1836)

Giantscale mullet

Diagnostic features: D.IV+I,8; A. III, 9; P.15; V. I,5; Ls.26-31. Adipose eyelid covers 1/3rd of iris; no teeth in lower jaw; tongue toothed; no pectoral axillary scale; dorsal spines strong; second dorsal origin on vertical through middle of anal fin base. Body greenish-brown above, silvery below; all fins dusky.

Habitat: Demersal. Inhabit shallow coastal waters, mangroves, estuaries, lagoons and rivers. Feed on algae, diatoms and other organic matter. Attains 30 cm Total Length.

Distribution: Widespread in Indo-Pacific.

Remarks: Frequently encountered in fish catches.

189. Liza parsia (Hamilton, 1822)

Goldspot mullet

Diagnostic features: D. IV+I,8; A. III, 9; P.15; V. I,5; Ls.31-36. Head moderately wide, flattened on top; adipose eye lid covers most of the posterior iris; lips thin, lower lip with symphysial knob; pectoral axillary scale rudimentary or absent; caudal fin slightly forked. Body greenish-brown. Flanks and belly white to silvery; a golden spot on upper portion of operculum; edge of dorsal fins dusky; caudal fin base yellowish.

Habitat: Demersal. Schooling fishes of shallow coastal waters, creeks, lagoons, estuaries and mangroves. Attains 25-30 cm Total Length.

Distribution: Widespread in Indo-Pacific.

Remarks: Most common and abundant. Commercially important fish.

190. Liza subviridis (Valenciennes, 1836)

Greenback grey mullet

Diagnostic features: D. IV+I,8-9; A. III, 9; P.15-16; V. I,5; Ls. 27-32. Body robust, head flattened on top; adipose eyelid covering iris; lips thin, lower lip with symphysial knob; pectoral axillary scale rudimentary or absent; caudal fin slightly forked. Back of body dark greenish, flanks and belly white; caudal fin edged with black.

Habitat: Demersal. Occur in schools in shallow coastal waters, estuaries and lagoons. Attains 30 cm Total Length.

Distribution: Persian Gulf to Australia.

Remarks: Good food fish. Fairly abundant in catches.

191. *Liza tade* (Forsskal, 1775)

Tade grey mullet

Diagnostic features: D.IV+I, 8; A.III, 9; P.15; V. I,5; Ll.31-33. Body slender and elongate; adipose tissue covers most of iris; pectoral fins without axillary scale; caudal fin forked. Body pale olive, flanks and belly silvery; 5-7 indistinct longitudinal lines on sides.

Habitat: Demersal. Inhabits estuaries, lagoons and even enter freshwater rivers. Attains 25-30 cm Total Length.

Distribution: Indo-west Pacific.

Remarks: Common fish in the cathches.

192. *Liza vaigiensis* (Quoy & Gaimard, 1824)

Diamond-scale grey mullet

Diagnostic features: D. IV+I, 8; A. III, 9; P.16; V. I,5; Ls. 24-27. Body robust; head broad and flat; adipose eye lids vestigial; pectoral bent forward reaches eye; pectoral fin with no axillary scale; caudal fin slightly emarginated. Body olive-brown on back, silvery on sides, yellowish white on belly; scales on upper side with brown blotches; fins yellowish-white, margins dusky; pectoral fin black.

Habitat: Demersal. Inhabit shallow coastal waters, estuaries and lagoons. Attains 60 cm Total Length.

Distribution: Widespread in Indo-west Pacific.

Remarks: Fairly common in catches. Good food fish.

193. Rhinomugil corsula (Hamilton, 1822)

Corsula mullet

Diagnostic features: D. IV+I, 8; A. III, 9; P.16; V. I,5; Ls. 48-52. Body stout, head moderate, concave between eyes; eyes without adipose eye lids; mouth ventral and protrusible. Body dull olive-brown, silvery below; fins with golden tinge.

Habitat: Demersal. Inhabit rivers, estuaries, lagoons and mangroves. Attains 35-40 cm Total Length.

Distribution: Coasts of India to Myanmar.

Remarks: Caught in small quantities.

194. Valamugil cunnesius (Valenciennes, 1836)

Long-fin mullet

Diagnostic features: D. IV+I, 8; A. III, 9; P.15-16; V. I,5; Ls. 30-35. Body moderately robust; adipose eye lids well developed; maxilla exposed when mouth shut; pectoral fins long, equal to slightly shorter than head length, with a long axillary scale. Body dark grey, flanks and ventral side silvery; a dark spot on base of pectoral fin.

Habitat: Demersal. Inhabit shallow coastal waters, estuaries, lagoons and mangrove areas. Attains 40 cm Total Length.

Distribution: Widespread in Indo-west Pacific.

Remarks: Caught small quantities. Good food fish.

*195. **Valamugil seheli*** (Forsskal, 1775)

Bluespot mullet

Diagnostic features: D. IV+I, 8; A. III, 9; P.18; V. I,5; Ls. 38-42. Head wide and flattened; adipose eye lids feeble, a rim around eye; pectoral fins long, reaching to vertical from second spine of first dorsal, axillary scale long; caudal fin forked. Body greenish above, silvery below; upper rows of scales with dusky spots forming indistinct bands along body; first dorsal, anal and pelvic fins white; pectoral fin dull yellow with a blue axillary spot.

Habitat: Reef associated. Inhabit shallow coastal waters, estuaries, lagoons and mangrove areas. Attains 35-45 cm Total Length.

Distribution: Widespread in Indo-west Pacific.

Remarks: Caught occasionally in Chilika Lake.

196. *Valamugil speigleri* (Bleeker, 1858)

Speigler's grey mullet

Diagnostic features: D. IV+I, 8; A. III, 9; P.16-17; V. I,5; Ls. 37-40. Body moderately robust; adipose eye lid well developed; pectoral fin slightly shorter than head length, its axillary scale long. Body dark green above, flanks and ventral side silvery; margin of first dorsal black, other fins dusky; black spot at axil of pectoral fins.

Habitat: Demersal. Inhabit coastal waters, estuaries and lagoons. Attains 50-60 cm Total Length.

Distribution: Widely distributed from Pakistan to Western Central Pacific,

Remarks: Fairly common in the catches.

Family: SPHYRAENIDAE

Key to the species of Family Sphyraenidae

1(a) Preopercle smoothly rounded; body with 20 vertical dusky cross bars .... *Sphyraena jello*

1(b) Preopercle obliquely rounded; body with 15 acutely angled cheverons on sides .... *S. putnamiae*

197. *Sphyraena jello* (Cuvier, 1829)

Banded barracuda

Diagnostic features: D. V+I, 9; A. II, 8; P. 12-13; V. I, 5; Ll. 130-140. No fleshy tip at the end of lower jaw; preopercule rounded, no produced flap; caudal fin tri-lobed. Body purplish above, silvery below with 15-20 vertical dark bars extend onto the lateral line; caudal fin light yellow.

Habitat: Pelagic. Coastal waters, also enters estuaries and lagoons. Attains 130 cm Total Length.

Distribution: Widely distributed in Indo-west Pacific.

Remarks: Good food fish. Taken commercially in small quantities. Frequently encountered.

198. *Sphyraena putnamae* Jordan & Seale, 1905

Sawtooth barracuda

Diagnostic features: D.V+I, 8; A. II, 7; P. 12-14; V. I, 5; Ll. 123-136. A fleshy tip at the end of lower jaw; pre-opercule obliquely rounded, opercle rounded with two weak, flattened spines. About 15 acutely angled cheverons on sides of body.

Habitat: Reef associated. Shallow coastal waters, enters estuaries and lagoons. Attains 80 cm Total Length.

Distribution: Tropical Indo-Pacific.

Remarks: Good food fish. Taken commercially in small quantities. Frequently encountered.

Family: **POLYNEMIDAE**

Key to the species of Family Polynemidae

1(a) Free pectoral filaments are four; lower lip absent; teeth extending on exterior part of jaws ....*Eleutheronema tetradactylum*

1(b) Free pectoral filaments are 5-7; lower lip well developed; no teeth on exterior part of jaws .... 2 (*Polydactylus*)

2(a) Upper pectoral filament reaches to anal fin; lateral

line with 70-75 scales; caudal fin deeply lunate with lobes ending in filaments .... *P. indicus*

2(b) Upper two pectoral filaments longest, reaching to ventral fin; lateral line with less than 65 scales; caudal fin forked with equal lobes 3

3(a) Pectoral fin with 6-7 free filaments; lateral line with 48-50 scales; pectoral fin not black; large black blotch at beginning of the lateral line .... *P. sextarius*

3(b) Pectoral fin with five free filaments; lateral line with 60-65 scales; pectoral fin black; body with dusky narrow stripes along scale rows .... *P. plebeius*

199. Eleutheronema tetradactylum (Shaw, 1804)

Foufinger threadfin

Diagnostic features: D.VIII+I-II, 13-15; A. II, 15-17; P. 12-15 +4; V.I,5; Ll. 75-85. Body elongate and comprssed; snout projecting, mouth large; pectoral fin inserted low on body, its rays branched, lower four rays free and filamentous; airbladder absent; caudal fin forked. Body silvery green above, yellowish white on sides and abdomen; dorsal and caudal fins yellowish, dusky at margins; pectoral filamentous rays white.

Habitat: Pelagic. Coastal waters, also enters estuaries and lagoons. Attains 25-30 cm Total Length.

Distribution: Indo-west Pacific, from Pakistan to Australia.

Remarks: Good food fish. Frequently caught in the Chilika Lake.

200. Polydactylus indicus (Shaw, 1804)

Indian-threadfin

Diagnostic features: D.VIII+I, 13-14; A. II-III, 11-12; P. 14-15 +5; V.I, 5; Ll. 70-75. Body oblong, slightly compressed; mouth large with small teeth in jaws; upper filamentous pectoral ray longest and extends nearly to anus; caudal fin deeply lunate, with pointed lobes ending in filaments; airbladder large. Body golden-olive, dark above with faint dusky stripes along sides of body; fins yellowish.

Habitat: Demersal. Inhabits coastal waters, estuaries, lakes and also enters rivers. Attains 25 cm Total Length.

Distribution: Widespread in Indo-west Pacific.

Remarks: Its flesh is highly esteemed. Caught fairly in large quantities.

201. *Polydactylus plebeius* (Broussonet, 1782)

Common threadfin

Diagnostic features: D.VIII+I, 13; A. II, 11-12; P. 15-18 +5; V. I,5; Ll. 60-65. Snout projecting, mouth large; eyes large 3.8-4.0 in head length; pectoral rays unbranched, upper two filamentous rays reaching to tip of pelvic fin; airbladder elongate, narrow and simple. Body golden-olive with a few narrow dusky stripes along scale-rows; pectoral fin black; dorsal and caudal fins grey edged.

Habitat: Demersal. Inhabit shallow muddy bottoms of coastal waters, estuaries and lakes. Attains 45 cm.

Distribution: Widely distributed in tropical Indo-west Pacific.

Remarks: Found abundant in catches. Commercially important fish.

202. *Polydactylus sextarius* (Bloch, 1801)

Black-spot threadfin

Diagnostic features: D.VIII+I, 12-13; A. II-III, 12-13; P. 13-15 +6; V. I,5; Ll. 44-50. Body slightly compressed; mouth small and inferior; upper part of pectoral rays branched, the upper two filamentous rays extending to tip of pelvic fin; caudal fin lobed. Body greenish-olive, silvery on sides and below; a large black spot at beginning of the lateral line; inner side of operculum dusky; fins yellowish.

Habitat: Demersal. Inhabit shallow sandy shores, estuaries and lakes. Attains 30 cm Total Length.

Distribution: Indo-west Pacific.

Remarks: Fairly common in fish catches. Good food fish.

Family: SIGANIDAE

Key to the species of Family Siganidae

1(a) Scale rows between lateral line and base of 2nd to 4th dorsal spines more than 29; upper half of body and head with numerous blue spots; ventral part with narrow irregular bluish-gray wavy stripes form a reticulum ....*Siganus javus*

1(b) Scale rows between lateral line and base of 2nd to 4th dorsal spines less than 29; sides of body with extensive vermiculating lines .... *Siganus vermiculatus*

203. *Siganus vermiculatus* (Valenciennes, 1835)

Vermiculate Rabbitfish

Diagnostic features: D. XIII, 10; A. VII, 9; P. 15-16; V. II, 3. Body moderately deep and ovate; dorsal profile of snout steep; fin spines are stout; caudal fin emarginated. Body bluish white with irregular vermiculate dark brown bands on body except ventrally spotted with brown; head with narrow brown bands; caudal fin with small brown spots; a row of brown spots above base of soft dorsal fin; dorsal and anal fins dusky; iris golden yellow.

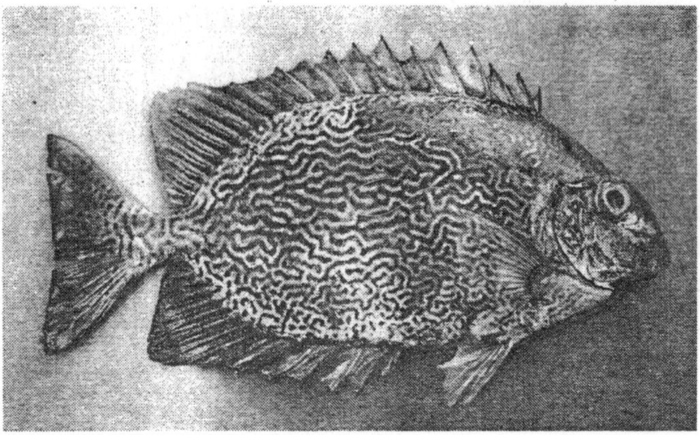

Habitat: Reef associated. Found in murky waters of shallow coasts, estuaries, lakes and mangrove areas. Attains 40 cm Total Length.

Distribution: Widespread in Indo-west Pacific.

Remarks: Very good food fish, important component in commercial catches. It is an ideal fish for aquaculture.

204. *Siganus javus* (Linnaeus, 1766)

Spiny Rabbitfish

Diagnostic features: D. XIII, 10; A. VII, 9; P. 17-18; V. II, 3. Dorsal fin spines are slender; anal fins spines stout; caudal fin emarginated. Body bluish white above, light below with numerous blue spots on head, nape and upper half of body; ventral part of body with narrow irregular bluish grey wavy stripes form a reticulum; dorsal and anal fins yellow; caudal fin dusky with a large black patch in the middle.

Habitat: Benthic. Found in small groups from brackish waters to coastal areas. Attains 50 cm Total Length.

Distribution: Indo-west Pacific.

Remarks: Good food fish. Frequently found in catches.

Family: SCOMBRIDAE

Key to the species of Family Scombridae

1(a) A single pair of oblique keds near end of caudal fin; dorsal and anal finlets 5 each; gillrakers very long, visible when mouth is opened, 30-46 gill rakers on lower arm of 1st arch; 1st dorsal with 8-10 spines .... *Rastrelliger kanagurta*

1(b) Two small keels with an additional mid-lateral keel on either side of caudal peduncle; dorsal and anal finlets 9-10 each; gill rakers normal; 8-12 on lower arm of 1st arch; 1st dorsal with 15-17 spines ....*Scomberomorus lineolatus*

205. *Scomberomorus lineolatus* (Cuvier, 1831)

Streaked Spanish mackerel

Diagnostic features: D.XV-XVII+19-20+ 8-10 finlets; A.18-19+8-10 finlets; P.21; V.I,5. Body elongate and strongly compressed; 8-12 gill rakers on lower arm of first arch; lateral line with a wavy pattern to below second dorsal fin and gradually bent downward towards caudal keel; intestine with two folds and three distinct limbs. Body bluish-grey on back, sides silvery with spots and dashes.

Habitat: Coastal pelagic fish, enters estuaries and brackish water lakes occasionally.

Distribution: Coasts of India to Thailand.

Remarks: Uncommon. Commercially important. Good food fish.

206. *Rastrelliger kanagurta* (Cuvier, 1816)

Indian Mackerel

Diagnostic futures: D. IX+12+5 finlets; A. 12+5 finlets; P. 19; V. I, 5. Body fusiform; gillrakers are long and visible when mouth is opened; two dorsal fns widely separated. Body blue green above, sides silvery with golden tint; narrow dark longitudinal bands on upper part of body; two rows of small dark spots on upper back; a black spot near lower margin of pectoral fin; dorsal fin yellowish with black tips; caudal and pectoral fins yellowish; ventral fin dusky.

Habitat: Pelagic. Found in coastal waters and adjacent to estuaries and lakes in small schools. Attains 35 cm Total Length.

Distribution: Widely distributed in Indo-Pacific.

Remarks: Commercially important pelagic fish. Caught fairly in large numbers.

Family: BLENNIIDAE

207. *Omobranchus zebra* (Bleeker, 1868)

Zebra blenny

Diagnostic features: D.XII, 18020; A. II, 20; P. 14; V. I, 2. Body elongate gill opening not extending below bi-pored lateral line tubes 1 to 4, extending posteriorly to below level of 2-4 dorsal fin spines. Four broad drak bands on head and eight broad drak bands on body in males; these bands faint or absent in females.

Habitat: Demersal. Found in coastal marine, mangroves and brackish waters. Attains 6.5 cm Total Length.

Distribution: Indo-West Pacific: India, Malaysia, Indonesia, Singapore and Philippines.

Remarks: No commercial value.

Family: ELEOTRIDAE

Key to the species of Family Eleotrididae

1(a) Angle of preopercle with a single ventrally directed spine; scales in longitudinal series 60-68; numerous horizontal dark lines on body; fins spotted in young .... *Eleotris fusca*

1(b) Angle of preopercle without spine; scales in longitudinal series 29-30; several dark longitudinal lines on body; pectoral fin base with 1-2 black spots ... *Butis butis*

208. ***Butis butis*** (Hamilton, 1822)

Duckbill sleeper

Diagnostic features: D.VI+I, 8-9; A. I, 8-9; P.18-20; LS. 25-30; PD.20-25. Depth 5.0 -6.0 times in statndard length; maxilla extends to front edge of eye; head depressed with bony serrations above each eye; top of head, cheeks and opercle scaled; anterior nostril short; axilla ends under front edge of eye; adults with small auxillary scales between larger body scales; bony serratins or crests on head in inter-orbital and around eyes. Body dark grey with several dark longitudinal lines; caudal black with light margin dorsally; pectoral base with 1-2 black spots.

Habitat: Demersal. Coastal waters, estuaries and enters freswater. Attains 14 cm Total Length.

Distribution: Tropical Indo-west Pacific.

Remarks: Considered trash fish.

209. ***Eleotris fusca*** (Schneider, 1801)

Dusky sleeper

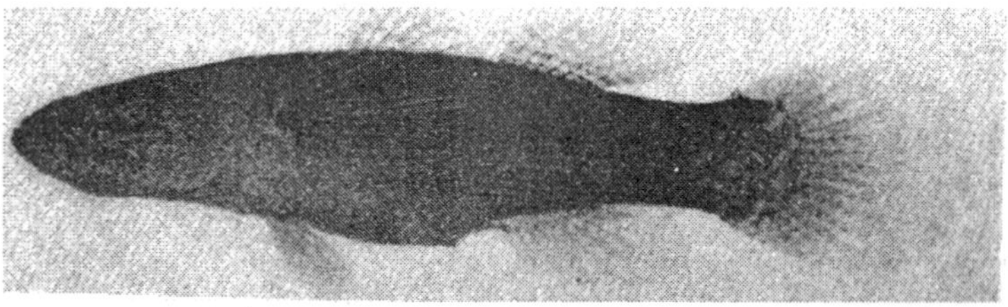

Diagnostic features: D.VI+I, 8-9; A. I, 8-9; P.17-19; LS.53-68; PD.38-50. Body oblong, head depressed, snout blunt; top of head, lips thick; cheeks and opercles scaled; interorbital scales minute; anterior nostrils a short tube; pectoral rays mostly branched; no head pores; a single downward curved spine at angle of preopercle. Head, body and fins dark brown to black; numerous dark horizontal lines on body; fins spotted in young.

Habitat: Demersal. Inhabit shallow coastal, estuaries and lakes. Attains 25 cm Total Length.

Distribution: Tropical Indo-West Pacific.

Remarks: Not considered as food fish.

Family: **GOBIIDAE**

Key to the species of Family Gobiidae

1(a) Body very elongate, mouth vertical or oblique; dorsal and anal fins continuous with caudal; dorsal and anal anal fin rays more than 40 2

1(b) Body not elongate; mouth oblique oblique or horizontal; Dorsal and anal fin rays not continuous with caudal; dorsal and anal fin rays less than 20 3

2(a) Anal fin rays 35; mouth vertical; a row of three barbells on each side below head; caudal fin pointed; body covered with rudimentary scales or naked; colour brownish olive .... *Tenioides buchanani*

2(b) Anal fin rays 39-46; mouth oblique; no barbells below head; caudal fin rounded; body covered with well developed scales; colour reddish .... *Trypauchen vagina*

3(a) Caudal fin lanceolatus or oblongus and pointed 4

3(b) Caudal fin rounded or obtuse or oblongus and pointed 13

4(a) Tongue bilobed .... 5 (*Glossogobius*)

4(b) Tongue not bilobed, rounded or emarginated or truncate 7

5(a) Lateral scale series 24-25; no ocelli in 1st dorsal fin; no markings on fin .... *G. mas*

5(b) Lateral scale series 29-36; ocelli present or absent on 1st dorsal; fins spotted 6

6(a) Two ocelli on 1st dorsal fin; caudal fin slightly rounded .... *G. biocellatus*

6(b) No ocelli on 1st dorsal, but some times with dark spot posteriorly; caudal fin obtuse ....*G. giuris*

7(a) First dorsal with 5 rays; 2nd dorsal with 30 rays; scales minute; lateral scale series 200 .... *Pseudopocryptes elongates*

7(b) First dorsal with 6 rays; second dorsal with less than 30 rays; lateral scale series less than 100 8

8(a) Lateral scale series 75-79; pectoral fin with free silky rays .... *Parapocryptes rictuosus*

8(b) Lateral scale series below 68; pectoral fin without free silky rays 9

9(a) Lateral scale series 50-65; eyes with small tentacle at upper margin may be present .... 10 (*Oxyurichthys*)

9(b) Lateral scale series less than 30; eyes without tentacle 11

10(a) Lateral scale series 50-55; no tentacle on eye but a black triangular spot in iris at the upper part; pectoral fin rounded .... O. *microlepis*

10(b) Lateral scale series 52-65; tentacle on upper margin of eye; pectoral fin obtuse ... . O. *tentacularis*

11(a) Tongue emarginated; caudal fin pointed ....Drombus globiceps

11(b) Tongue truncate; caudal fin lanceolate .... 12 (*Oligolepis*)

12(a) Body brownish with numerous dark blotches along back; dark brown bar below eye to hind end of jaw .... *O. acutipennis*

12(b) Body yellowish with narrow 7-11 yellow bands on flanks; black spots on head ... . *O. cylindriceps*

13(a) Tongue bilobed 14

13(b) Tongue not bilobed 16

14(a) First dorsal fin rays 6; lateral scale series 30-43; caudal fin rounded .... 15 (*Bathygobius*)

14(b) First dorsal fin rays 5; head and nape naked lateral scale series 27; caudal fin truncate .... *Gobiopterus chuno*

15(a) Lateral scale series 38-40; body grayish with dusky spots; dorsal and caudal fin spotted .... *B. ostreicola*

15(b) Lateral scale series 29-36; body dusky with scattered spots; fins dark with dusky margin .... *B. fuscus*

16(a) Caudal fin obtuse or rounded; lateral scale series 25-60; 1st dorsal fin spines normal or filamentous.................. 17

16(b) Caudal fin wedge shaped; lateral scale series 30; no fleshy flaps on inner edge of shoulder; 1st dorsal fin spines filamentous .... *Bathygobius nunus*

17(a) Lateral scale series 50-60; eyes close together and above dorsal profile .... *Priophthalmus barbarus*

17(b) Lateral scale series less than 45; eyes normal in position 18

18(a) Head, cheek and operculum naked; 1st dorsal fin spine filamentous; lateral scale series 28-29 ....
Amoya madraspatensis

18(b) Head, cheek and operculum scaled; lateral scale series 25-45 19

19(a) Predorsal scales more than 15 .... 20 (*Acentrogobius*)

19(b) Predorsal scales 6-10 23

20(a) Predorsal scales 15-16 .... *A. cyanomos*

20(b) Predorsal scales 25-30 21

21(a) Predorsal scales 25; a broad papillae on each side of chin; brilliant blue spots on nape and behind pectoral fins

.... *A. masoni*

21(b) Predorsal scales 25-30; no papillae on chin; no blue spots on nape 22

22(a) Lateral scale series 34-38; predorsalscales 30; body dark green above, laterally with green spots; caudal fin with black spots .... *A. viridipunctatus*

22(b) Lateral scale series 42; predorsal scales 25-30; body olivaceous with black spots; caudal fin edge dark .... *A. griseus*

23(a) Predorsal scales 6-8; middle of the 1st dorsal fin ray longest; cheek scaled; body with numerous minute spots; 1st dorsal fin with black blotch; caudal fin base with two black spots .... *Pseudogobius javanicus*

23(b) Predorsal scales 8-9; cheek naked; body yellow with 4-5 oval blotches on flanks .... *Stigmatogobius minima*

210. Acentrogobius cyanomos (Bleeker, 1849)

Diagnostic features: D.VI+I, 10; A.10; P.18; V.I,5; C. 11; Ll. 28-31; PD. 15-16. Cheeks swollen, no warts on cheeks; no crest or tentacles on head; a short pair of barbels below symphysis of mandible; second and third dorsal spines filiform; caudal fin slightly rounded. Body dull olive with with light bluish spots on scales; deep blue spot on the shoulder; second dorsal and anal fins dark with reddish outer edge.

Habitat: Demersal; amphidromous. Found in marine and backfish waters. Attains 11.5 cm Total Length.

Distribution: Indo-West Pacific: India, Thailand, Malaysia and Indonesia. Reported from Bangladesh

Remarks: Trash fish. No commercial value.

211. *Acentrogobius griseus* (Day, 1876)

Grey goby

Diagnostic features: D.VI+I, 10; A.10;.P.17; V.I,5; C. 14; Ls. 42; PD. 25-30. Body elongate and compressed; lower jaw longer, cleft of mouth oblique; numerous rows of warts on cheek and opercle; no barbels on chin; dorsal spines ending in filamentous prolongations; caudal foin wedge shaped, the central rays being the longest. Body olivaceous with black spots; base of first dorsal yellow with three or four horizontal brown bands and a dark mark at its posterior extremity; second dorsal yellow with dark edge; anal, ventral and caudal fin edges dark.

Habitat: Demersal; amphidromous; Inhabits freshwater, brackish and coastal marine waters. Attains 8.5 cm Total Length.

Distribution: Asia: India.

Remarks: Considered trash fish.

212. *Acentrogobius masoni* (Day, 1873)

Diagnostic features: D.VI+I, 10-11; A.I, 9; P.19; V.I,5; C. 12; PD. 25. Body slightly elongate, profile of head bluntly rounded, cleft of mouth oblique; a broad papilla on each side of chin; numerous wart like glands along the opercle, nape and madibles; dorsal fin spines filiform; caudal fin wedge-shaped. Body olive with numerous brilliant blue spots on nape and behind pectoral fin; pectoral fin yellow with black margin, rest of the fins black.

Habitat: Demersal; amphidromous; Occurs in brackish and coastal marine waters.

Distribution: Indian Ocean.

Remarks: Considered trash fish.

213. *Acentrogobius viridipunctatus* (Valenciennes, 1837)

Diagnostic features: D.VI+I, 10; A.I, 9; P.18-19; V.I,5; C.15; Ls. 34-38; Pd. 30. Body elongate, head little comprssed. Mouth oblique; lower jaw prominent; maxilla extend to below middle of eye; teeth filiform in many rows; outer row enlarged; head scaled above behind eyes and on upper part of pre-opercle and opercle. Body dusky green above, lighter below; laterally with green spots; a dark stripe on first dorsal; second dorsal with two longitudinal dark bands; caudal with black spots.

Habitat: Demersal. Inhabits mangroves, estuaries and lagoons. Attains 8-10 cm Total Length.

Distribution: Indo-west Pacific.

Remarks: Considered as trash fish.

214. *Amoya madraspatensis* (Day, 1868)

Diagnostic features: D.VI+I, 9; A.I, 9; P.17; V.I, 5; C. 13; Ls. 28-29; PD. 82. Cleft of mouth oblique; eye diameter 4 times in head; cheeks and operculum naked; dorsal fin spines flexible, its first ray filamentous; caudal fin rounded. Body olivaceous with irregular brownish blotches and dots; five to eight vertical narrow black lines pass from back to abdomen; fins grey, first dorsal with two rows of black blotches, second dorsal irregularly blotched; pectoral and anal unspotted; ventrals tipped with black; caudal fin with small dots in rows.

Habitat: Demersal; amphidromous; Found in fresh; brackish and coastal marine waters. Attains 7.5 cm Total Length.

Distribution: Eastern Indian Ocean and Western Central Pacific.

Remarks: Considered as trash fish.

215. *Bathygobius fuscus* (Ruppell, 1830)

Dusky-frill goby

Diagnostic features: D.VI+I, 9; A.I, 8; P.17-19; LS. 29-36; PD. 14-16. Small goby, body elongate and somewhat compressed; lips thick; teeth in several rows in jaws; longitudinal rows of mucous canals on cheek; maxilla extend to below posterior part of eye; upper three pectoral rays free from membrane; pre-pelvic region scaled; caudal fin obtuse, equal to head length. Body dusky with scattered spots; sides with faint blotches; fins dark with dusky margins.

Habitat: Demersal. Inhabits mangroves, estuaries and lagoons. Attains 8-10 cm Total Length.

Distribution: Indo-Pacific.

Remarks: Considered as trash fish.

216. *Bathygobius ostreicola* (Chaudhuri, 1916)

Diagnostic features: D. VI+I,9-10; A. I, 8-9; P.I,17-18; Ls. 38-40. Body elongate, head compressed; mouth oblique; tongue rounded; upper three or four pectoral rays free and silky; predorsal scl rudimentary. Body grayish with ark spots; two or there faint blotches below dorsal fins; dorsal and caudal fin spotted; anal fin dusky.

Habitat: Amphidromous; demersal. Occurs in freshwater, marine, backlist waters and estuaries. Attains 5.5 cm Total Length.

Distribution: East coast of India.

Remarks: Considered as trash fish.

217. *Brachygobius nunus* (Hamilton, 1822)

Bumblebee goby

Diagnostic features: D. VI+I,9; A. 9; P.17; V. I,5; C. 15; Ls. 30; L.tr.7. Body depth 5 times in total length; eyes small; cleft of mouth oblique; dorsal fin spines with filamentous prolongations; caudal fin wedge shaped. Body reddish brown with seven black bands, first through eye, the second over opercle the rest on the body, these bands extend on to the dorsal and anal fins.

Habitat: Demersal; amphidromous. Occurs in estuaries, mangroves, tidal creeks and freshwater streams. Attains 3.0 cm Total Length.

Distribution: India, Myanmar, Thailand, Malaya, Indonesia and Borneo, also reported from Bangladesh.

Remarks: Considered as trash fish.

218. *Drombus globiceps* (Hora,1923)

Bighead goby

Diagnostic features: D. VI+I, 10; A.I, 9; P.17.Ls.26-27; PD.7-8. Body elongate and slightly compressed; snout short and rounded; eyes large, about 3.3 times in head; Back and flanks yellowish-green; belly reddish-yellow; head and body with brown spots; body with pearl like blue spots; 1st dorsal with black spot behind the fifth ray; 2nd dorsal and caudal fin with a white stripe.

Habitat: Demersal; amphidromous. Inhabit fresh, brackish and marine waters. Attains 4.0 cm Total Length.

Distribution: India, Indonesia and Papua New Guinea.

Remarks: Considered as trash fish.

219. ***Glossogobius biocellatus*** (Valenciennes, 1837)

Sleepy goby

Diagnostic features: D.VI+I, 9; A.I,8; P.17-19; Ls. 29-33; PD.13-16. Body elongate, head compressed; tongue bilobed; branchiostegal membranes forms a free fold across isthmus; iris with a lappet; caudal fin rounded. Body dark brown to black, with small black spots in longitudinal rows; 2-3 broad saddles on back and side; 1st dorsal with two black ocelli; ventral with dark cross bands.

Habitat: Demersal. Inhabit freshwater and brackish waters. Attains 10 cm Total Length.

Distribution: Indo-Pacific.

Remarks: Consumed locally.

220. ***Glossogobius giuris*** (Hamilton, 1822)

Tank goby

Diagnostic features: D.VI+I,9; A.I, 8; P.19-20; LS. 29-36. Body elongate, head compressed; tongue bilobed; branchiostegal membranes attached to sides of isthmus; caudal fin rounded; iris without lappet. Body olive to dusky green above, lighter below; 5-6 large blotches on body; dorsal with small spots forming longitudinal stripes.

Habitat: Demersal. Inhabit fresh and brackish waters. Attains 50cm Total Length.

Distribution: Widespread in Indo-west Pacific.

Remarks: Common in fish catches. Locally consumed.

221. *Glossogobius mas* (Hora, 1923)

Diagnostic features: DVI+I,7; A.7; Ls. 24-25. Body slender with flattened head; snout bluntly pointed, slightly longer than eye diameter; head 2.7 in standard length; ; eyes small situated on dorsal surface, 5.2 in head length; mouth oblique and wide; tongue deeply notched; caudal fin lanceolate. Body reddish brown, center of scales whitish, while edges black; no markings on fins

Habitat: Demersal; brackish and marine waters. Attains 4.5 to 5.5 cm Total length.

Distribution: Indian Ocean: India.

Remarks: Considered as trash fish.

222. *Gobiopterus chuno* (Hamilton, 1822)

Diagnostic features: D.V+I,-8; A. I,9-10; P.13-15; Ls.27-30. Body transparent in life; elongate and compressed; mouth oblique; teeth in jaws uniserial; head naked. Body greenish yellow; tip of lower jaw brownish; fins hyaline.

Habitat: Demersal; amphidromous. Inhabit rivers and brackish waters. Feed mainly on zooplankton. Attains 3.5 cm Total Length.

Distribution: India, Myanmar, Malay Peninsula, Sumatra and Indonesia.

Remarks: No commercial value.

223. ***Oligolepis acutipennis*** (Valenciennes, 1837)

Sharptail goby

Diagnostic features: D.VI+I,11; A.I,11; P.20-21; LS. 25-27. Head rounded; pre-opercular pores present; maxilla not reaching past eye; caudal fin lanceolate. Body brownish with numerous dark blotches along back; a series of eye size faint blotches on mid-side, the last spot is at caudal base; fins dusky, often spotted; dark brown bar from below eye to hind end of jaw.

Habitat: Demersal. Muddy coastal, estuaries and brackish areas. Attains13 cm Total Length.

Distribution: Widely distributed in Indo-west Pacific.

Remarks: No commercial value.

224. ***Oligolepis cylindriceps*** (Hora, 1923)

Diagnostic features: D. VI+I,9; A. I,9-11; P. 17; Ls. 25. Body elongate and copmpressed; mouth oblique; no barbels; dorsal fins separate; caudal fin lanceolate. Body yellowish with narrow 7-11 dark yellow bands on flanks; round black spots on head; 1st dorsal with minute spots, second fin variegated; anal fin dusky; ventral fins dark.

Habitat: Demersal; occurs mostly in brackish waters. Feed on zooplankton, crustaceans, insects. Atrtains 3.5 cm Total Length.

Distribution: India to Malaysia.

Remarks: No coomercial value.

225. ***Oxyurichthys microlepis*** (Bleeker, 1849)

Maned goby

Diagnostic features: D.VI+I,12-13; A.I,13; P.20-22; Ls. 42-50; PD.15-20. Body moderate, head large, 3.3-3.8 in standard length length; tongue largely fused to floor of mouth, tip free; ventral a disc; pectoral base and pelvic naked; no bump on eyes; pre-dorsal with low crest; caudal twice head and lanceolate. Body violet; vertical fins pink; 1st dorsal with two blue lines, 2nd with blue spots; pectoral orange with violet spots; ventrals orange.

Habitat: Demersal. Found in mangroves, estuaries, lagoons and sand and mud bottoms of shallow coastal areas. Attains 13 cm Total Length.

Distribution: Widespread in Indo-west Pacific.

Remarks: Considered as trash fish.

226. ***Oxyurichthys tentacularis*** (Valenciennes,1837)

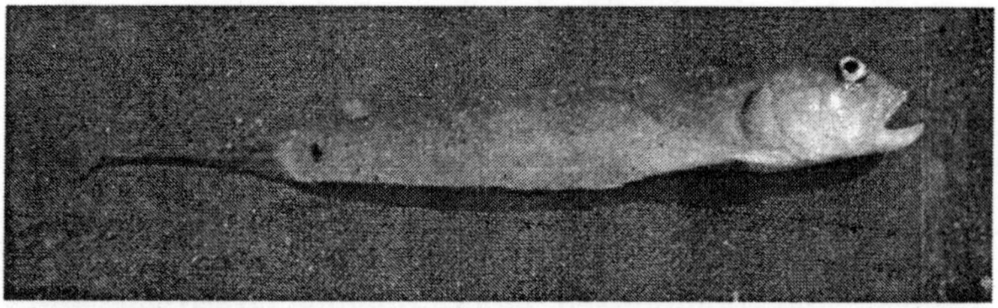

Diagnostic features: D.VI+I, 12; A.I,14; P.18-20; V.I,5. Body very elongate with a pair of ocular tentacles; mouth oblique; lower jaw prominent; maxilla extends to below posterior part of eye; longitudinal mucous canal on cheek; median line of head and nape naked; caudal fin long and pointed. Body reddish green above, paler below; scales of back and sides with red spots; 1st dorsal fin spotted with three longitudinal rows of reddish-violet spots; 2nd dorsal with oblong reddish violet spots; pectoral fin orange; ventral and anal fins violet; caudal fin with oblique reddish streaks.

Habitat: Demersal. Inhabitat shallow coastal areas, estuaries and backwaters. Attains 10-13 cm Total Length.

Distribution: Widely distributed in Indo-west Pacific.

Remarks: Considered as trash fish.

227. ***Parapocryptes rictuosus*** (Valenciennes,1837)

Diagnostic features: D. VI+19-27; A. 19-28; P. 20; V. 1,5;

LS.75-79. Body elongate and compressed posteriorly, head sub-cylindrical; lower jaw slightly longer; dorsals continuous at their bases; caudal fin pointed and very long. Body greyish above, lighter below with faint oblique bands from the base of dorsal fin half way to abdomen, a black spot surrounded by yellow ring on the last few dorsal rays; inside of mouth with black spots.

Habitat: Demersal; amphidromous. Brackish and marine. Attains 16.0 cm Total Length.

Distribution: Indian Ocean: India.

Remarks: Considered as trash fish.

228. *Periophthalmus barbarus* (Linnaeus, 1766)

Mudskipper

Diagnostic features: D.IX+I,11-13; A. I, 11-12; P.16-20; LS. 50-60; PD. 22-23. No frenum uniting pelvic fins; inner rays of ventral fins unite at the base by narrow membrane. Body blackish brown above, lighter below; first dorsal with pale margin; infra-marginally black band with broken white line, most of the fin grey-brown; second dorsal fin margin brown, below it a dark band between two white lines; caudal fin spotted.

Habitat: Demersal. Found in mangroves, estuaries, lagoons and sand and mud bottoms of shallow coastal areas. Attains 9-10 cm Total Length.

Distribution: Indo-West Pacific.

Remarks: Considered as trash fish.

229. *Pseudapocryptes elongates* (Cuvier, 1816)

Diagnostic features: D. V+I,30-31; A. I,25-28; P.16-18; Ls.200. Body very elongate; head subcylindrical; upper jaw slightly prominent; teeth in jaws uniserial; caudal fin pointed, longaer than head. Body light greenish above, lighter below; with brown markings on back and cheeks; fins yellowish; second dorsal fin spotted; pectoral fin on basal half with red spots; caudal fin barred.

Habitat: Demersal; amphidromous. Found in fresh, brackish and coastal waters. Attains 20.0 cm Total Length.

Distribution: India to Tahiti and north to China.

Remarks: No commercial value.

230. *Pseudogobius javanicus* (Beeker, 1856)

Diagnostic features: D.VII, 7; A. I, 7-8; P.15. Ls. 27-28; PD. 6-7. Transverse scales 7; Maxillary extends to the vertical of anterial half of eye, upper jaw prominent; lips thin; snout obtuse, overhanging the upper lips; head scaled above behind eye and opercle; scales on head, breast and belly cycloid; on lateral side of body ctenoid; pectoral and ventral about as long as head. Colour when fresh greenish and somewhat transparent. Body with numerous minute spots; 1st dorsal with a black blotch; caudal fin base with two vertical black spots.

Habitat: Benthopelagic; amphidromous. Inhabit sea, estuaries and rivers. Feed on small fishes and invertebrates Attains 6.0 cm Total Length.

Distribution: Indo-West Pacific: India to Australia and northward to China.

Remarks: Trash fish.

231. *Stigmatogobius minima* (Hora, 1923)

Diagnostic features: D.VI+I,7; A.I,7-8; P.15; Ls. 25-26; PD.8-9. Body elongate; mouth slightly oblique; teeth in several rows in jaws. Body pale yellow with four or five oval blotches on flanks; soft dorsal and anal fins with a black band on outer half; caudal fin slightly dusky.

Habitat: Demersal; amphidromous. Occurs in brackish water areas. Attains 2.0 cm Total Length.

Distribution: India: Chilka lake in Orissa and Godavari estuary in Andhra Pradesh.

Remarks: No commercial value.

232. ***Taenioides buchanani*** (Day, 1873)

Burmese gobyeel

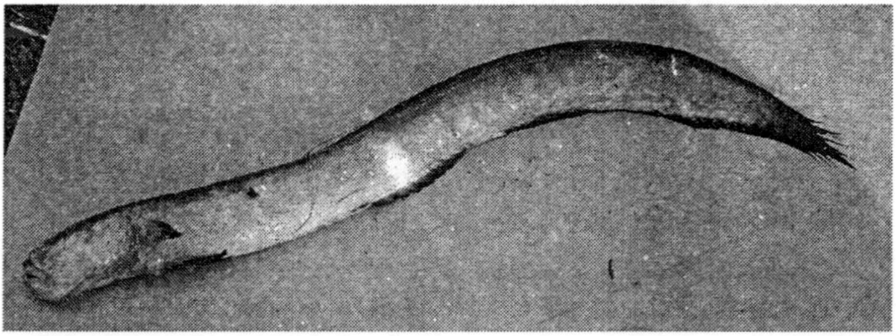

Diagnostic features: D.VI+42; A. 36; P. 18-19; V. I,5; C.17. Body oblong; eyes distinct; lower jaw prominent; posterior nostril opens just before eye, the anterior one, which is tubular, close to the front edge of snout; a pair of minut barbels below the symphysis of lower jaw, and still a small pair behind them; caudal fin elongate and pointed;. Body brownish-olive, reddish inferiorly; pectoral and ventral fins yellowish; dorsal and anal fins blackish.

Habitat: Demersal; amphidromous. Brackish and marine. Attains 30.0 cm Total Length.

Distribution: Indian Ocean: east coast of India and Myanmar. Reported from Bangladesh

Remarks: No commercial value.

233. *Trypauchen vagina* (Bloch & Schneider, 1801)

Comb goby

Diagnostic features: D.VI, 40-49; A. I, 39-46; P.15-18; I, 5. Body compressed and elongate; eyes very small, covered by skin; mouth oblique, lower jaw prominent; maxilla extends to behind eye; teeth in jaws many rows and pointed; head, nape and breast naked; body covered with cycloid celes; pectoral fin half of head length; caudal fin rounded and equal to head length. Body reddish.

Habitat: Demersal; amphidromous. Inhabits shallow coastal areas, creeks and mangroves. Attains15-18 cm Total Length.

Distribution: Widespread in Indo-west Pacific.

Remarks: Considered as trash fish.

Family: **TRICHIURIDAE**

Key to the species of Family Trichiuridae

1(a) Ventral fin absent; lateral line nearer to ventral profile of body; dorsal fin rays 110-117 .... *Lepturacanthus savala*

1(b) Ventral fins present; appearing as a scale-like structure; lateral line almost on mid-line of body; dorsal fin rays 123-131 .... *Eupleurogrammus glossodon*

234. *Eupleurogrammus glossodon* (Bleeker, 1860)

Bleeker's Ribbonfish

Diagnostic features: D. III,123-131. P.I,10. Body extremely elongate and compressed, ribbon-like, tapering to a point; mouth large, sharp canine teeth in jaws, those in front of upper jaw are fang-like; caudal fin absent; anal fin reduced to separate spines which are buried in flesh, its origin below 31st to 37th soft dorsal rays,; pelvic fins reduced to a wing-like structure. Body silvery-white.

Habitat: Benthopelagic. Inhabits shallow coastal waters, estuaries and backwaters. Attains 50 cm Total Length.

Distribution: Coasts of India to East Indies.

Remarks: Caught in large quantities. Consumed fresh or salt-dried.

235. *Lepturacanthus savala* (Cuvier, 1829)

Small-headed ribbonfish

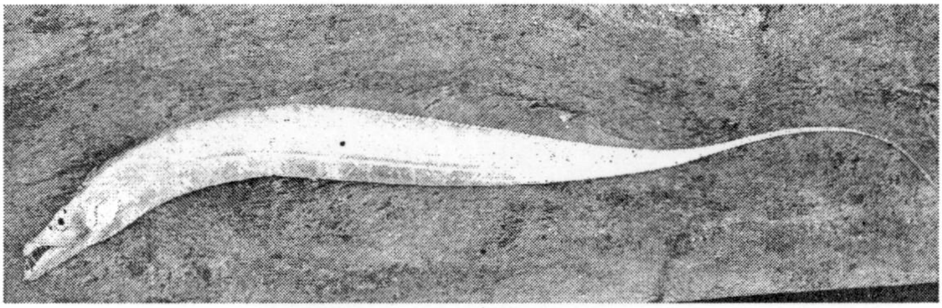

Diagnostic features: D.III, 110-117. Body extremely elongate and compressed, ribbon-like, tapering to a point; mouth large, lower jaw considerably prolonged, sharp canine teeth in jaws, those in front of upper jaw are fang-like; caudal fin absent; anal fin reduced to separate spines, are not buried in flesh; pelvic and caudal fins absent. Body silvery-blue with metallic reflections; fins yellowish white.

Habitat: Benthopelagic. Inhabit shallow coastal waters, estuaries and backwaters. Attains 75 cm Total Length.

Distribution: Indo-West Pacific, from coasts of India to Australia.

Remarks: Caught in large quantities. Commercially important fish. Consumed fresh or salt-dried.

Family: ANABANTIDAE

236. *Anabas cobojius* (Hamilton, 1822)

Gangetic koi

Diagnostic features: D. XVI-XVIII, 9-10; A. IX-XI, 9-11; P.13-15; V.I, 5; Ll.25-28. Body elongate and fairly deep; depth 2.2-2.8 in standard length; snout 10.5-12.5 in standard length. Body greenish, pale yellow on belly; more than four vertical bands on sides, disappear with age; a dark spot at base of caudal fin; dorsal fin edge dusky; fins yellowish.

Habitat: Benthopelagic. Found in lakes, ponds, ditches and paddy fields also enter brackish waters of less saline. Able to live out of water for a long period. Attains 30 cm Total Length.

Distribution: India and Bangladesh.

Remarks: Highly commercial fish. Good food fish, consumed fresh.

237. *Anabas testudinus* (Bloch, 1792)

Climbing perch

Diagnostic features: D. XVI-XX, 8-10; A. IX-XI, 8-11; P.15; V.I, 5; Ll.28-32. Body oblong and compressed; 4-5 scale rows between eye and rear margin of preoperculum.; body depth 3.0-

3.5, snout 5.7-7.7 times in standard length; Color dark to pale greenish, pale below, head with longitudinal stripes ventrally; posterior margin of opercle with a dark spot; iris golden reddish..

Habitat: Demersal; potamodromous. Found mostly in canals, lakes, ponds, swamps and estuaries. Tolerate extremely turbid and stagnant waters. Feed on macrophytic vegetation, shrimps and fish fry. Attains 25.0 cm Total Length.

Distribution: India to China.

Remarks: Important food fish in SE Asia, considered tasty.

Family: **OSPHRONEMIDAE**

238. ***Colisa lalia*** (Hamilton, 1822)

Dwarf gourami

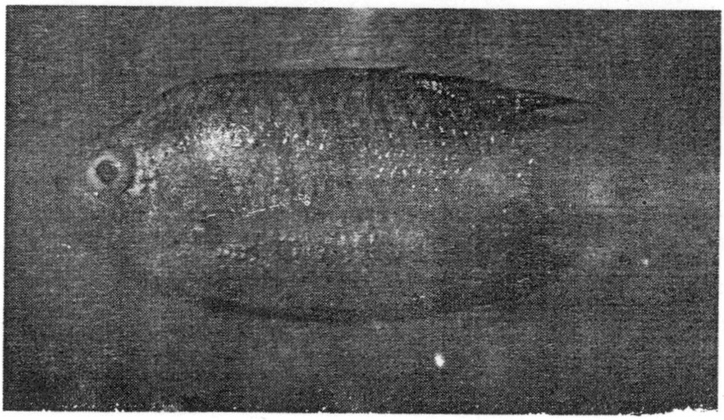

Diagnostic features: D.XV-XVIII, 11-20; A.XV-XXII,11-20; P.10; V.1; Ll.26-28. Head and body compressed; mouth terminal, cleft small; soft parts of dorsal and anal fins not produced; caudal fin slightly emarginated. Body scarlet and light blue vertical bands; the bands extend onto dorsal, anal and caudal fins.

Habitat: Benthopelagic; freshwater. Occurs in sluggish or standing water in canals, lakes and swamps. Carnivorous, feeds on fish, frogs, snakes, insects, earthworms and tadpoles. Attains 9.0 cm total length.

Distribution: Pakistan, India and Bangladesh.

Remarks: Aquarium pet, highly commercial.

239. *Colisa fasciata* (Bloch and Schneider, 1801)

Banded gourami

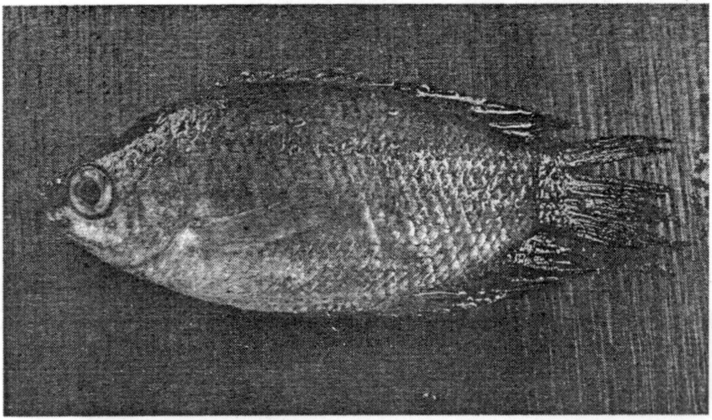

Diagnostic features: D.XV-XVII,9-14; A.XV-XXIII,14-19; P.10, V.1; Ll.29-31. Body elongate and strongly compressed; mouth small, slightly protrusible; upper lip papillose; preorbital serrate in young specimen; caudal fin slightly notched or cut square. Color greenish with oblique orange or bluish bars backwards from the back to the anal fin; dorsal; and anal fins with alternating dark and pale spots or bars; the anal fin with red margin.

Habitat: Benthopelagic; occurs in large rivers, estuaries, ditches, ponds and lakes, generally prefer weedy environment. Attains 12.5 cm Total Length.

Distribution: Pakistan, India, Nepal, Bangladesh and upper Myanmar.

Remarks: Aquarium pet. Widely marketed around the world.

Family: **CHANNIDAE**

Key to the species of Family Channidae

1(a) Predorsal scales 12-13; 4-5 scales between orbit and angle of preopercle; dorsal fin rays 28-33 .... *Channa punctatus*

1(b) Predorsal scales 15-22; 9-17 scales between orbit and angle of preopercle; dorsal fin rays 35-55..............................2

2(a) Predorsal scales 18-20; anal rays; anal rays 23-29; several dark vertical bands below lateral line ....*C. striatus*

2(b) Predorsal scales 15-16; anal rays 28-36; 5-6 dark oval blotches on flanks; large black ocellus on caudal fin base; numerous white spots on body and fins... *C. marulius*

240. ***Channa punctata*** (Bloch, 1793)

Spotted snakehead

Diagnostic features: D.29-32; A.21-23; P.17; V.6; Ll.37-40. Body subcylindrical anteriorly; haed depressed; predorsal scales 12; five scale rows between orbit and angle of preopercle. Back greenish, yellowish on sides and abdomen with dark stripe on side of head; many bands pass from back downwards to middle of body; fins spotted; dorsal, anal and caudal fins with narrow light edge and dark basal; band.

Habitat: Benthopelagic; potamodromous. Found in ponds, swamps, brackish water and ditches. Prefers stagnant waters in muddy streams. Feed on worms, insects and small fish. Attains 30 cm total length.

Distribution: Afghanistan, Pakistan, India, Sri Lanka, Nepal, Bangladesh, Myanmar and Yunnan in China.

Remarks: Good food fish. Consumed resh.

241. *Channa marulius* (Hamilton, 1822)

Great snakehead

Diagnostic features: D.45-55; A.28-36; P.18; V.6; Ll.60-70. Body elongated, subcylindrical anteriorly; abdomen rounded; haed depressed; predorsal scales 15-16; 10 scales between orbit and angle of preopercle; a black white-edged ocellus on basal portion of caudal fin present.

Habitat: Benthopelagic; potamodromous; freshwater. Attains 180 cm Total Length.

Distribution: India to China, south to Thailand and Cambodia.

Remarks: Commercial and gamefish fish; good aquaculture species.

242. *Channa striata* (Bloch, 1793)

Snakehead murrel

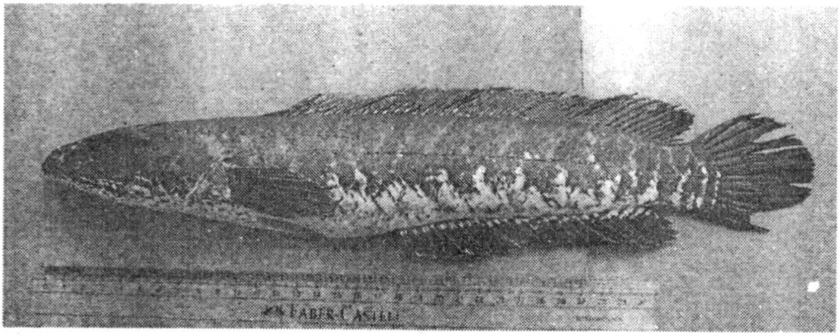

Diagnostic features: D. 38-43; A. 23-27; P. 17; V.6; Ll. 50-57.Body sub-cylindrical; head depressed; caudal fin rounded; scales large; predorsal scales 18-20; nine or ten between orbit and angle of preopercle. The dorsal surface and sides is dark and mottled with a combination of black and ochre, and white on the belly.

Habitat: Benthopelagic; potamodromous. Inhabits ponds, streams, rivers and brackish water lakes. Prefer stagnant and muddy waters. Survives dry season by burrowing in bottom mud of lakes, canals and swamps as long as skin and air-breathing apparatus remain moist and subsists on the stored fat. Feed on fish, frogs, snakes, insects, earthworms, tadpoles and crustaceans. Attains 100 cm total length.

Distribution: Pakistan, India to Thailand and south China.

Remarks: Highly commercial fish and consumed fresh; good aquaculture species and also aquarium pet.

Family: **MASTACEMBELIDAE**

Key to the species of Family Mastacembelidae

1(a) Dorsal fin spines 32-40; dorsal fin merged with caudal fin; rostrum relatively small; no rostral tooth plates; rim of anterior tubular nostril with two broad-based flaps .... *Mastacembelus armatus*

1(b) Dorsal fin spines below 32; dorsal fin separated from caudalfin; rostrum relatively large, ventral surface lined with tooth plates; rim of anterior tubular nostril with six finger-like projections .... 2 (*Macroganathus*)

2(a) Concave ventral surface of rostrum with paired tooth plates; dorsal fin rays 44-45; no spines on pre-operculum; pre-orbital spine absent .... *M. aral*

2(b) Rostrum rounded; no tooth plates; dorsal fin 30-42; preopercel with 2-5 spines; preorbital spine strong .... *M. pancalus*

243. *Macrognathus aral* (Bloch & Schneider, 1801)

One-stripe spinyeel

Diagnostic features: D. 13-32/ 42-56; A. 3/43-54; C.10. Body eel-like, compressed and elongate, snout long with a concave prolongation of the upper jaw consisting of a paired series tooth plates; rim of anterior tubular nostril with six finger-like projections; body covered with minute scales; caudal fin rouned, separated from dorsal and anal; lateral line present. Body light with brownish stripe from snout to caudal end.

Habitat: Benthopelagic. Found in fresh brackish waters and deltas of large rivers, ponds and slow flowing rivers with vegetation. Nocturnal, feed on insects and worms. Attains 60 cm Total Length.

Distribution: Widely distributed in Pakistan, India, Sri Lanka, Bangladesh, Nepal and Myanmar

Remarks: Minor commercial value; good food fish.

244. *Macrognathus pancalus* (Hamilton, 1822)

Barred spinyeel

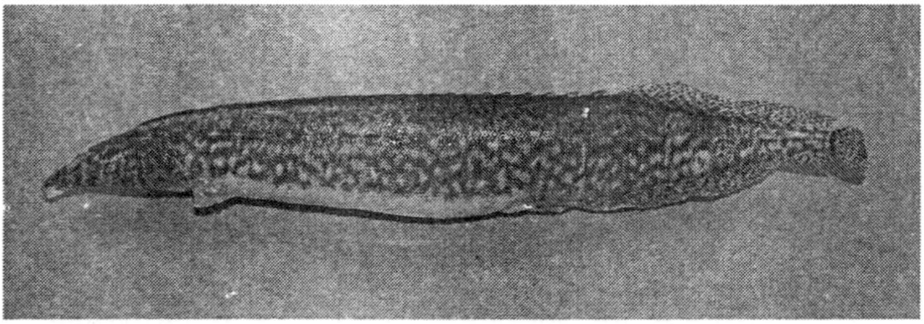

Diagnostic features: D. 24-26/30-42; A. 3/31-46; P.19; C.12. Body slightly long and compressed, eel-like; snout long with a concave prolongation of the upper jaw; no tooth plates on rostrum. Body olive green back, yellowish beneath; sides of body with yellowish spots; fins yellow with black spots.

Habitat: Benthopelagic. Inhabit shallow waters of rivers and estuaries. Attains 18cm Total Length.

Distribution: Pakistan, India, and Bangladesh, also reported from Nepal.

Remarks: Minor commercial value, good food fish, consumed fresh.

245. *Mastacembelus armatus* (Lacepede

Zig-zag eel

Diagnostic features: D.32-39/67-82; A. 3/67-85; C. 14-17. Body eel-like, compressed and elongate; snout long without tooth plates on the under surface; mouth inferior, cleft narrow; rim of anterior nostrils with two finger-like fimbriate and two flaps. Body dull brown becoming lighter on abdomen, with 1-3 dark, longitudinal zigzag lines, more or less connected to form a reticulated pattern, restricted to the dorsal two thirds of the body; a row of black spots along the base of dorsal fin.

Habitat: Demersal; potamodromous. Found in streams, rivers and in coastal marshes; Feed on insect larvae, worms and some submerged plant material. Attains 85 cm Total Length.

Distribution: Pakistan to Viet Nam and Indonesia.

Remarks: Economic ally important species, both food and aquarium trades.

Order: Pleuronectiformes

Family: **PARALICHTHYIDAE**

Key to the species of Family Paralichthyidae

1(a) Anterior rays of dorsal fin longer than those that follow; 23-25 gill rakers on lower arm of 1st arch; three dark conspicuous large ocelli arranged in the form of a trianagle .... *Pseudorhombus triocellatus*

1(b) Anterior rays of dorsalfin not prolonged; 9-13 gill rakers on lower arm of 1st arch; two blotches on lateral line .... *P. arsius*

246. *Pseudorhombus arsius* (Hamilton, 1822)

Large-tooth flounder

Diagnostic features: D.74-76; A.58-61; P.11-13; V.5; Ll.67-80. Body oval and compressed; both eyes are on left side; scales on eye side ctenoid, on blind side cycloid; first dorsal ray inserted over anterior nostril; gill rakers 9-13 on lower arm of first arch. Body light brown with dark spots and rings on eye side; a large dark spot at the junction of straight and curved parts of lateral line and two smaller ones on lateral line at posterior part of body and near anterior end of caudal fin; median fins with scattered dark spots.

Habitat: Demersal. Found on sand bottom and muddy coastal waters, estuaries and lagoons. Attains 35 cm Total Length.

Distribution: Widespread in Indo-west Pacific.

Remarks: Frequently caught in the lake. Good food fish.

247. *Pseudorhombus triocellatus* (Bloch, 1801)

Threespot flounder

Diagnostic features: D. 66-72; A. 49-56; P.11-12; V.5; Ll. 67-74. Body oval and compressed; both eyes are on left side; gill rakers long and slender, about 23 on lower arm of first arch. Ocular side brownish with indistinct dark spots and markings; three large ocelli arranged in the form of triangle; dorsal, anal and caudal fins with dark spots and blotches.

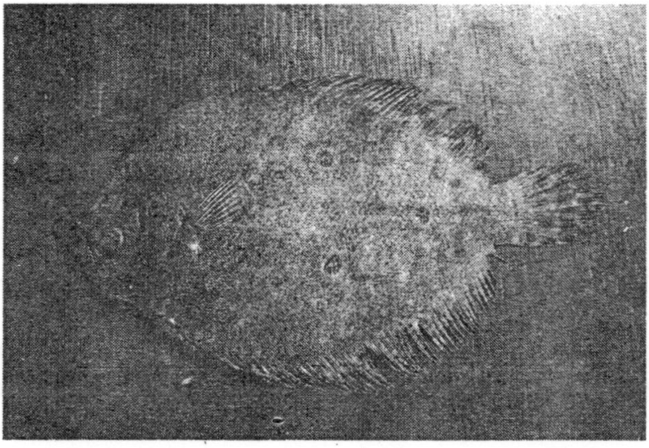

Habitat: Demersal. Found on sand bottom and muddy coastal waters, estuaries and lagoons. Attains 30 cm Total Length.

Distribution: East coast of India, Sri Lanka to Malay Archipelago.

Remarks: Frequently caught in the lake. Good food fish.

Family: CYNOGLOSSIDAE

Key to the species of Family Cynoglossidae

1(a) Scales 11 or 12 between lateral lines; dorsal fin rays 126-138 ; anal fin rays 97-114 .... *Cynoglossus lingua*

1(a) Scales 16-19 between lateral lines; dorsal fin rays 90-100; anal fin rays 72-78 ... ... *C. puncticeps*

248. *Cynoglossus lingua* (Hamilton, 1822)

Long-tongue sole

Diagnostic features: D. 126-138; A. 97-114; C. 10. Body flat and very elongate; anterior nostril tubular; snout obtusely pointed; rostral hook short; pectoral fins absent, only left ventral fin present. Ocular side reddish brown, sometimes with irregular brownish black patches; a large black blotch on operculum.

Habitat: Demersal. Found on sand bottom and muddy coastal waters, estuaries and lagoons. Attains 15-20 cm Total Lemgth.

Distribution: Widespread in Indo-west Pacific.

Remarks: Frequently caught in the lake. Good food fish.

249. *Cynoglossus puncticeps* (Richardson, 1846)

Speckled tongue-sole

Diagnostic features: D.90-100; A.72-78; C.10. Body flat and elongate; interorbital space narrow; anterior nostril tubular; snout rounded; pectoral fins absent, only left ventral fin present. Ocular side yellow-brown with distinct irregular brown blotches; lower side whitish; some rays of dorsal and anal fins dashed with dark brown.

Habitat: Demersal. Found on sand bottom and muddy coastal waters, estuaries and lagoons. Attains 18-25 cm Total Length.

Distribution: Widespread in Indo-west Pacific.

Remarks: Frequently caught in the lake. Good food fish.

Family: **SOLEIDAE**

250. *Solea ovata* (Richardson, 1846)

Ovate-sole

Diagnostic features: D. 58-67; A. 41-51. Body ovate and flat; eyes on right side; inter-orbital scaly; snout obtusely pointed;

dorsal and anal fins not confluent with caudal; both ventral fins present. Ocular side of body and fins olive-brown with spots and black blotches; deep black blotches on outer two-thirds of pectoral fins.

Habitat: Demersal. Found on sand bottom and muddy coastal waters, estuaries and lagoons. Attains 15-18 cm.

Distribution: Coasts of India to China.

Remarks: Occasionally caught in the lake. Good food fish.

251. *Brachirus orientalis* (Bloch & Schneider, 1801)

Oriental sole

Diagnostic features: D.62-68; A. 47-56; P. 7; V. 5; C. 16; Ll. 70-86. Body oblong, eyes on the right side; lips fimbriated or entire; upper jaw rather overlapping lower; nasal tube simple; right pectoral longer than left; dorsal fin commences on snout; scales ctenoid on both sdes. Body bluish slate colour on ocular side with narrow vertical bands, whitish on blind side; dorsal and anal fins dark, outer half of pectoral black.

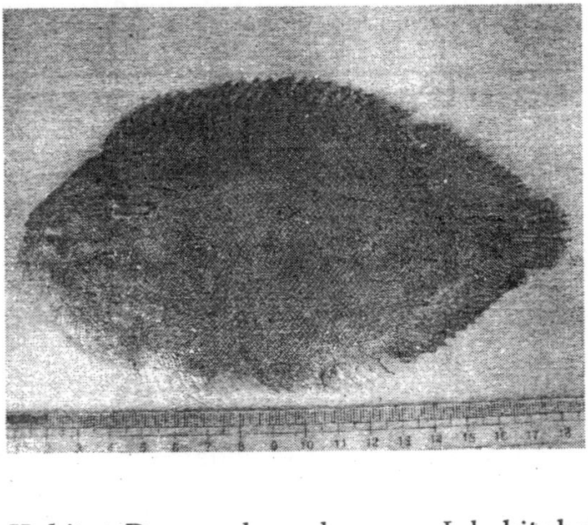

Habitat: Demersal; anadromous. Inhabit shallow sand and mud bottoms of coastal and waters brackish marine. Feed mainly on bottom-dwelling invertebrates, especially small crustaceans. Attains 30.0 cm Standard Length.

Distribution: Indo-West Pacific: Red Sea and Persian Gulf, then off the west coast of India and Sri Lanka, eastward through the Malay Peninsula and Archipelago to China and northern Australia.

Remarks: Marketed fresh, frozen and dried salted.

Order: Tetraodontiformes

Family: **TRIACANHIDAE**

252. ***Triacanthus biaculeatus*** (Bloch, 1786)

Black-finned Tripodfish

Diagnostic features: D. V+23; A. 21; P. 13-14; V. I. Body oblong and compressed; snout slightly concave; caudal peduncle depressed. Body silvery brown on snout and back, white below; membrane between first and second dorsal spines is black; dorsal, anal and pectoral fins light yellow; caudal fin yellowish orange.

Habitat: Demersal. Found on sandy coastal areas, estuaries and lagoons. Feed on a variety of benthic animals. Attains 30 cm Total Length.

Distribution: Widespread in Indo-west Pacific.

Remarks: Not edible fish. Dorsal and ventral spines are venomous. Ornamental fish.

Family: **TETRAODONTIDAE**

Key to the species of Family Tetraodontidae

1(a) Nasal organ a short rounded tube with a terminal opening; back with dark cloudy or reticulated markings; dark ocellus in front of dorsal and anal fins .... *Tetraodon cutcutia*

1(b) Nasal organ an upright sac with two openings or a

solid bifid tentacle, or a cup with fleshy lobes; colouration not as above 2

2(a) Nasal organ covered by a small sac with two nostrils...................... 3

2(b) Nasal organ not covered by sac 4

3(a) Interorbital space longer than snout; caudal peduncle depth subequal to its length; caudal fin truncate .... *Takifugu oblongus*

3(b) Interotbital space longer than snout; caudal peduncle depth half or less of peduncle length; caudal fin lunate .... *Lagocephalus lunaris*

4(a) Nasal organ a bifid tentacle with opposing surface of each tentacle with minute pits; single lateral line; white spots on back; belly with longitudinal brown stripes, curving upward on sides of head .... *Arothron reticularis*

4(b) Nasal organ in a depression with slightly raised margin, front and rear edges produced in to broadly rounded flaps; two lateral lines .... 5 (*Chelonodon*)

5(a) Nasal organ a depression with slightly raised margin, expanded in to a pair of triangular flaps; inter-orbital space flat and broad; dorsal fin rays 9-10; anal fin rays 8-10 .....*C. patoca*

5(b) Nasal organ cup-like with two rounded lobes at its tip; interorbital space concave; dorsal fin rays 14-16; anal fin rays 12-15 .... *C. fluviatilis*

253. *Arothron reticularis* (Bloch & Schneider,1801)

Reticulated puffer

Diagnostic features: D. 10-11; A. 10-11; P. 16-18. Body short and heavy; nostrils with two tentacles on each side; body covered with small spinules except around mouth; caudal fin rounded. Body brownish above, white ventrally; back, sides, caudal peduncle and caudal fin with white spots, sometimes fused to form reticulations; belly with dark longitudinal bands and ascending to cheeks and snout.

Habitat: Reef associated. Found around coastal, estuaries and mangrove areas. Feed on small invertebrates. Attains 35-40 cm Total Length.

Distribution: Widespread in Indo-west Pacific.

Remarks: Very common puffer but not edible fish. Good aquarium pet.

254. *Chelonodon fluviatilis* (Hamilton, 1822)

Blackspotted puffer

Diagnostic features: D. 14-16; A. 12-15; P. 22; C. 11. Body Body short, with the back broad; both jaws with median suture; nasal organ cup-like with two rounded lobes at its tip; gill opening not reaching below middle of pectoral fin base; caudal fin truncate with rounded corners; no lateral cutaneous folls along caudal peduncle; body wholly or partially covered with dermal spines. Body greenish olive above, sides and belly white; back and sides with large black blotches; one or two light bands, one crossing between eyes, another between the pectorals; abdomen with black spots and blotches; all fins yellowish, caudal fin edge black.

Habitat: Demersal, anadromous. Found in shallow coastal mud and rocky areas, estuaries and brackish lagoons. Occur on sand and mudflats. Feed on small invertebrates. Attains 20-28 cm. Total Length.

Distribution: Costs of India, Sri Lanka to Borneo.

Remarks: Not edible fish. Flesh is poisonous.

255. *Chelonodon patoca* (Hamilton, 1822)

Marbled puffer or Whitespotted puffer

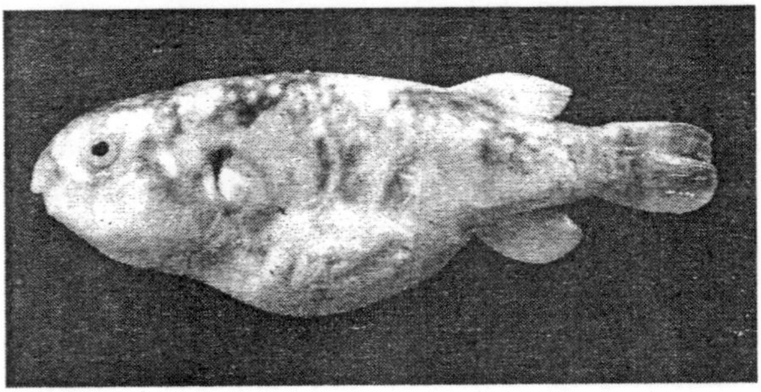

Diagnostic features: D. 9-10; A. 8-10; P. 16-17. Body short and robust; nostrils in a pit with flaps; small spinules on back and abdomen; caudal fin rounded. Body dark brownish grey with large round to ovate white spots; ventral part whitish; a broad yellow streak on lower sides of body; three narrow dark bars on back.

Habitat: Demersal, anadromous. Found in shallow coastal mud and rocky areas, estuaries and brackish lagoons and sometimes penetrates fresh water. Occur on sand and mudflats. Attains 35 cm. Total Length.

Distribution: Widespread in Indo-West Pacific: East Africa to the Admiralty Islands, New Britain and Trobiand Islands, north to China, south to northern Australia.

Remarks: Very common puffer. Flesh is very poisonous.

256. ***Lagocephalus lunaris*** (Bloch & Schneider1801)

Greenbacked blowfish

Diagnostic features: D. 11-13; A. 9-11; P. 18. Body and caudal peduncle slightly elongated; snout blunt, inter-orbital space flat; caudal fin emarginated. Body yellowish green above, silvery below; dorsal, pectoral and upper half of caudal fin white.

Habitat: Demersal. Found on sandy and rubble areas of shallow coastal waters, estuaries and lagoons. Attains 45-55 cm.

Distribution: Widespread in Indo-West Pacific.

Remarks: Common puffer. Flesh and viscera are highly poisonous.

257. ***Takifugu oblongus*** (Bloch, 1786)

Lattice puffer

Diagnostic features: D.12-14; A.10-12; P.14-16. Body slightly elongated; snout blunt, inter-orbital space flat; caudal fin truncated; lower lateral line along the ventro-lateral part of peduncle; nasal organ covered by a small sac with two nostrils; belly, top of head and front part of back with spinules. Body brown above with pale spots, yellowish white below; narrow dark bars on sides.

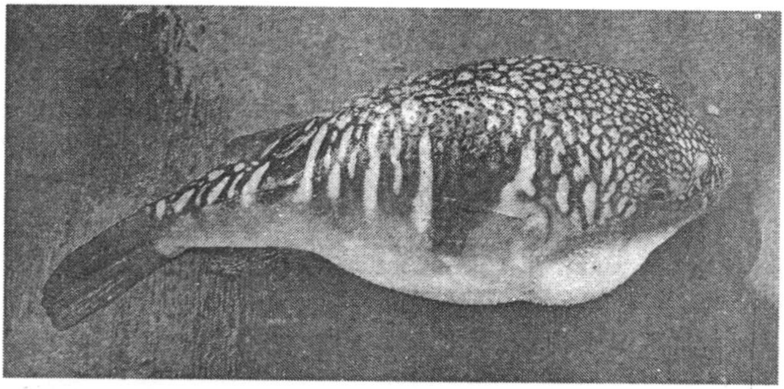

Habitat: Demersal. Found on sandy and rubble areas of shallow coastal waters, estuaries and lagoons. Attains 40 cm. Total Length.

Distribution: Widespread in Indo-West Pacific.

Remarks: Common puffer. Flesh and viscera are highly poisonous. Ornamental fish.

258. ***Tetraodon cutcutia*** (Hamilton, 1822)

Ocellated puffer

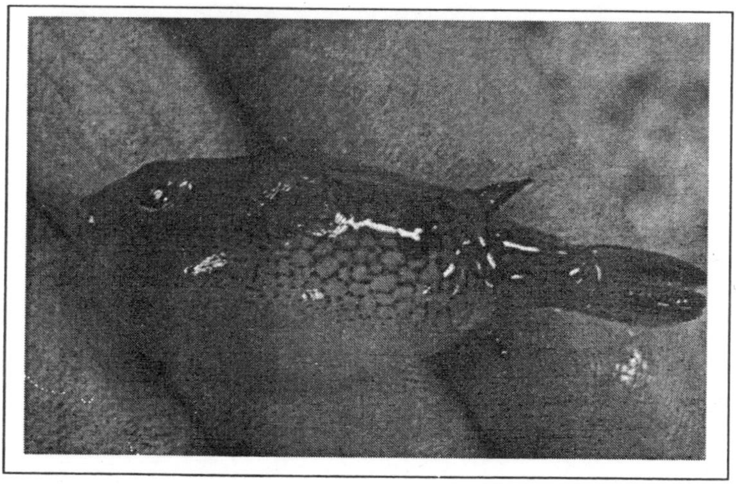

Diagnostic features: D.7-13; A. 8-12; P. 21; C.7. Body short, abdomen rounded, snout blunt, mouth terminal; one or two nostrils on each side in the form of short tube; both jaws with a midian sture; body covered with fine dermal spines or absent; upper lateral line not reaching end of tail, curved down above anal fin; ventral fins absent; all fins rounded. Body greenish above, white below; a light band across eyes; a large black ocellus on the side anterior the origin of dorsal and anal fins; back of body with greenish reticulations; a red spot on the throat.

Habitat: Demersal; potamodromous; fresh and brackish water, found in ponds, beels, canals and rivers. Attains 15 cm Total Length.

Distribution: Asia: India, Bangladesh, Sri Lanka, Myanmar and Malay Archipelago.

Remarks: Not edible, ornamental fish.

Select Bibliography

Chaudhuri, B.L. 1916a. Description of two new fishes from Chilkam Lake. *Rec. Indian Mus.*, 12(3):105-109.

Chaudhuri, B.L. 1916b. Fauna of Chilka Lake: Fish, Part I, *Mem. Indian Mus.*, 5(4):403-440.

Chaudhuri, B.L. 1916c. Fauna of Chilka Lake: Fish, Part II, *Mem. Indian Mus.*, 5(5):441-458.

Chaudhuri, B.L. 1917. Fauna of Chilka Lake: Fish, Part III, *Mem. Indian Mus.*, 5(6):491-508.

Chaudhuri, B.L. 1923. Fauna of Chilka Lake: Fish, Part VI, Mem. Indian Mus., 5(11):711-736.

Devasundaram, M.P. 1954. A report on the fishes of the chilka lake from 1948-50. Orissa Govt. Publ., 1-34.

Hora, S.L. 1923. Fauna of Chilka lake: Fish Part V. *Mem. Indian Mus.*, 5(11): 737-770.

Jayaram, K.C. 1981. *The Freshwater Fishes of India, Pakistan, Bangladesh, Burma and Sri Lanka: A Hand Book,* Zoological Survey of India,Calcutta, No. 2, 475 pp.

Jhingran, V.G. and A.V. Natarajan, 1966. Final report on fisheries of the Chilka lake (1957-65). *Bull. Cent. Inland Fish. Res. Inst. Barrackpore,* (8): page Var.

Jhingran, V.G. and A.V. Natarajan, 1969. A study of the fisheries and fish populations of the Chilka lake during the period 1957-65. *J. Inland Fish. Soc. India,* 1:49-126.

Jhingran, V.G. and A.V. Natarajan, 1991. *Fish and fisheries of India*. Hindustan Publishing Corporation, New Delhi, 327 pp.

Jones, S and K.H.Sujansingani, 1954. Fish and Fisheries of he Chilka lake with statistics of fish catches for the years 1948-1950. *Indian J. Fish.*, 1(1&2):256-344.

Koumans, F.P. 1941. Gobiod fishes of India. *Mem. Indian Mus.*, 13(3): 205-313.

Menon, M.A.S. 1961. On a collection of Fish from lake Chilka, Orissa. *Rec. Indian Mus.*, 59(1&2): 41-69.

Mitra, G.N. 1946. *Development of Chilka Lake*, Orissa, Govt. Press, Cuttack.

Misra, S. 1962. An aid to the identification of the common commercial fishes of India and Pakistan. *Rec. Indian Mus.*, 57(1-4): 1-320.

Misra, S. 1969. *Pisces: The Fauna of India and Adjacent Countries.* Vol.1 (2nd. Ed.), Managers Publications.

Rajan, S., S. Patnaik and N.C. Basu, 1968. New records of fish fauna of Chilka Lake. *J. Zool. Soc. India*, 20(1&2): 80-93

Roy, J.C. and N. Sahoo, 1957. Additions to fish fauna of the Chilika Lake. *J. Bombay nat. Hist. Soc.*, 54:944-953.

Talwar, P.K. and Kacker, 1984. *Commercial Sea Fishes of India. Hand Book*, ZSI, Kolkata., No.4, 997 pp.

Talwar, P.K. and A.G. Jhingran. 1991. Inland *Fishes of India and Adjacent Countries*, Vol.I, 541 pp & Vol.II., 543-1158 pp, Oxford & IBH Publishing Co. Pvt. Ltd., New Delhi.

Anodontostoma chacunda

Atherinomorus lacunosus

Atule mate

Caranx ignobilis

Caranx melampygus

Xenentodon cancila

Carcharhinus limbatus

Valamugil seheli

Catla catla

Channa punctata

Acentrogobius viridipunctatus

Glossogobius giuris

Oxyurichthys tentacularis

Periophthalmus barbarus

Taenioides buchanani

Channa striata

Colisa fasciata

Anabas cobojius

Macrognathus pancalus

Pseudorhombus triocellatus

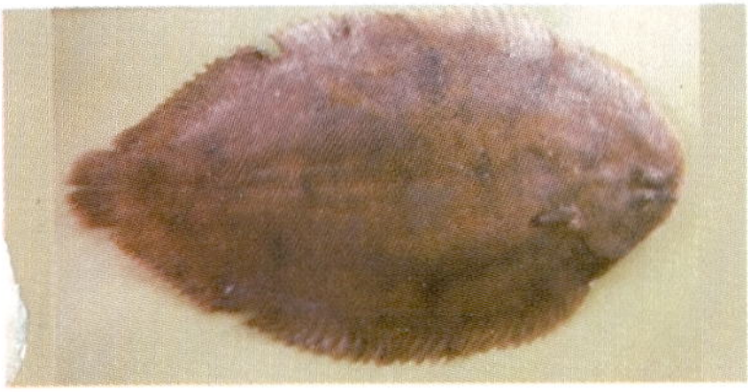
Brachirus orientalis

Arothron reticularis

Chelonodon patoca

Lagocephalus lunaris

Takifugu oblongus

Tetraodon cutcutia

Aetobatus narinari

Alectis indicus

Alpes djedaba

Ambassis commersoni

Parambassis ranga

Pastinachus sephen

Pelates quadrilineatus

Platycephalus indicus

Plotosus lineatus

Polydactylus plebeius

Pterois radiata

Puntius sophore

Rachycentron canadus

Rasbora daniconius

Lutjanus kasmira

Megalaspis cordyla

Megalops cyprnoides

Scomberoides lysan

Mugil cephalus

Nandus nandus

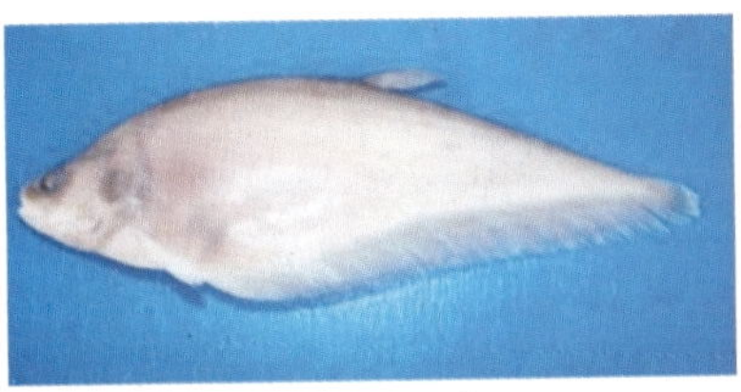

Notopterus notopterus

Stolephorus baganensis

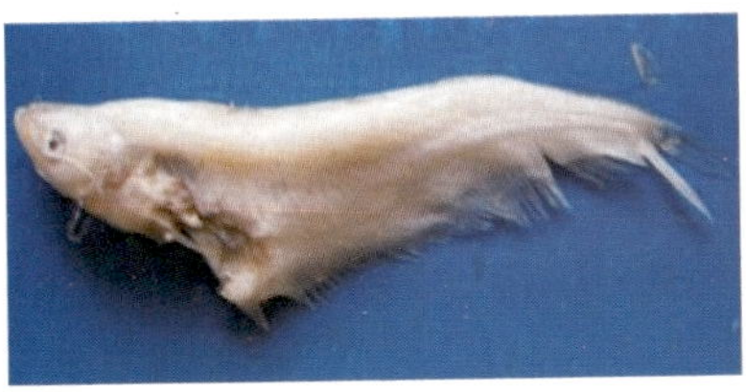

Ompok pabda

Oreochromis mossambicus

Ilisha melastoma

Johnius belangerii

Lates calcarifer

Leiognathus equulus

Lepturacanthus savala

Sphyraena jello

Liza parsia

Heteroneustes fossilis

Lutjanus argentimaculatus

Gerres oyena

Chanos chanos

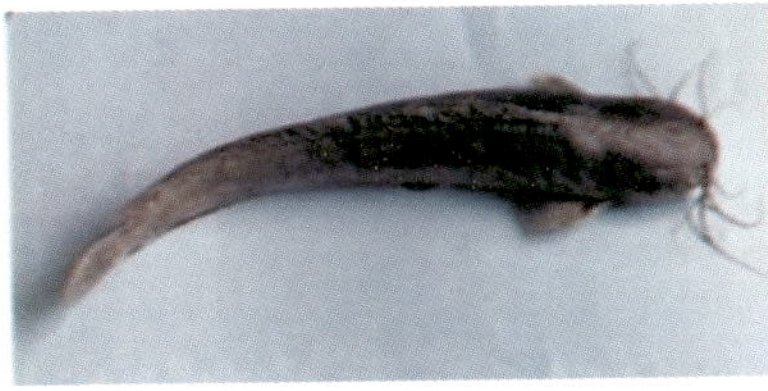

Clarius batrachus

Colisa fasciata

Whipfin majarra

Secutor insidiator

Echeneis naucrates

Eleotris fusca

Elops machnata

Epinephelus coioides

Escualosa thoracata

Rasbora rasbora

Rastrelliger kanagurta

Rhabdosargus sarba

Sillago vincenti

Rhinomugil corsula

Sardinella fimbriata

Sardinella longiceps

Scatophagus argus

Scoliodon laticaudus

Scomberoides commersonianus

Species Index